Ready for Regression

Hypnosis Practitioner's Guide to Preparing Clients for Successful Regression to Cause Hypnotherapy

Wendie Webber

Ready for Regression: *Hypnosis Practitioner's Guide to Preparing Clients for Successful Regression to Cause Hypnotherapy*

Wendie Webber

Copyright © 2025 Wendie Webber
All Rights Reserved.

All rights reserved. No part of this publication may be reproduced, distributed, or transmitted in any form or by any means, including photocopying, recording, or other electronic or mechanical methods without the prior written permission from the author, except in the case of brief quotations embodied in critical reviews and certain non-commercial uses permitted by copyright law.

The information given in this book should not be treated as a substitute for professional medical advice; always consult a medical practitioner. Any use of information in this book is at the reader's discretion and risk. Neither the author nor the publisher can be held responsible for any loss, claim, or damage arising out of the use, or misuse, of the suggestions made, the failure to take medical advice, or for any material on third-party websites.

ISBN Print Book: 978-1-0688514-7-6

wendie@tribeofhealers.com

Table of Contents

WHY REGRESSION? 1
    The Devil's Therapy 8
    Ready for Regression First Session 10
CHAPTER 1: What Tools Do You Need? 17
    Support the Client 18
    Support Yourself 20
    Emotional Release Work 26
    Skype or Zoom Sessions 29
CHAPTER 2: Set for Success 31
    Two-Part Protocol 33
    Three Ps 34
    The Intake 42
    The Educational Pretalk 46
    The Potty Break Protocol 47
    Session Worksheet 51
    Your Script 60
    Key Players 61
    Other Stuff 63
CHAPTER 3: Conditioning Phase 65
    Four Permissions 65
    Be Convincing 68
    Formalize the Induction 69
    Utilize Sounds 73

    Use Physical Relaxation 77

    Body Awareness Exercise 81

    Autosuggestion 88

CHAPTER 4: Modify the Elman Induction 95

    Test for State 103

    Deepen Immediately 112

    Body Tour 113

CHAPTER 5: Emerge (Not Really) 119

    Hypnotic Stare 120

    Time Distortion Test 121

    Test the Trigger 123

    Deepen Immediately 128

    What next? 131

    Conditioning Phase Checklist 137

CHAPTER 6: Preliminary Check In 139

    Two Important Questions 140

    What's the next step? 143

    Subsequent Session Checklist 144

CHAPTER 7: The Core Work 145

    Regression-to-Cause Hypnotherapy Tools 147

    Root Cause Theory 148

    Time is an Illusion 156

    Parts Theory 161

    Traumatic History 168

    Chemical Lids 173

CHAPTER 8: Ready for Regression Phase 177
    Strategizing 178
    Remember 181
    Hypermnesia Exercise 188
    Moment of Insight 191
    Age Regression 192

CHAPTER 9: Uncovering Procedure 197
    How to Respond 198
    The Six Basic Uncovering Questions 200
    Core Emotions 205
    Stages of Separation Distress 208
    Primary Emotions 209
    What's the story? 215
    What if Things Go Sideways? 220
    Insight is Not Enough 227
    Healing is in the Feeling 229

CHAPTER 10: Inner Child Work 235
    Childhood Needs 237
    Transmit Love 256
    Test Acceptability 266

CHAPTER 11: Introduce Forgiveness 279
    Buried Emotions Don't Die 282
    Repression 285
    Releasing 287
    Forgiveness 297

CHAPTER 12: Wrap Up Powerfully 307
    Revelation Wrap Up 308
    Zig-Zag 312
    Big Bucket of Pain 312
    Buttoning Up 315
    Quick Polishing Techniques 319
    Generalize & Integrate Change 323

CHAPTER 13: Debriefing 335
    Debriefing Doubt 337
    Set Up for the Next Session 346
    Two-Minute Coaching Session 349

CHAPTER 14: Preliminary Check-In 353
    Same, Better, or Worse? 355
    Poke a Stick Technique 356

CHAPTER 15: Get Lasting Results 365
    Do you always need to locate the ISE? 366
    The Backwash Effect 367
    Follow Up 372
    Testing in Hypnosis 374
    Testing in Daily Life 379
    Homework 384
    Keep the Contract Open 398

CHAPTER 16: Healing Trauma 401
    What to Watch For 404
    Tapping Techniques 408

Abreactions 414

Uncovering Tools 417

Titrating 419

Myoclonic Shaking 420

Abuse 425

The Aftermath of Abuse 433

Birth Trauma 444

Optional: Autosuggestions 454

CHAPTER 17: Why Diets Don't Work 455

CHAPTER 18: Conclusion 463

Time Management Tips 465

Ready for Regression Phase Checklist 467

Stand-Alone Protocols 468

Standard Regression Session Checklist 472

Wendie Webber 473

To regain our health, it is necessary for us to open up to all our feelings and sensations.
~ J. Konrad Stettbacher

WHY REGRESSION?

Regression is the "forbidden hypnotherapy". You've probably heard it said that regression is bad, regression retraumatizes the client, regression is unnecessary. Dangerous, even! Heck, I was taught this in my first hypnotherapy training! I continue to hear these things being expressed on social media hypnosis forums.

Clearly, some hypnosis practitioners have strong judgments against regression. Usually, it's because they either don't really know how it works, they lack the skill necessary to facilitate it effectively, or they're intimidated by the thought of having to deal with a traumatic memory. They're afraid of upsetting the client. I find this curious.

What's wrong with being upset? The reason the client is seeing you is *because* they're upset. Okay, don't get me started. Instead, let me share some of the things I have learned over many years of working with real clients who were struggling with real problems.

First, regression happens. People are going to regress whether you want them to or not. They're going to get triggered, they're going to experience uncomfortable feelings, and they're going to regress. Do you know what to do when that happens?

Situations in daily life can act as triggers for unresolved events from the past. This is because, when a painful event from the past doesn't get resolved, the subconscious mind holds onto that memory *as if* it was a present issue of concern. Because it doesn't get stored as a past event, the client is left vulnerable to re-stimulation by situations which are, in some way, a match to the past event that caused distress.

The situation responsible for causing unwanted thoughts, feelings, or behaviors hasn't been processed and brought to completion. As a result, the client continues to relive the undigested contents of that memory - maybe not consciously, but UN-consciously – every time they get triggered.

People who get triggered are going to get triggered again. And when they get triggered, they automatically re-experience the thought and emotional debris trapped in that unresolved memory. What's happening is a process of remembering the experience. This is accomplished by mentally re-assembling all the parts of that memory. As this happens, aspects of memory are brought to conscious awareness. It's not bad or wrong. It's just how the mind works.

But when a person doesn't know how to deal with an uncomfortable emotion, they'll try to avoid the feeling. That never works. Putting a lid on your emotions will only make things worse because it traps the feeling inside. This is why emotional problems tend to get worse over time. With nowhere to go, the internal pressure starts to build up and the feelings grow stronger.

Avoiding feelings and emotions is the problem. Memories are made up of impressions including thoughts, feelings, emotions and sensations. When a person gets triggered, that information gets uploaded into conscious awareness in the present moment. Often, unexpectedly.

Unfortunately, what comes to the surface is usually fragmented. As a result, it doesn't make sense to the conscious mind. This makes it even more distressing. But the cause of the problem is not what triggered the client. It's an unresolved situation that occurred earlier in life which involved an experience of overwhelm.

The subconscious mind must protect. The subconscious mind works tirelessly to find answers to questions and solutions to problems. When we get stuck, it doesn't relinquish its protective function. It continues to do what it was designed to do by trying to find a solution. The problem is that the subconscious mind only has the resources that were available to the person at the time of the traumatic event. If that happened to be an event in childhood, that's where they're still stuck.

When the subconscious mind is still trying to find a solution to whatever happened in a past event, it ruminates. This can generate habitual worrying, bad dreams and more. Like a hamster on a wheel, the mind keeps running the event, over and over again. This just compounds the problem by reinforcing the perception of being stuck, unable to fix it, having no way out, feeling scared, or whatever happens to be the client's subconscious "truth."

Regression therapy allows us to get the mind out of the spin. It's a way to locate where the pattern got started and identify the thoughts and feelings that are running the wheel.

Every problem is the result of a life experience. The "seed planting" event of any problem is what we call the Initial Sensitizing Event (ISE). It's what caused there to be a problem, in the first place. We strive to locate this event because it's going to be the one with the least emotional charge. This makes it easier for both you and the client.

Often, the ISE turns out to be no-big-deal. But even when it was, the client survived it. They're still here. The problem is that the subconscious mind doesn't know this, yet. As a result, it's still protecting the client's younger self!

Do you need to find the ISE when there are so many alternative methods available?

Not every therapy is suitable for every client. Surface issues respond beautifully to surface techniques. Deeper issues are emotional issues which require a deeper technique. This is one of the benefits of having a full complement of therapeutic tools. If what you're doing isn't working, or fails to achieve a lasting result, you can employ a deeper technique like regression therapy.

Regression therapy is ideally suited to working with emotional issues because feelings don't come out of nowhere. When a client habitually responds to situations with the same uncomfortable thought, feeling, or behavioral responses, it's because something happened to trigger them. "That feeling" isn't coming out of what's happening *now*, however. The client has felt that feeling *before*! Does this mean that they're being retraumatized? Hardly! All that is happening is they are experiencing an emotion from the past - again.

It's perfectly normal and natural to experience feelings and emotions. Feelings and emotions are how the subconscious mind communicates with the conscious mind! But when a problem has time to grow and develop, it can build up a big head of steam. This translates into emotional intensity in the here and now.

Identifying the causal event allows you to deal with the problem at its inception. And because the ISE is the weakest link in the chain of events contributing to the problem, resolving the problem at the ISE tends to be much easier on the client (and you).

Is there even such a thing as the ISE?

All change is based on belief. We are working with beliefs, not truth or facts. If the client believes that a specific event, or series of events, is responsible for causing the problem, then resolving that experience will allow them to accept and believe that they no longer have the problem.

Rather than trying to process a whole lifetime of reinforcing events (which is what's happening every time a person gets triggered in daily life) you can pull the plug on the whole pattern by clearing the pattern within the event that caused it.

The client's mind naturally knows how to connect to *every time* they ever felt that way or thought that thought. And the adult consciousness of the client has greater maturity and resources than were available during the causal event. Why not use them?

Why bother with regression when there are far more reliable ways which avoid false memories?

All memory is false. Studies in Memory Reconsolidation have shown that every time you review an event, you reinterpret that event. That's what we do in a regression session. We're utilizing a natural process. We're taking mature adult consciousness back to reevaluate events in childhood. This is helpful because the Child often lacks the ability to make sense of what's happening.

Regression hypnotherapy is not forensic. We're not going back to find the truth of what happened. We're looking into how the event was interpreted by the client *at that time*, and how impressions made during that event are still impacting the client *now*. The reason we want to do this is because the conscious mind doesn't have access to all the information.

You can guide a client back to a consciously remembered event and the subconscious will reveal elements of the event that the client has no conscious recall of. The memory is still there. But parts of it can get blocked. This is called repression.

Why take a person back to a traumatic event when you can use an imagined event to achieve the same result without causing them to feel upset?

Everybody has trauma. It either makes you stronger or it knocks you down. Some people need a little help getting back up again. But trauma is not what most people think. Dr. Robert Scaer[1] defines trauma as *the perception of threat while in a state of helplessness.* Children are helpless. This is why, so often, the underlying cause is found in an event in childhood.

Often, the ISE turns out to be no big deal to *adult* consciousness. The problem often has to do with the fact that the Child was feeling overwhelmed, lacked the maturity to cope with the situation, or needed support in making sense of that experience. It is because these things were lacking that the Child formed some erroneous beliefs.

---

[1] Robert C. Scaer, MD. The Body Bears the Burden: Trauma, Dissociation, and Disease.

Our beliefs determine our self-image and our expectations of self, others, and life. Because our core beliefs form in childhood, resolving one issue can transform a person's entire life in ways you never imagined.

The subconscious doesn't distinguish between real and imagined. But research in Memory Reconsolidation[2] shows that when you create an imagined event, you are creating a false memory. This is because creating an alternative event, such as a happy experience, does not extinguish the original memory of traumatization. This establishes two conflicting memories which generate cognitive dissonance.

The objective of regression therapy is not to change memories. If something happened, we can't change that. Nor should we try. What we *can* do is empower our clients to face what happened to them and then change how it *feels*. This results in greater resilience. If you can achieve this by another means, that's wonderful! But if the client has already tried everything, and your techniques have failed to achieve a lasting result, regression might be the next logical step.

Granted, regression is not for everyone. Like root canal surgery, it's good for certain issues. But it's seldom the first intervention a person should try. It's when nothing else works that regression becomes a worthwhile option.

Regression hypnotherapy is certainly not about retraumatizing or installing false memories. It's exactly the opposite. Done correctly, regression therapy is an empowerment process that can put an end to the cycle of re-traumatization that the *client* has been doing to him or herself. Anyone who is retraumatizing clients with regression is not

---

[2] Bruce Ecker, Robin Ticic, Laurel Hulley. Unlocking the Emotional Brain: Eliminating Symptoms at Their Roots Using Memory Reconsolidation

practicing therapeutic hypnosis. It takes advanced training to facilitate regression hypnotherapy effectively. If you're not trained in regression to cause, go get trained.

The purpose of Ready for Regression First Session System is to lay the foundation for regression to happen easily. Knowing the steps can help you to feel more confident moving forward with the healing process. Clients need to be prepared to face painful truths. After all, *it's their mind!*

While some people will be ready to dive into the pain of their past, others are going to need more time to achieve a lasting result. That's okay. Regression hypnotherapy is not a single-session approach. It's a *client-centered* approach which often requires multiple sessions. Realize it's not up to you. The *client* decides the time it takes.

The Devil's Therapy

The Devil's Therapy provides a three-phase, seven-step protocol for facilitating effective regression hypnotherapy. Phase 1 is all about setting up for regression to happen easily. This involves the intake process, educational pretalk, followed by the **Ready for Regression First Session**.

In chapter 1, we'll look at how to set up for regression hypnotherapy by getting your tools ready. While the focus is on in-person sessions, tips for working online are also provided.

In chapter 2, we'll look at the pre-hypnosis session set up including the Three Ps, Session Confirmation Checklist, Intake process, Educational Pretalk, Potty Break Protocol, and the key information you need to gather into your Session Worksheet.

The Intake Process

The intake process is a preliminary uncovering procedure which can provide important clues which can help you to guide the healing process effectively. It also allows you to customize your educational pretalk by making it relevant to the needs and expectations of the client. For this reason, the intake comes before your pretalk.

In my first hypnosis certification course, I was taught not to waste time talking to the client's conscious mind. The idea was that the conscious mind doesn't have the answer, the subconscious mind is where you need to go to get the answers. All true. But . . . The real timewaster in a session is having to wrestle with an uncooperative client.

If you don't give the client enough time to feel heard, the conscious mind has the power to block you. The conscious mind must be willing to step aside, hand over the reins, and let *you* run the show, while the subconscious mind needs to know that you can be trusted to protect the client. This is the purpose of your intake process.

The intake process is covered in-depth in **Ditch the Script**: *Get Everything You Need from the Client for Successful Hypnotherapy and Set Up to Wrap Up with Results*. This includes how to:

- Qualify your clients with six Critical Questions
- Facilitate the intake process
- Conduct Intake Assessments
- Identify Symptoms Resolution Keys
- Set up for your session wrap up
- Set up for forgiveness work
- Set up for the next session

Educational Pretalk

Hypnosis is essentially an agreement between you and the client that says, "I lead, you follow." You need the client to be willing to follow your instructions. But most people don't know much about hypnosis and what they *do* know is often contaminated with misinformation. The purpose for a *hypnosis* pretalk is to resolve any fears or misconceptions the client might have because these things can prevent a person from entering the state of hypnosis.

The educational pretalk for *regression hypnotherapy*, however, needs to be more comprehensive because the therapeutic contract is not merely an agreement to allow hypnosis to happen. You need an agreement that allows feelings and emotions to be a part of the process.

Because regression hypnotherapy is not a passive process, the client must be willing to be an active participant in their own healing processes. The goal of educating the client for regression hypnotherapy is, therefore, to establish a contract based on informed consent.

The educational pretalk is covered in-depth in **Radical Healing**: *Hypnosis Practitioner's Guide to Harnessing the Healing Power of the Educational Pretalk.* This includes how to establish contracts for the first session; hypnosis; regression to cause; allowing and releasing feelings and emotions; mind-body healing. In addition, there are chapters on teen hypnotherapy; resistant/analytical clients; palliative clients.

Ready for Regression First Session

Phase 2 and 3 of the Devil's' Therapy follows the completion of the set up phase. These same processes will be used in the Ready for Regression Session to *prepare* a client for regression to cause therapeutic hypnosis. Phase 2 is where the core work of regression hypnotherapy takes place. This is the Transformation Phase which includes regression to the causal event, the uncovering procedure, emotional release work, and inner child work. Phase 3 focuses on ensuring a lasting result. This is the Verification Phase which utilizes testing and integration techniques followed by forgiveness work.

In the Ready for Regression First Session, you will learn how to create your ideal client for regression therapy by:

- Guiding the client into hypnosis
- Proving that hypnosis is safe
- Proving that hypnosis is happening
- Conditioning the client for a rapid induction
- Introducing the client to the core work of regression hypnotherapy
- Assessing and training the client to be an active participant in their own healing.

As hypnotherapists, we are change-makers. We're paid to facilitate a change. Hypnosis is actually the least important part of the therapeutic process. But most clients think they're paying for the hypnosis. This is why you need to educate them[3] about the process. The client is only *hoping* that hypnosis will help them to achieve their desired goal. They don't yet believe it. You need to provide proof that hypnosis happened because nothing is going to happen without the client's belief.

The last thing you need is to have delivered a stellar first session and then have the client emerge and say, "I don't think I was hypnotized!" That little bit of doubt can sabotage your success.

---

[3] Radical Healing: Hypnosis Practitioner's Guide to Harnessing the Healing Power of the Educational Pretalk

Providing proof that hypnosis happened will make it easier for the client to believe that the changes they want can and will happen. The easiest way to prove that hypnosis is safe is to use relaxation hypnosis in the first session.

Relaxation hypnosis allows you to focus on making the client's first experience working with you a pleasant experience. This will help to instill in the client a sense of confidence and positive expectations regarding future sessions. And because relaxation hypnosis is slow, it affords you the time to observe the client's responses and evaluate what needs to happen next. You can then use the pleasant feelings of relaxation as *evidence* that hypnosis is truly happening.

Conditioning Session

Regression hypnotherapy takes time. In a regression therapy session, you need to get the client into hypnosis quickly so that you can get to work on their issue. That's what they're paying you for. Using the client's first session to condition the client to go into hypnosis will save you gobs of time in subsequent sessions.

Conditioning a client is easy. In the Ready for Regression First Session System, you will learn a permission-based approach to facilitating the Elman Induction[4]. The Elman Induction is great because it works for everyone and has all the tests and convincers built into it. You'll learn how to guide the client into a state of somnambulism, utilize covert and overt tests, and install a trigger for rapid re-induction.

In chapter 3 and 4, we'll look at the induction process including the four Permissions, how to formalize the induction, utilize sounds, physical relaxation, and autosuggestion. We'll explore how to tweak the

---

[4] Dave Elman. Hypnotherapy

Dave Elman Induction to make it fail-safe. We'll also look at covert testing, overt-testing, and setting up an effective Convincer. In chapter 5, you'll learn how to install a trigger for rapid re-induction. Once you have conditioned the client for hypnosis, you'll be all set up for the next session.

While the goal is to complete both the Conditioning Session and the Ready for Regression Session in a single session, the Ready for Regression First Session is designed to give you total time control in the first session. Should you find that you're short on time, you can easily wrap things up following the Conditioning Session. The next session would then begin with a preliminary check-in before continuing with the Ready for Regression Session.

Ready for Regression Session

Before you start diving into the regression work, you can use the first session to train your clients and prepare them for the deeper work of regression to cause hypnotherapy. Regression gives us access to the event that caused that uncomfortable feeling in the first place.

This is why we follow the feeling back. We want to get to the root of the problem. It's the emotional charge trapped in that event that is holding the pattern in place. Releasing the feelings trapped in that event will help to restore internal peace and harmony. But before we start bringing up uncomfortable feelings and emotions, you need to make it safe for the client to allow those things.

There's always going to be resistance to "going there." Nobody wants to face uncomfortable memories and feelings. After all, those feelings don't feel good! But avoidance is always a big part of the problem. Why not use your first session to prove to the client that it's safe to "go there"? The approach you're about to learn allows you to assess the needs of the clients *before* guiding them into painful events from the past. This gives you the opportunity to get rid of unnecessary resistance while teaching the client how to work with you in a regression session. Not only will this give you an easier client to work with, but it will also help you to feel more confident guiding the process.

In the Ready for Regression Session, you will introduce your client to the tools and techniques of regression therapy. In chapter 7, we will explore the core work of regression to cause hypnosis. We'll look at the primary tools we use, root cause theory, parts theory, conscious versus subconscious time, traumatic history, and the problem with antidepressants.

In chapter 8, you will learn how to convert a simple memory exercise into real regression. Chapter 9 follows with the uncovering procedure and how to utilize the six basic uncovering questions of regression hypnotherapy effectively. Other topics include core emotions, separation distress, and what to do when your session goes sideways. In chapter 10, we'll dive into Inner Child Work, including childhood programming, bonding issues, utilizing dual consciousness, assessment keys, and how to provide what the Child most needs. In chapter 11, we'll look at forgiveness work, who needs to be forgiven first, releasing anger, and healing the pain of childhood.

Chapter 12 looks at how to wrap up your sessions powerfully, how to button up a session when there's still work to be done in an event, and how to generalize and integrate change. Chapter 13 covers the debriefing process following the first session and how to set up for the next session. Included is a two-minute coaching session you can use in every session with clients.

What's the best next step for this client? That's the only question you ever need to answer. Chapter 14 looks at how to utilize the results of your two-minute coaching session to identify the next step in the client's healing process. Included is the Poke-a-Stick Technique to quickly find a Bridge for regression.

Throughout the Ready for Regression First session process, you'll have opportunities to gather up positive resources to support the client on their healing journey and, based on what you discover through the process, formulate a strategy.

Chapter 15 focuses on how to ensure a lasting result by testing the results both in session and between sessions, and by keeping the Contract open. Chapters 16, 17, and 18 provide bonus content related to healing trauma including core needs, tapping techniques, dealing with abreactions, additional uncovering tools, working with abuse, how to process the birth experience, and why diets don't work. Finally, chapter 18 concludes with time management tips and a regression session checklist for subsequent sessions.

By the end of the Ready for Regression First Session, your client will have experienced much more than just hypnosis and you'll have a client who is truly ready for regression. You'll have a client who can:

- Return to the state of hypnosis quickly and easily,
- Follow your instructions to regress into past events,
- Respond quickly during the uncovering procedure,
- Be a source of loving support for the Inner Child,
- Forgive Inner Child and Parent Parts

Let's get started!

The Devil's Therapy Series

Book 1: The Devil's Therapy: *Hypnosis Practitioner's Essential Guide to Effective Regression Hypnotherapy*

Book 2: Ditch the Pitch: *Simple Proven Client Attraction Strategies for Hypnosis Practitioners Who Don't Love Digital Marketing*

Book 3: Ditch the Script: *Get Everything You Need from the Client for Successful Hypnotherapy and Set Up to Wrap Up with Results*

Book 4: Radical Healing: *Hypnosis Practitioner's Guide to Harnessing the Healing Power of the Educational Pretalk*

Book 5: The Devil's Little Black Book: *Regression Hypnotherapist's Troubleshooting Guide with Tips, Tricks & Even Scripts to Tweak Your Therapeutic Technique*

Book 6: The Dream Healing Practitioner Guidebook: *A Healer's Guide to Uncovering the Secret Messages of Your Dreams*

Book 7: Ready for Regression: *Hypnosis Practitioner's Guide to Preparing Clients for Effective Regression Hypnotherapy*

CHAPTER 1:
What Tools Do You Need?

They don't teach you this in hypnosis school but there are two sides to your hypnotherapy business. There's the practice side of hypnosis and then there's the business side. If you're in business for yourself, you need to take care of both. The business side is everything you do to support yourself in making a living. The practice side is everything you do to guide your clients to achieve their results. This begins with creating a space that makes it safe for the client to allow healing to happen.

When I had a commercial office, a man came in to see what I was all about. I was on the phone, so I invited him to have a look around, and while he waited, he spent considerable time looking over my certificates which were displayed in the hallway. When I got off the phone he said, "It looks like you know what you're doing." After a brief conversation, he decided to become a client.

His decision on whether to trust me was based on his first impressions. This is always true. Often the first impression a person gets is over the phone. But if you're seeing clients in the privacy of your office, your session space tells a person – consciously or unconsciously - whether it's safe to trust you. It is a non-verbal suggestion that speaks volumes about you, what you care about and about how credible you are. Ultimately, your healing space has two functions. It should (1) provide a safe place where the client can allow healing to happen, (2) support *you* in feeling confident guiding the client through a healing process.

Support the Client

Your healing space should be focused on meeting the needs of the client. Healing happens *when we let it*. Your healing space needs to be a safe place for the client to allow healing to happen. Step back and look at your space through the eyes of a total stranger. What's your first impression? Is it neat and clean? Does it smell fresh? Everything in your room is a suggestion. What is it saying?

Remember, you're working with the client's subconscious mind. The subconscious mind's primary concern is safety. That needs to be *your* primary concern as well. Make sure your healing space is a safe space for the client to be with you. Get rid of the clutter. Clear out the distractions. Anything that doesn't serve the healing process doesn't belong there. For example, family pictures are appropriate for an executive office, but your session room needs to be about the healing.

Look around. Is your session room neat and clean? Does it provide adequate privacy? Are your certificates framed professionally? Are they hanging straight? A dollar-store frame hanging slightly askew doesn't say much about your value. Consider investing a few extra bucks in having your certificates matted and framed. You're worth it.

What about plants and crystals? If your clientele is metaphysical, there's nothing wrong with having a few crystals and gemstones around. But if you're running a general practice, make sure they're decorative and not demanding. Any plants in your session room should be vibrant and healthy. Dead or dying plants are bad feng shui and don't suggest positive outcomes. You can get silk plants that look very lifelike. They're inexpensive and don't require any upkeep. This might be an alternative if you don't have a green thumb.

When working from home, you need to be very conscious of things like cooking smells, pets, kids, and the state of your bathroom. Take steps to protect your client's confidentiality and ensure that you won't be interrupted when in session. I have a "Do Not Disturb" sign that goes on the front door. When the client arrives the sign goes up, pets go out, and the phone is turned off. Also, no cooking bacon on those days!

Make sure the bathroom is within easy reach of your session room. It needs to be neat and clean, too. Stow away personal items like toothbrushes and hair gel, close the shower curtains across the bathtub to reduce clutter, and make sure the toilet and sink are clean.

Another way you can create a space for healing is by using an essential oil diffuser in your hypnosis session room. I use Young Living Essential Oils because they're pure. The one I use a lot is called Thieves. The reason I use it is because it has anti-bacterial, anti-viral, and anti-infectious properties. Diffusing essential oils is an easy way to protect both yourself and your clients from airborne "bugs". It must work because I can't remember the last time I came down with a virus.

Apparently, Thieves wards off the Bubonic plague! That's how it got its name. During the Middle Ages, the Black Plague shut down all international trade. There were four French spice traders who took to looting and *they never got sick*. Before going into homes and looting the bodies of plague victims, they rubbed their bodies with certain oils and spices. When they eventually got caught stealing, they were able to obtain a lighter sentence in exchange for sharing the recipe with the king. If you want to protect yourself and your clients from the plague, or just make the place smell really good, invest in a diffuser. The volcano types are very reliable and inexpensive. Make sure you choose therapeutic grade essential oils. These oils are free of toxic carriers and synthetics and can bring another level of healing into your sessions.

Thieves essential oil contains cloves, cinnamon bark, rosemary, lemon, and eucalyptus. When you diffuse Thieves into the air it's delicious. It is said to have an uplifting and energizing effect. Energetically it's used to cleanse and purify a space. It's also supposed to get rid of negative emotions and vibrations. I like that. But honestly, I just like how it smells.

Support Yourself

Your session room should also support *you* in guiding the healing process. You need to think about what tools and resources *you* need to guide the healing process effectively. Do you have everything you need? Are they within easy reach when you're working with a client? For example, when you're just starting out you rely on scripts and protocols. There's just too much stuff to keep in your head.

It's okay to use cheat-sheets. These can help you to stay on track in session and being consistent in your sessions will help you to get more consistent results. But your scripts and protocols need to be out of sight of the client. You need your clients to be 100% confident in your skill and ability. If they sense that you're using a script they may doubt your expertise. That could cost you in terms of rapport and they might not trust you enough to let you guide them.

All it takes is a little bit of doubt to sabotage your success. You need to be discreet when using a script or a protocol. Your scripts and protocols should be within easy reach without being obvious to the client.

When I was learning regression hypnotherapy, I needed a way to keep me consistent in my sessions with clients. I was still learning the various processes and didn't feel confident that I could remember all the steps involved. I wasn't comfortable just 'winging' it with clients. The solution was to build myself a session manual. This started out as a binder with different sections in the order I typically used them. For example, the first section held my inductions and deepening techniques. The next section was preliminary techniques. What followed were different sections for specific regression protocols and polishing techniques.

As I continued to learn and evolve, so did my session manual. For example, when I was studying with Gerry Kein, it was an Omni-Hypnosis manual. When I was studying with Cal Banyan, it became a 5-PATH manual. When I moved onto regression hypnotherapy it became a Regression Hypnotherapy manual. This became quite a substantial binder! I didn't want it to be out in the open where clients could see it because I didn't want clients to think I was just reading a script. That's *not* what I was doing! Still, I needed something to guide me so that I could feel confident facilitating the process. That's what my session manual gave me.

I just needed a place to keep my session manual that wasn't obvious to the client, yet easily accessible to me while I was working in session. The solution I came up with was a workstation. We have workstations for computers. Why not for hypnotherapy sessions? What I had built was essentially a bookshelf with a few custom features. For example, it had task lighting above the first shelf where the binder sat. The task lighting allowed me to turn down the lights in the session room and still be able to see my protocol or session notes. However, I made a mistake in installing halogen lights in the workstation. It didn't take long to realize halogens get hot. (Put two people in a closed room with a couple of halogen lights, add some pillow whacking, and your room gets suh-mokin!) I swapped out the halogens for cool fluorescent lighting, instead. Much better.

When I went digital, I moved all my scripts and protocols onto my tablet and organized them into a library. This was even better than using a binder because it allowed me to switch to different sections very quickly. Instead of the bulky binder, all I needed was a stand for the tablet. Because the tablet needed to be at eye level, the stand sat on top of the workstation, freeing up the inside top shelf where my session manual used to go. This created the perfect place for me to keep the client's working papers. For example, client file, session notes, etc.

Think of your session manual as training wheels. Once you have internalized the processes you won't need it anymore. Until then, the session manual can help you stay on track in a session, feel more confident guiding a process and, as a result achieve better/more consistent outcomes.

Create Your Own Manual

Think about how you can organize your scripts and protocols in a way that supports you in your sessions. This will help you to feel more confident while you're learning the various processes. When the time is right, the training wheels will come off all by themselves. You'll have internalized the processes so well that it will just come automatically. That's when you'll really start to rock in your sessions.

The key is to find what works best for you. It might be easier to create a manual system first, then switch over to digital format, as I did. After all, everything high-tech started out as a manual system. I used a simple binder system for years. But if you want to use a tablet the same guidelines will apply.

Start by creating sections for your scripts and protocols. Put them in the order you would normally use them. For example:

1. Inductions and deepeners
2. First session protocol
3. Regression protocols
4. Forgiveness protocols
5. Specific protocols
6. Scripts, polishing techniques, etc.

If you're using a binder, separate each section with a big tab. This will make it easier for you to work on the fly because everything will be in a logical order and clearly visible to you. With a glance, you'll be able to see what you need. You'll be able to change from one section to another and still stay present to the needs of the client. For example, shifting from a dialogue process to a forgiveness protocol.

It's important for you to be able to see your scripts from a distance or in low light. Printing all your scripts and protocols in 14-point font or larger will make it easier for you to see. If you set your margins at ½ inch, you'll get more print on the page. This will save on paper and means less page-turning during a session. If you're using a digital system, narrower margins will allow more text to be displayed on the screen.

Clients are hyper-alert in hypnosis. The sound of paper rustling can be distracting. If you're using a manual system, slide your pages into plastic page protectors. The page protectors stop the rustling noise that paper makes, allowing you to turn the page quietly without the client's awareness. This will allow you to operate in 'whisper mode'.

Session Notes

When you're using a multi-session approach to healing, it's important to keep good notes during sessions. This will give you a record of the client's healing process and provide all the information you need for creating suggestions when it comes time to wrap up your sessions. You don't need anything special for session notes. All I use is a clip board and three-hole punched, lined school paper. When I'm not using the clipboard, it just sits off to the side on the shelf where it's within easy reach.

Tip: Buy two clipboards. That way, if you need the client to fill out forms, or write a check, you can give them a firm surface to write on while they're sitting in the chair.

Big Clock

During sessions, you need to keep your eye on the clock to ensure that your session ends on time. You'll need a *big clock* if you want to conduct the time distortion test. Some clients wear glasses. When you emerge them, they won't be able to see the clock. This can mess up your test. Put the clock somewhere obvious. When the client opens their eyes, you want them to see it right away. Even if you're not doing a time distortion test, the client will often look at the clock and say, "Woah!" That's when you can say, "Time flies when you're in Lah-Lah Land..." You can tell them about how time distortion is one of the signs of hypnosis. This makes a nice Convincer.

Appointment Cards

Clients are sometimes groggy following a session. Sometimes they're discombobulated. If you don't give them a written reminder, they could forget their next appointment. No-shows cost you! Invest in appointment cards[5].

Blanket

A blanket isn't just for warmth; it's a suggestion of comfort and safety. If a client is wearing shorts or a short skirt, a blanket can provide a sense of security by giving them a way to cover up. As a result, they won't be distracted by feeling self-conscious or exposed. That will only get in the way. A blanket can also be used to signal when the hypnosis is about to begin. Just pull out the blanket and say, "Let's get comfy, shall we?" This tells the client that the induction is about to begin.

When choosing a blanket, make sure it's washable. Micro-fleece is very durable and comfortable. It's easy to wash and cozy-warm. Buy two. That way you can rotate them weekly through the laundry and you'll always have a clean one on hand.

Twin-Sized Sheet

Clients who come in wearing shorts or a dress will stick to a leather chair. That's not comfortable. Tossing a twin-sized sheet over the chair will prevent them from sticking. Obviously, if you have a fabric chair, this won't be an issue. But people are going to come in wearing hair grease and skin grease and perfume, and they'll leave it behind on your chair. It's much easier to launder a sheet than it is to get the chair cleaned.

---

[5] You can get inexpensive appointment cards at Vistaprint.com

Emotional Release Work

Giving an uncomfortable feeling a way out will get the client rapid relief. If you're going to incorporate emotional release work into your hypnotherapy sessions, you need to set things up in a way that works for you. Remember to make sure the tools you need are placed within easy reach of your chair. For example, I'm right-handed so my chair is on the right-hand side of the client. That's what works best for me. Tucked behind the client's chair, kind of out of sight, is a big, sturdy pillow. When it comes time to start releasing feelings and emotions, I just reach down, pull out the pillow, and place it gently in the client's lap. Mwah-hah-hah ...

Pillow

The purpose of pillow work is to *discharge* the energy that's been trapped inside. You're giving the feeling a way *out* while, at the same time, giving it a place to go – into the pillow. This understanding makes it safe for the client to let it out and let it go.

Make sure that your clients understand that pillow work is not about hitting or punching. Hitting and punching are about aggression. This is about *releasing* the energy that's trapped inside. That's what's causing internal pressure and pain.

For Pillow Therapy you need a sturdy pillow - the firmer, the better. Some pillows are stuffed with poly-fill which is too soft. It just smooshes and slimes around. You need something solid and firm to absorb the impact. I have several pillows in the office to choose from, including a futon bolster. The bolster is especially useful for "heavy hitters" because a futon is very dense and can really take a beating. The client can even put it between their knees, if they want to. This secures the pillow when they want to really go to town on it. Generally, the bigger your pillow is, the better. Give the client a nice big target area to hit. This ensures that they won't hurt themselves, making it safe for the client to really let loose.

Plastic Bat

You'll get clients with arthritis or shoulder issues. They'll have problems with pillow-releasing because they can't get those big movements that really help to move things out. Physically, they're too stiff or, because they're afraid they're going to hurt themselves, they hold back. The solution is to give them the bat.

Tucked in next to the pillow I keep a plastic baseball bat. It's very light weight. A Nerf bat works, too. The bat is very handy for clients who have neck and shoulder issues because it gives them some leverage. It also makes a very satisfying "whack" sound when it meets the pillow. I did this with an arthritic 80-something client who had some anger coming up. She wasn't comfortable hitting the pillow, so I gave her the bat. I then encouraged her to go to town on the pillow by giving her permission to get all that stuff out so she wouldn't have to carry it around inside anymore. The bat gave her a safe way to do that. Once she let herself go, she just *loved* it.

Tennis Ball

From time to time, you're going to get a client who has long fingernails. If you ask them to make a fist, their nails are going to dig into the palms of their hands, and they'll bleed all over your pillow. I learned this the hard way. When a person is focused on the emotions they're feeling, they're in *deep* hypnosis. This produces analgesia. As a result, they won't notice that their nails are slicing into the palm of their hand.

The solution is to keep a racquetball or tennis ball in your office. Then, when it's time to do releasing work with a client who has six-inch claws, it's no problem. Just pull out your tennis ball, place it into the palm of her hand, tell her to make a fist around it, then place her fist into the pillow, pump her hand up and down a couple of times, while giving the suggestion to "get it out." Not only will this protect her hands when she starts releasing the energy into the pillow, it will save you having to launder the pillow.

Large Bowl

Having a large bowl close at hand is about being prepared for any eventuality. From time to time, you'll get a client who starts releasing some pretty nasty stuff. Some clients will say that they feel like they are going to vomit. I've never actually had someone vomit, but some have needed to spit up. Recognize that this is the body trying to get it out. That's good.

If the client starts to gag, gently place the bowl in their lap and encourage them to get it all out! They'll be surprised at how quickly they feel better, simply by allowing that feeling to be expressed.

Essential Tools Checklist

1. Is the space large enough to be comfortable?
2. Are your credentials displayed discreetly?
3. Do you have a large, sturdy, comfortable client chair?
4. Do you and the client have water?
5. Have you provided tissues?
6. Is there a wastepaper basket within reach of the client chair?
7. What kind of operator chair works best for your style of therapy?
8. What kind of workstation will accommodate your working papers?
9. How will you manage your scripts and protocols during a session?
10. What kind of task lighting do you need in a session?

11. Do you have a large clock that clients can see without their glasses?
12. Do you have several blankets that are easy to launder?
13. Are you set up for emotional release work?
14. Do you have a large, firm pillow?
15. Do you have a lightweight bat?
16. Do you have a racquetball or tennis ball for clients with long nails?
17. Do you have a bowl – just in case?

Skype or Zoom Sessions

Some hypnosis practitioners facilitate sessions online via Skype or Zoom. This is fine if all you're offering are direct suggestion sessions, but I would not recommend it for regression hypnotherapy sessions if you're just starting out. Get your feet wet working with actual clients before you go virtual. You first need to develop your observation skills in sessions, and it is very difficult to see subtle changes when you're viewing the client through a monitor (even the 30" screen I use.) Plus, there are always technical issues to deal with. For example, dropping the signal, screen pixelated, screen freezing, etc.

When you're just starting out, you don't need more problems to deal with. You need to keep the focus on the client. Go easy on yourself by working with flesh and blood clients, first. Then, when you feel confident guiding the process, you can add to your revenue-stream by offering virtual hypnotherapy sessions. The greater your skill, the higher your success rate will be. And the higher your success rate, the more referral business you will attract[6].

When you're facilitating Skype or Zoom sessions, your client needs to prepare the space prior to the call. Be sure to provide them with

---

[6] To learn simple, proven strategies you can use to promote your hypnotherapy services, get Ditch the Pitch: *Digital Free Client Attraction Guide for Hypnotists*

instructions on how to set up for their distance session with you and provide a checklist of things they need to take care of ahead of time. For example, they will need to take steps to make sure they won't be disturbed during the session by phones, kids, pets.

It's best to test the connection prior to the session. Check the audio. Headphones with a microphone can help to eliminate echo while providing better quality sound. This will make it easier for you and the client to hear each other. Check to ensure the lighting is sufficient to allow you to observe changes in the client's facial expressions, emotions, breathing, etc.

Remind the client to be prepared for their session with water, a light blanket, a firm pillow, and a sturdy chair to sit in. Then, when it comes time for their appointment, before beginning the session, check the audio/video quality, again.

Skype or Zoom Session Checklist

1. Do you have pens and paper ready for note taking?
2. Has the client completed all the necessary forms?
3. Is audio and video working on both ends?
4. Can you clearly hear and see the client?
5. Is the client in a safe and comfortable position where they will not be disturbed during the session?
6. Does the client have a blanket, pillow, and drinking water ready?
7. Did the client go to the bathroom?

CHAPTER 2:
Set for Success

Regression therapy can seem really complicated sometimes. This is because there are so many processes involved, and far too many things to pay attention to in a regression session. Plus, no two clients are ever alike. Fortunately, the only thing you *ever* need to focus on is set up. What's the next logical step for the client? Identify the next step and all you need to do is set up for it to happen. This simple method can put you in the driver's seat for your sessions!

I call my first session a "S.E.T for Success" Session. S.E.T. stands for Satisfy, Educate, and Train. Those are my three objectives for the first session. First, I want to *Satisfy* the client's expectation to be hypnotized. Second, I want to *Educate* the client about how the mind works, how hypnosis works, and how we will work together to get the results the client wants. Third, I want to *Teach* the client how to be successful working with me while in a state of hypnosis. This will allow me to evaluate the client's readiness to proceed with regression therapy.

If you're a well-established hypnosis practitioner, you may not need to do this because, when you're an experienced therapist, you have several things working for you. First, you have prestige. You've built your reputation for results. Second, you're recognized as an expert. You're seen as an authority. Third, your confidence level is high. You have plenty of experience to fall back on and you know what to expect in a session. This allows you to pretty much do things your way. Clients are more likely to follow your instructions when you have prestige, authority, and confidence. But when you're just starting out you don't have these things working for you.

When you're just starting out, you're more likely to be struggling with your confidence. You're still working on increasing your skill level and building your reputation. You question your own credibility because you don't have years of experience to back you up. If this sounds like where you're at, you'll appreciate being able to ease into things while you build your confidence and skill.

The Ready for Regression First Session approach gives you the time you need to observe and strategize. This makes everything that follows much easier because, by preparing the client to take the next step, you have effectively prepared yourself. You'll know what you're dealing with before you dive into potentially shark-infested water by allowing you to assess how cooperative the client is going to be.

Success is always in your set up. Before you ask the client to take the next step, make sure the client is ready to take that step. Then set up for it. This is what your first session should give you. All you ever need to know is - what's the next step? Once you know what the next step needs to be, all you need to do is set up for it. This is true at every phase of the healing process.

What does the client need to know or do to allow the next step to happen? For example, how much resistance is there? How much internal pressure is there? Does the client question everything, or are they willing to follow your instructions without thought? The answers to these questions will tell you what the next step needs to be for *that client*.

Some clients will be ready to dive right into their feelings. They'll be on-board and gun-ho to get to the root cause of their presenting issues. The next logical step for these clients is regression hypnotherapy. But other clients will need more preparation to be ready for the regression work. Some will need to be educated further about the process. Some will require ego-strengthening before they're ready to face painful events from the past. But you won't know any of this until you have conducted a preliminary assessment. This is the purpose of the Ready for Regression First session.

Two-Part Protocol

The Ready for Regression First session is broken down into two distinct phases which are designed to work back-to-back in the first session. However, some clients are going to need more time during the intake process. That's okay. There's no need to feel pressured to get it all done in a single session. That's never helpful. Having a two-part protocol means that each phase can be facilitated as a stand-alone session. This gives you time control in the first session, putting you back in the driver's seat of your sessions.

The Conditioning phase is designed to set up for future sessions by teaching the client how to enter a state of hypnosis, provide proof to the client that hypnosis is happening, then install a trigger for a rapid induction. This will give you a push-button client. In subsequent sessions, being able to get the client into hypnosis quickly and easily will free you up to focus on the client's issue. That's what they're paying you for!

Even if the client has experienced hypnosis with someone else before, this is their first experience with *you*. The objective is to make their first session with you a positive and memorable experience. You can do this very easily by simply showing the client the power of their own mind.

Knock their socks off and they'll be excited about continuing to work with you. They'll also be much more willing to "go where you need them to go" and "do what you need them to do" when you ask them. This is where the second phase comes into play. **The Ready for Regression Phase** is designed to provide a safe experience of regressing into past events. This allows you to assess the needs of each client before diving into their "stuff". Not only will you have a better idea of how best to proceed, but you can also train your client in readiness to face uncomfortable memories and emotions from the past. You can then effectively create a program that is best suited to the client.

Three Ps

I have a simple routine I follow for every session. When the client arrives for their session, I extend my hand. I want to shake the client's hand because it's a stress test. This isn't as telling in winter, but if it's mid-summer and the client's hands are cold, you'll know that their body is in a stress response.

After welcoming the client, I put the do-not-disturb sign on the door and lead the client into the session room. On the way to the session room, I point out where the bathroom is located so they'll know where it is when they need it. (I don't require the client to go to the bathroom before we begin. I have a more strategic use for a bathroom break which I call the Potty Break Protocol.)

Once we're in the session room, I invite the client to take a seat in the "big chair." Once they're settled, I'll point out the glass of water waiting for them on the side table. Then, I'll say, "Before we begin let's take care of business first."

You can easily create the *perception* of separation between the business side and the healing side of your practice by taking care of the Three Ps before you begin focusing on the client's problem.

P1: Privacy

Take care of privacy, first. Remember, hypnosis requires the client's focused attention. But the healing process does not begin with the hypnosis. It begins as soon as you start discussing the client's problem with them. Before you do that, make sure you're not going to be disturbed by reminding the client to put their phone on airplane mode. Clients will forget their phone is on. It's a daily part of their life. It's always in their handbag or in their pocket. They don't think about it. But even if it's set to vibrate, they're going to hear it. They're attuned to it. If it goes off, it's going to be a distraction. Taking care of privacy will ensure the client's focus is where it needs to be.

P2: Payment

Get the money out of the way before you start exploring the client's issue. A lot can happen during a session. It's too easy to get sidetracked and forget to collect payment. Clients are often groggy following a session. They're still processing. The last thing they should be thinking about is paying bills. Following a hypnosis session, when the client opens their eyes, they're not fully emerged yet. This is a valuable part of a session during which suggestions to reinforce success can be delivered while the client comes back to Planet Earth.

Asking for payment interrupts the process. Once you begin the healing process you want to keep the client focused on *that*. People tend to remember whatever happened *last* in the session. Keep the client's attention on what just happened in the session. What just happened? Something amazing. And something wonderful is *about* to occur as a result. That's why they're seeing you, right?

That's where you want the client's focus to be. If you suddenly shift their attention away from the reason that they're seeing you onto *you* getting paid, you're no longer someone who is helping them to create positive change. You're no longer a healer. You've changed hats. Now you're a businessperson. Obviously, if you're in business for yourself, you need to take care of the business. But this isn't the time to ask for payment. It's simply not the best note to end your session on. Instead, take care of the business *first* by collecting payment before you begin the session. That way you won't risk interrupting the healing relationship you worked so hard to develop.

The best way to handle payment is to set it up before the client arrives for their first session. You can do that while you're scheduling the first session. Just tell the client what to expect in the first session. Let them know that payment is expected *before* the session begins. If possible, get them to pay for the session ahead of time. That's one less thing you'll have to take care of before beginning the healing work.

P3: Paperwork

Before you begin the hypnosis session you need to take care of any preliminary paperwork. For example, if you need a doctor's referral, collect that for your files first. You should also have the client sign a release form before you begin the hypnosis.

When I schedule a client in for their first session, I send them a letter to confirm their appointment. Included with this letter is a Contact Form with instructions for the client to fill it out beforehand and bring it with them to their first session.

The reason I am sending this out in advance is because having the client complete it ahead of time will save time in the first session. It also gets them thinking about their session before they arrive. This can stir up subconscious material so that, by the time they arrive, it's right on the surface. If you send this out for the client to complete before they arrive for their session, all you need to do is collect it when they arrive for their session.

Session Confirmation Checklist

- What is the date and time of their appointment?
- How do they get to your office?
- What is your phone and email contact information?
- How long does the first session take?
- What is the purpose of the first session?
- Do you provide a waiting room?
- Do you have a client bill of rights?
- What are your qualifications?
- What is your fee structure? Taxes? Package rates?
- What is your cancellation policy?
- What payment methods do you accept?
- When is the payment due?
- Have you included a Client Contact Form?
- Have you included a release statement?
- How can the client prepare for their first session?

Dear (Client),

This will confirm your first appointment at [time, day, date].

Your first hypnosis session will take (X) hours. During this time, we will discuss your goals and how we can work together to help you successfully achieve them. I'll ask you to tell me briefly about yourself and your personal history. I will then teach you what you need to know to be successful with hypnosis in the healing process. This informational session is extremely important as it will lay the foundation for your success as we work together.

How long will it take? Everyone is an individual. To ensure positive, permanent change it is necessary to address the many aspects of the problem. Some issues can be cleared up in as few as two sessions, while deeper issues may take much longer. For most issues 4 - 6 sessions are usual. After your first session you may wish to take advantage of one of the session packages offered in the fee schedule (see attached).

The length of sessions can vary. Sometimes continuing a session for another 10 or 15 minutes can save a great deal of time in the long run for the client. In some cases, stopping the session at a particular time may be inappropriate because the issue being dealt with is emotional, and the client needs some time to debrief before leaving. As a result, sometimes I will run a little late. Please excuse me if I do.

Please **print out the included forms** and bring them with you to your first appointment. Filling them out in advance will free up time so we can accomplish more during your first session. I have also included an informative article to help you get the most out of your first hypnosis session. I look forward to seeing you soon!

Yours truly,
[Your Name]
Certified Hypnotherapist

Client Contact Form

This form is to be completed prior to the initial session:

Date: _____

NOTE: *All information will be kept strictly confidential except that which we are legally obliged to report, such as threat of injury to self or others. If you are in any way uncomfortable with any of these questions, feel free to skip them. Please be aware that the more you tell me about yourself, the more I may be of assistance to you. It is an honor to assist you.*

Name: _____

Date of Birth (MM/DD/YY): _____

Address: _____

Postal Code: _____

Email(s): _____

Day Phone _____ Eve Phone _____

Mobile/Cell: _____

How may I contact you? Home ____ Cell ____ Email ____

Personal Status: Married _____ Single _____ Divorced _____

Names and Ages of Children:

Name of Spouse/Partner: _____

Current occupation: _____

Do you enjoy your work?   Yes __ No __

Who referred you? _____

Have you ever had a hypnosis session? Yes _____ No _____

Was it a positive experience? Yes _____ No _____

Reasons you are coming for hypnosis:

How long has this been a problem? _____

When did it start? _____

Any previous efforts to solve the problem? Yes ____ No _____

If yes, what were the results?

Do you have a spiritual path or practice that can assist you in transforming your issue? Yes _____ No _____

MEDICAL:

Have you had any prolonged illness? Yes _____ No _____

If yes, when?

Do you have any current health problems?

Yes _____ (please list) No _____

Are you being treated by a physician/psychologist/psychiatrist?

Yes _____ No _____ If yes, for what?

Doctor's name & Clinic:

List any medications you are currently taking:

Anything else you would like me to know?

RELEASE STATEMENT:

I have received and read this Client Bill of Rights and understand what I have read. I hereby authorize (Hypnotherapist) to hypnotize me for the purposes outlined in this intake form and for future purposes that I may request. I understand that the success of my hypnosis therapy depends greatly on my desire to create change in myself and my willingness to follow instructions. I understand that (Hypnotherapist) is neither diagnosing nor treating specific health issues or challenges and, because the results of my sessions depend greatly upon my own serious participation, that (Hypnotherapist) cannot offer any guarantee of the success of my treatment. I am aware however, that (Hypnotherapist) will do everything reasonably in (his or her) power to ensure my success.

_____   _____
Signature   Date

The Contact Form provides me with their address, phone number, email. It asks for a brief statement of why they're coming to see me and provides a place for them to list any medications they might be taking. That way, if they need to look at the prescription label, they can do that while they're still at home. The Contact Form also includes a release form for the client to read and sign before they come in.

Once you have taken care of the 3 Ps of privacy, payment and paperwork, you can turn your full attention to the client's problem. To do that, just say, "Now that we've got the *business* out of the way, let's talk about *you*." And you're ready to begin the intake process. This marks the beginning of the client's healing journey.

The Intake

The intake is where you take a history of the client's problem and identify the key information you need to guide the client through the healing process. Don't start educating the client about the process. It's too soon for that. When a person has been struggling with a problem for too long, they have a powerful need to be heard. This is especially true if they have been through the medical mill.

Let the client talk in the first session. Realize they need you to hear their story. You know it's not the whole story. But both the subconscious mind and conscious mind need safety. You can *satisfy* both these needs simply by listening. If you don't take the time to listen, the conscious mind is just going to try to run the show. You don't want that.

Once you have satisfied this important human need to be heard, your client will be much more willing to let their subconscious mind reveal the rest of the story. That's what your intake process is setting up for.

(If you want to learn how to facilitate a strategic intake process, get **Ditch the Script**: *Get Everything You Need from the Client for Successful Hypnotherapy and Set Up to Wrap Up with Results* which includes 10 Strategic Intake Questions, Intake Assessments, Symptom Resolution Keys, and a whole lot more).

Intake Questions

1. How does the client describe the problem?
2. How long has this been a problem?
3. Attempts to resolve – past or present?
4. Areas of life being impacted by the problem?
5. Spiritual practice/belief?
6. Childhood Family System?
7. Significant other (including any ex's)?
8. Medications? Recreational?
9. What do they hope to accomplish by working with you?
10. Anything else?

Sleep

During your preliminary intake, be sure to ask how your client is sleeping. According to sleep-expert, Dr. Rubin Naiman, there are over 60 million insomniacs out there. That's 60 million people who have trouble getting to sleep or staying asleep.

Sleep deprivation is a BIG problem. It impairs memory, concentration, and attention span. It drains your energy. And it worsens any underlying health problem. Research shows that persistent depression, anxiety, and PTSD may be signs of an underlying sleep disorder.

Poor *quality* sleep is the biggest issue for most people. If you have a client who does not sleep well night after night, does not wake up feeling refreshed and rested, and lacks the energy they need to get through the day, they're not getting enough sleep. If you can fix the sleep quality problems, they'll start to get the sleep they need naturally.

Sleep problems can be caused by breathing issues like sleep apnea or by unresolved emotional issues. It's best to rule out any physical causes first. But the most common culprit is a busy mind. It's an inability to turn the mind off. Instead of slowing down and nodding off at the end of the day, the client's mind keeps yammering on. They worry, fret, plan, or ruminate over events of the day. This mind chatter is often chaotic. And lack of emotional closure at the end of the day keeps the mind spinning.

Many troubled sleepers are either out of touch with their emotions or they don't know how to manage their emotions during the day. The most common emotion they wrestle with at bedtime is anxiety. According to Dr. Naiman, what wakes us up is not what keeps us awake. Going to war is the problem. When sleep doesn't come some self-sabotaging behaviors can develop. Things like obsessing over the time: clock watching, time monitoring, and counting the number of hours they've slept.

Time is the territory of the conscious mind so guess where they're hanging out? In their *thinking* mind which is keeping them awake! This can lead to frustration, or anger, or fear over the problem of sleep. Some people become obsessed with physical sensations of tension, or feeling antsy, or too hot or too cold. All or which just compounds the problem by keeping the mind spinning.

Many of your clients are going to have sleep issues and not even realize it. Sleep affects energy, cognition, and emotional state. And sleep deprivation contributes to every problem we deal with. It can contribute to or even *cause* weight problems, and it inhibits the body's ability to heal. It makes pain worse. It's the leading cause of pain due to accidents – both on the highways and in the workplace.

Sleep Medicine expert, Dr. Barry Krakow, says that the clients who come to you for help with insomnia need to understand what the overriding problem is. Their brain is moving too fast to sleep. And the reason it's so busy is because they don't *want* to go to sleep. They're not *ready* to go to sleep because their day is not done yet. They're preventing sleep from happening.

Now, you can't make a person sleep any more than you can make them relax. But there is much the client can do for themselves to put themselves back in charge of their sleep routine. A good place to start is to stop the war. Stop trying to get to sleep. Instead, get up and do something to finish the day, preferably something pleasurable.

The first step is to get out of bed. They have learned to associate *not* sleeping with the bed. Bed is for sleeping. Not mental activities like thinking and worrying and planning. Forget about trying to sleep. Try means fail. If the mind is still active, get up and do something enjoyable. For example, read a book, watch a funny movie, play solitaire, write in a journal, work on a jigsaw puzzle. Then, as soon as they start to feel sleepy – go to bed.

This is important. They are *not* to fall asleep on the sofa, or in the chair, or anywhere except the bed. These simple strategies can yield significant improvement after a week. But the client must be willing.

According to Dr. Krakow, sleep issues often have unresolved emotions at their root. If behavioral changes fail to resolve the issue, the next logical step would be to identify the underlying emotions. It's just like dealing with a weight loss problem. But even the smallest improvement can be used as proof that change is possible. As you take care of the underlying emotions trapped inside, the client will get a new lease on life.

During your preliminary intake process ask your client about their sleep. Assess both the quality and the quantity of sleep. Do they sleep well every night? Do they wake feeling refreshed and rested? What's their energy like throughout the day? This will provide the information you need to educate the client about the value of sleep. At the end of each session, you can then incorporate suggestions for sleep while you're emerging them. For example, suggestions for deep and restful sleep, waking feeling refreshed and rejuvenated, and having plenty of energy throughout the day.

The Educational Pretalk

What follows the intake process is the educational pretalk. Your intake provides the information you need to personalize your pretalk. The purpose of your pretalk is to remove fears and misconceptions. This allows the client to make an informed decision to let you guide the healing process. The goal is to establish a therapeutic contract for both hypnosis and regression hypnotherapy. (If you want to learn how to educate your clients for regression hypnotherapy, **Radical Healing**: *Hypnosis Practitioner's Guide to Harnessing the Healing Power of the Educational Pre-Talk* will show you how to use your pre-talk to get rid of resistance and make your client a partner in the healing processes of regression hypnotherapy).

The Potty Break Protocol

The purpose of the Ready for Regression First Session is to create your ideal client for regression hypnotherapy by making it safe for the client to "go there." If you want the client to regress easily, you need to get rid of the unknowns. This is where the Potty Break Protocol comes in. Before you begin guiding the client into hypnosis, take advantage of the natural break that occurs between the educational pretalk and beginning the induction.

The perfect time to take a little break is right after you have established the Therapeutic Contract, and right before you begin the hypnotic induction. This is because, in the first session, you're going to be asking the client to relax into hypnosis. To do that, they need to be comfortable. But when the body relaxes the *bladder* relaxes. That can get uncomfortable, making it a distraction. We want to do away with any potential distractions.

There's a more strategic purpose for taking a potty break here. The intake process and the pre-talk are conversational, making it seem more like a counseling session. You need to do away with that perception because, in a moment, you're going to be asking the client to set aside thinking and pay attention to feelings and emotions. Feelings and emotions are how the subconscious mind communicates. If the client is busy thinking, analyzing, and trying to figure things out, it will prevent them from entering hypnosis.

A lot has happened in the session, already. The client has opened up to you and shared personal information about themselves and their issue. They've been remembering situations and people from the past. They've probably bumped into a few uncomfortable emotions in the process. They've also been learning about how the mind works, and how they are to work with you to achieve their therapeutic goal. Realize that's a lot to take in! The client is still processing this information. A strategically placed potty break will give the client a few minutes to prepare - mentally *and* physically - before you begin guiding them into the subconscious level of mind. It also gives you a few minutes to set up for the next part of the session.

While the client is out of the room you can get organized. You can sort out your paperwork, turn down the lights a little to change the mood, turn on some music, if that's something you use, and get out a blanket for the client. If you want to pull out a script or a protocol, the best time to do that is while the client is out of the room. That way they won't know you're using a script in the session.

You don't really need a script because the best suggestions will always come from the client. This is the purpose of your Session Worksheet (more on this in a minute) but sometimes having a script can be useful. Sometimes you just know that you have the perfect script that's ideal for a particular client. If so, while they're out of the room you can pull out your script and you'll be good to go.

Client File System

When you're facilitating multiple hypnotherapy sessions you need a system for managing your client files that keeps you organized while keeping your clients' information confidential. I have a very simple system that is easy and inexpensive. It organizes all your session working papers. It also keeps the client's information secure to protect their privacy.

Instead of using a paper folder, I use a clear-front Duo Tang folder. A Duo Tang folder has three embedded metal prongs that bend through holes in the paper to keep it in place. This keeps all your confidential paperwork securely in place. If you happen to drop a file everything inside it stays intact. The folder is 8 ½ X 11. This fits nicely into a letter-size filing cabinet which is less costly than a legal-sized filing cabinet. As a result, this can help to keep your costs down.

The clear plastic front cover means that you can put your client Contact Form in the front allowing you to see the client's name and contact information, without having to open the folder. Nice, right?

I use a five-compartment file organizer to store current client files. I see clients Tuesday to Saturday, so the top shelf is for Tuesday clients, the next shelf is Wednesday clients, and so on. This allows me to organize a whole week of scheduled clients ahead of time. When I wrap up the first client on Tuesday, their file moves to the bottom of the pile on the Tuesday shelf. This brings the next client's file to the top. By the end of the day the first client's file is back on top and we're ready for next week. If I have a *new* client coming in, I create a folder for them in advance and file it on the day they're scheduled to come in.

The beauty of this client file system is that it's simple. It only takes a few minutes to assemble a file. Put together a dozen or more files ahead of time and you'll be ready to take on a dozen new clients. Having a paperwork system prepared ahead of time can reduce a lot of stress when you're busy. You can always let a stack of new client files act as an incentive to go out and get new clients!

Everything in your client file is organized in chronological order from front to back. Your Client Contact Form goes right in front. Your intake form comes next. After that, your session notes are stored in order by date.

Session Notes

For session notes all you need is a package of three-hole-punched school paper. You can stock up for a whole year at Walmart for pennies when the back-to-school sales are on.

Session Forms

I have a few forms that I use in every session. These stay loose in the back of the file. I just clip them to the inside back cover with a paper clip and everything is organized into one neat, orderly file system. For example, the Session Summary Sheet helps you to keep track of the client's appointments, record what techniques/processes you used with them, make notes of the highlights of the session and where you left off, record comments about what to address in the next session, and confirm that they paid.

Session Summary

Name: _____

Handouts: _____

Techniques: _____

Date	#	Session Highlights/ Notes for Next Session	Paid

When the client comes back from the bathroom tell them, "Okay, I have everything I need. Now that we've got all the talking out of the way, here's what's going to happen, from now on …." Then, tell them what the next session will look like. What's going to happen in the next session? First, you're going to ask them to do a little check-in to see how things went. Normally, this only takes a few minutes. (There's no need for chit-chat.) Then you'll go straight to work with the hypnosis.

Sending the client out for a short potty break before you begin the induction virtually creates a new session. This sets you up for future sessions because, when the client comes back from the bathroom, it will be *as if* you were beginning a fresh new hypnosis session - which you are. From now on this is precisely how ever sessions will go. This is when you fill out your Session Worksheet.

Session Worksheet

Your Session Worksheet holds onto the three critical pieces of information that you need to reference when you're doing the regression work. You will be referring to this information in every session. At the end of each session, you can then use your Session Worksheet to create targeted suggestions that are relevant to the client's healing. These are the suggestions that have an impact on the client.

The three important pieces of information are What, How, and Why? This is the key information you need to guide the healing process. You can use it to create suggestions at the end of each session.

Therapeutic Goal

When the client comes back from their potty break, ask them to tell you, in their own words, what their goal is. The client's Therapeutic Goal tells you *what* they want to accomplish. *What* does the client want to accomplish by doing this work with you? This is the client's therapeutic goal. You're about to begin a journey together. What's the destination? Where does the client want to achieve? What does the result look like? For example, "We've talked about a lot of things.... What I'd like you to do now is . . . in a nutshell . . . tell me what you wish to accomplish through us doing this work together?"

Remind the client about their reason for seeing you. Ask, then listen. You want a statement in the client's own words. Remember - whatever words the client uses have power. Write it down exactly as they say it. This Statement gives you your **Therapeutic Goal**. For bonus points, read the goal statement back to the client and ask them to rate how it feels. For example, "On a scale of one to ten, where ten is *absolute conviction*, how true does this statement feel?"

Conditions for Change

The Conditions for Change list gives you a list of changes that the client recognizes will contribute to them achieving that goal. You can use this information to plot a course toward their destination. *How* are they going to get there? How will they achieve their objective? What actions or behaviors are going to contribute to creating this change? For example, if you are working on a behavioral issue such as weight loss the client already knows what they *should* be doing. They just haven't been able to do it. That's why they need your help. You can make it easier for them to take appropriate action. But you can't do it for them.

There are things the client needs to either stop doing or start doing that will contribute to their success. What are they? You don't have to figure anything out. The client usually knows what needs to change for them to achieve their goal. Ask, "What would *need* to be true for that (therapeutic goal) to happen?" For example, if they want to lose weight, they know that they need to change their dietary habits. They usually know where they have a problem. (Sugar is a common issue for many people.)

The purpose of defining the Conditions for Change is to make the *client* responsible for making these changes. Ask your client to give you a list of specific actions or behaviors that *they believe* are necessary to realize their goal. What needs to change? What do they need to be doing? Let the client tell *you* because this gives you a list of strategies that the client is already invested in. Their belief in these strategies gives them power.

The Conditions for Change list can also give you a way to test the client's expectations. Are they expecting you to wave your magic wand and *make* them change? Hypnosis isn't magic. Conditions for Change need to be realistic. If the client says that what needs to happen is for them to be able to eat two large pizzas and a gallon of ice cream at every meal, there's a problem. You can't override the laws of Nature.

Another unrealistic expectation to watch for is the requirement that someone *else* change before the client can be happy. This is a subtle block that can prevent them from being successful. Clearly, this is something you would need to address before starting to work on their issue. For example, I had a weight loss client who was married to an alcoholic. She was adamant that she would *not* lose weight until her husband stopped drinking. That's a problem because it's an unrealistic expectation.

It's also a grievance. If the client's ability to have what they want is dependent on *someone else changing*, guess who has all the power? That "Someone" needs to be forgiven before the client can take charge of their life. This is someone to make note of because the client is holding this person responsible for the problem. My client basically believed that she was fat because her husband was an alcoholic. She was stuck in victim mode. To let go of the problem the client needed to take back her power.

To do that, she needed to let go of the grievance and let hubby be however he chose to be. So, I told her, "*He* isn't in the chair. If *he* needs to change, he'll have to book his own appointment. The only person that can change right now is YOU because *you're* the one in the chair." She got it.

Session Worksheet

Therapeutic Goal: _____

Conditions for Change:

    1. _____
    2. _____
    3. _____

Benefits of Change:

    1. _____
    2. _____
    3. _____
    4. _____
    5. _____
    6. _____
    7. _____

Most Important Benefit: _____

Why?

If the client's issue depends on their changing certain behavior, create a list of what new behaviors will contribute to their success. For example, a weight loss client might tell you they need to stop having three helpings at dinner. What action would be most do-able?

Not every issue requires behavioral changes. If they're dealing with a physical or emotional issue, their Conditions for Change list can give you guidelines for creating positive change. You can also use the Conditions for Change list to formulate suggestions for change, establish milestones leading to the client's final achievement, and test your results. For example, my client's Conditions for change involved situations in daily life that generated significant stress.

Because she was constantly getting into fights with her husband, her unresolved anger was driving her to over-eat. She was even picking fights in a futile attempt to get her husband to meet her needs. In this case, the Condition for Change had to do with changing her response to her husband's behavior. This provided both a milestone to achieve and a way of testing the results.

As we released the internal anger and anxiety, she began to feel more calm and in control in her daily life. The need to constantly struggle with her husband to get her needs met started to melt away. As a result, the fighting with hubby stopped. When she stopped demanding that *he* change to make her happy, she started to find other ways to satisfy her own needs. That's when her husband started trying to sabotage her success in an attempt to reinstall the old, familiar pattern.

So long as she was out-of-control and picking fights, her husband was able to dismiss her behaviors as irrational and needy. This observation proved to be useful feedback as it allowed us to identify where the client's triggers were. We then used these feelings to guide the process and get to the underlying issue which, no surprise, had nothing to do with hubby. This turned the tables on her relationship and put the client back in charge of her own life.

Some Conditions for Change will be small, easy changes to make. Others will be more challenging. If you start with something small, you'll find it easier to get a quicker result. This can help to build client motivation by giving the client a taste of success. Sometimes, it's just the boost they need to be ready to tackle more difficult challenges.

Sometimes the best place to begin is to help the client to experience some instant success. This will pave the way for greater successes. Positive results will increase motivation to achieve the larger goal. But if there's a lot of internal pressure, pushing up from inside, it might be better to tackle a larger goal right away. Taking down the bigger issue will have more impact on the client's overall life and will give your client a better bang for their therapeutic buck.

If the client has a BIG goal, you can chunk it down into smaller, easier-to-achieve milestones. Think in terms of increments of change. Positive actions can be lined up as milestones toward the client's ultimate goal. For example, if a person has 100 pounds to lose, that's a longer-term goal. A shorter-term goal of, say, the first 20 pounds, is a milestone that gets the client moving in the right direction. Some weight-loss programs call this a "quick-start". They take advantage of the client's higher motivation at the beginning of a program to get some quick wins.

As one milestone is achieved, you can then celebrate success. Use it to bolster enthusiasm and motivation to continue with the process of creating positive change.

Nothing builds success like success. Successfully achieving one change will give the client permission to allow more change. By establishing increments of change you can make it easier for the client to achieve and hold onto their successes.

Your approach will depend on what's most appropriate for the client. Simple issues often respond well to suggestions alone. Emotional issues, however, require a deeper approach. For example, I had a weight client who ate candy every night. She knew she needed to stop this behavior. She just couldn't do it.

The problem wasn't the behavior. The behavior was a subconscious solution to the real problem which was *driving* the behavior - anxiety. Sugar calms anxiety. You can't just suggest that away. Trying to suggest away an emotion won't get you long-term results. And this client was *not* going to accept a suggestion to just stop eating candy. She had already been through Cognitive Behavioral Therapy (CBT) and counselling. The mere thought of giving up the candy generated *more* anxiety!

Her Condition for Change, which was to stop eating the candy every night, took on a different function. Instead of trying to install a new behavior which the client was highly resistant to accepting we used this behavior change to test the results. This gave us a way to measure her progress. The client knew that when the *real* problem was resolved she'd find it easy to do what, consciously, she *wanted* to do - give up the candy. In other words, when the problem was resolved, the behavior would fall away on its own. And it did. She stopped binging on candy every night. When that happened, we knew the issue was resolved. A year later she was fifty pounds lighter - physically and emotionally.

Remember, the client knows what needs to change. When they are unable to make those changes on their own, instead of trying to *make* them change, you can use their Conditions list to test the results. This will provide the proof the client needs to know that the problem has really and truly been resolved – for good.

Benefits of Change

The client's Therapeutic Goal tells you *what* they want. Their Conditions for Change tell you what needs to happen so they can have it; that's the *how*. The Benefits list tells you the motivating factor. That's what's in it for them. *Why* do they want to create this change? The client's motivating factor is the benefits of change. What benefits does the client hope to enjoy as a result of having made this change?

Human beings are motivated to seek pleasure and avoid pain. The client's list of benefits should define the rewards that they'll enjoy for doing the work necessary to create those changes. Where are those rewards?

The power to create those changes is in their Benefits List. Ask, "How will your life improve once you have realized your goal?" How will the client know they have arrived at their destination? How will they feel when they look in the mirror and realize they have made this change? What will other people think? How will they respond differently in certain situations in life?

Ask the client to give you a list of as many benefits of making this change as they can come up with - at least seven. The more the better. Each benefit is a reminder of *why* the client is taking this journey with you. Why is it worth it to do the work necessary to make this change? This gives you a list of motivating factors.

Watch out for "won't power." Some clients will try to give you a list of all the things they *won't* have to put up with anymore. They'll say, "I won't have to do X anymore." Or "I won't have to deal with Y anymore ..." Or "I won't feel so *bad* all the time." Nuh-uh! Don't let them get away with that. "Won't power" won't get them what they want.

What you're looking for is a list of specific *positive* benefits. These form the basis of positive suggestions you can deliver at the end of a session. It's the *rewards* of change that help to keep the client inspired and moving in the direction of their heart's desire. That's *"will"* power.

When a client gives you a "won't" list, what this tells you is that the client has been stuck for too long. They're in the habit of focusing on what they *don't* have. The problem with this habituated point of view is the compounding effect. It's self-reinforcing. The more they focus on what they don't want, the more they reinforce that reality in their own mind.

The client's listed rewards need to have some juice in them because the rewards of change are emotional. When the client imagines experiencing that benefit, it should give them a little spark of excitement. This is because the rewards of change are not external. They're internal. They should feel hopeful and conjure images of better times to come. These are the pictures and images of who the client becomes because of making those changes. This means they need to be specific.

Watch out for, "I'll be happy." This just isn't specific enough to create change. What does "happy" *look* like? How will they know when they *have* it? Think in terms of health, relationship, sleep, mood, etc.

Ask your client to give you at least seven benefits - more if possible. Then, once you have completed the Benefits List, go back over the list and review it to get a felt sense of each benefit. Invite your client to close their eyes and just listen as you read their Benefits list back to them. As they hear each benefit being read back to them, have them notice how it feels.

Remember, each benefit on their list should have a little "spike" of pleasure to it. If it doesn't, it's not sufficiently motivating. As you read through the list, often what happens is that their subconscious mind will start coming up with other benefits that can be added to the list. The more the merrier!

Once you have reviewed their Benefits list, ask the client to *feel* the answer to this question. "Which of these benefits *feels* most important?" What's their most important benefit? Bonus points for asking, "Why?"

Your Script

Your Session Worksheet becomes your script providing all the information you need to craft suggestions that are specific to the client. These suggestions will pack a punch when you deliver them because they came *from the client*. They're not coming out of some generic script. They're specifically what your client knows and wants.

The client's Therapeutic Goal reminds the client of what they truly want. This is where they're going. When it comes time to do your session wrap up, come back to this and remind the client *why* they're doing this work with you. This will help to keep them committed to the process. How did they realize this change for themselves? Easily.

The Conditions for Change tells you *how* the client is going to get where they're going. This gives you a way to establish milestones of achievement and to test the results.

The Benefits List reminds the client *why* they are taking this journey with you. It provides all the reasons for doing the work necessary to create the change they want. During your session wrap up, remind the client that all the rewards are waiting for them. It's just a matter of time. Ask, "How much better is life for having made those changes? What are some of the *other* rewards you can look forward to enjoying?"

Remember, benefits should have juice in them! Emotion is the motivating factor that will keep the client committed to achieving their goal. How proud do they feel about having made this change?

See what I mean? You won't find this in any generic script. When you use your Session Worksheet to create suggestions, you'll be speaking directly about *the client's* hopes and dreams. You'll be conjuring up pictures of what it looks like to have achieved what they *want* and what it feels like to have succeeded. This stuff is GOLD because you get it from the client. That's where the answers lie.

Key Players

There are people in your client's life who have contributed to the problem they've come to resolve. This will be revealed by the uncovering procedure during the regression work. But many are often revealed during the intake process. While you're conducting the intake process, you can use the back of your Session Worksheet to create a list of key players. You can then use this list to keep track of the forgiveness work as it's processed.

Who does the client talk about? Some of these people may serve as positive resources. Others may be contributing to the client's issue. They're all part of the client's Story. As such, they are relevant to the issue. For example, Mom and Dad. What are their names? Does the client have siblings? What are their names? What about significant others such as a grandparent, ex-spouse, teacher, etc.

Make a note of the person's name, whether that person is alive or dead, and how the client would rate the quality of their relationship with that person. I place a plus or a minus sign next to each name. (-) For example, if the client's relationship with that person was positive, I would put a plus sign next to their name. This person would then represent an internal resource available to the person.

If the relationship is (or was) conflicted in some way, I would put a plus and a minus sign next to their name. (+/-) For example, the client may realize that they love a parent, but for some reason they don't get along. Or it may be that the relationship has changed.

Maybe the relationship was conflicted in childhood but as adults they get along. Make a note! Just because the client is consciously okay with that person, doesn't mean there isn't still a conflict at the subconscious level of mind.

If there is a person who hurt the client in some way, I would put a double negative next to their name. (-/-) For example, clients might tell you that they were abused by a parent or a sibling. Realize they're still carrying the pain of those experiences. The forgiveness work will be especially powerful in freeing the client from the control those relationships have had over them.

Keeping a list of key players gives you an easy-reference sheet with all the information you need to facilitate the healing process. Should the client go back into an event involving one of the people on your list, you don't have to try to remember who they are. With a glance, you'll be able to see who that individual is and whether they have angel or demon status in the client's life.

Other Stuff

The back of the worksheet is a convenient place to keep any other relevant information the client might share. As you move through the healing process you can continue to add information. For example, other players or sources of support might be revealed through the process. Or the client may have *insights* that can be reinforced as internal resources.

When the client experiences positive changes between sessions, make a note of them. You can use them later as evidence of success. Adding the client's realizations and recognitions to the back of your Session Worksheet will allow you to use them as reminders that the client is moving in the right direction. This can help increase motivation while reinforcing all the changes that are occurring. At the end of each session, you can use it to wrap up your session with suggestions that are relevant to each client.

Once you have completed the intake process, established the therapeutic contract, and filled out your Session Worksheet with the key information needed to guide the process, you're ready to guide the client into hypnosis.

Key Players List

	Name	Notes:
Mom	Mary (-)	
Dad	Bill (+)	
Sibling	Ralph (+/-)	
Spouse	Mike (-)	Alcoholic, divorced
Child	Jenny (15), Mark (10)	

Situational Triggers:

Other fears or limiting beliefs:

CHAPTER 3:
Conditioning Phase

The client's first session with you is the most important session because this is where you lay the groundwork for the client's success. Regression hypnotherapy is an interactive process that can take time. You can save yourself gobs of time in subsequent sessions by conditioning the client for a rapid induction in the first session. Having a client who can enter hypnosis quickly will give you more time to work on their problem. That's what they're paying you for, right?

Four Permissions[7]

Before you begin the induction process, there are several permissions you need to establish. You only need to do this in the client's first session, and it only takes a couple of minutes. Once you have established the permissions, they will be implied and automatically carried over into future sessions.

---

[7] Inspired by Marilyn Gordon, Center for Hypnotherapy & The Life Transformation Company.

Safety is the subconscious mind's Prime Directive. You need to make it safe for the client to go where you need them to go. Asking permission provides safety because it implies choice. You're not controlling them. You're asking them if it's okay. This makes it safe to just let things happen.

1. Okay to Touch?

You need the client's permission before you touch them. Safety is Rule #1. This begins with respecting the client's boundaries. Never assume. Ask. Make sure the client is okay with you touching them. Then, tell them *where* you might touch them during a session.

If the client says, "no" - honor their wishes. Find some alternative techniques that don't require physical touch.

If you're prohibited by law from touching your clients, or facilitating sessions online, obviously, you don't need to include this. But many of the techniques we use for therapeutic hypnosis involve the use of physical touch. For example, a kinesthetic deepener such as a shoulder press, rocking the forehead, or a hand-drop requires that you touch the client's shoulder, forehead, or wrist.

2. Okay to Let Things Happen?

Nothing is going to happen without the client's permission. You need to let the client know what to expect during the session. Not knowing simply generates anxiety.

Remove all the unknowns before you begin the induction by letting the client know *what might happen* while they're in hypnosis. Then, obtain their permission to *let those things be a part of the process*. I tell the client, "During the session, I might touch you on the forehead … I might snap my fingers …I might lift and drop your hand … Is that okay?" This is because these are some of the things that will typically happen in a session. We use all of them in the Ready for Regression First Session. For example, we use touch as a deepener. Snapping the fingers is used for testing and deepening during the session. We use a hand-drop.

If you tell the client in advance, they won't have to think about it.

3. Okay to Get What You Need Today?

Tell the client that hypnosis will happen. There's no need to do or try. For example, I say, "Some people *go into hypnosis very deeply*. Some go into a lighter state. Most people are somewhere in the middle. But whatever happens, *you'll get what you need today*. Okay?"

Notice how this sets up the expectation that hypnosis will happen? There's no option for it *not* to happen. The only option is light, medium, or dark roast! If the client is still holding onto a little performance anxiety or questioning whether they can go into hypnosis, this lets them know that there's no wrong way to do it. This removes all the pressure of getting it right.

4. Ready?

You need the client's permission to proceed with the hypnosis. The final permission confirms that the client is ready to begin. Here, the client is giving you their consent to hypnotize them. Let the client know that the session won't take very long. Remind them that, as you guide them to relax the mind and body together, they'll have full awareness and full control, and that no matter what happens they'll get what they need. Then offer the client a blanket.

The best time to offer the client a blanket is when you're ready to begin the induction. A blanket isn't just for warmth. It's a suggestion for comfort and safety. It's maternal. It shows that you care. You can use this in every session to mark the beginning of the hypnosis. When it's time to begin the induction, just pull out the blanket and say, "Let's get started. Ready?"

The four permissions are about establishing compliance. You're eliciting an agreement from the client to cooperate by setting up a yes-frame. Okay?

1. Okay to touch?
2. Okay for these things to happen?
3. Okay to get what you need today?
4. Okay to begin?

Be Convincing

Before you emerge the client from hypnosis, there should be no doubt in your client's mind that they were hypnotized. The client needs to believe that they were hypnotized because the change they want is supposed to happen through the hypnosis. If the client opens their eyes and says, "Yah, I was relaxed but I don't think I was hypnotized", you've got a problem. It's very difficult to convince a person once they've made up their mind. Make sure the client is confident that they have received what they paid for.

There's an old saying ...*A man convinced against his will is of the same opinion still.* If they're not convinced that they were hypnotized, they're going to question the whole process. Now there's doubt. Doubt can sabotage your best work. Even if you did a kick-ass job in the session, doubt has the power to hijack your whole session. As a result, the client won't get the benefit. If you've got a client who is skeptical, or thinks they can't be hypnotized, or has experienced hypnosis before and doesn't believe that they were hypnotized, set up for a Time Distortion test before you begin the induction. This will give you an easy way to prove to a client that they were, indeed, hypnotized.

Once the client gives their permission to proceed, pull out your blanket, and get them settled comfortably in the chair. Set up the expectation that *the session will be short* by casually suggesting that this first session won't take very long; only take a few minutes. Then, create the conditions for the client to realize this for themselves by asking them to make note of the time *because* you'll be asking them about it later.

Instruct the client to look at the clock and tell you what the time is. Then, *write it down*. If they say it out loud, they're more likely to remember it. Writing it down also ensures that *you* won't forget. Remember you will be using this at the end of the session to prove to the client that they were in hypnosis. You can't do that if you don't remember what time you started!

Formalize the Induction

An induction is a ritual. Formalizing the induction means giving it a clear beginning and a clear ending. This will let the client know when the hypnosis is starting and when it's coming to an end. This can then be used to provide the client with proof that the hypnosis happened.

Formalizing the induction also puts you in charge of the session right from the get-go by teaching the client to follow your instructions before you even get them into hypnosis. For example, if your first suggestion is to "close your eyes" don't just tell the client, "Close your eyes and let's begin." That's too wishy-washy. Make it a ritual with clearly defined steps. For example, I have a simple set of instructions that I use to begin every induction. It's always the same five steps[8].

1. Look at my hand.
2. Take a nice deep breath in, really fill up your lungs . . .
3. Hold it, hold it, hold it ….
4. Now as you exhale, relax and close your eyes,
5. And let the body begin to relax.

Five steps and it becomes a very useful procedure. The first four steps are just getting the eyes to close. But what this does is *formalize* the entire process. First, it gets the client to follow your instruction, "Look at my hand."

If the client accepts the first suggestion, they're more likely to accept the next suggestion… And the one after that… Notice how you're establishing compliance right from the start? And you're doing this in a very step-by-step manner.

I've had clients who would close their eyes before I tell them to. Usually, it's because they've experienced hypnosis before. So, they *think* they know what it's all about. Nuh-uh! When that happens, I make them start over. This may seem like a trivial thing. But here's the problem. You haven't even started the induction and already the client is taking over.

---

[8] Inspired by Gerald Kein, Omni-Hypnosis.

They're not following instructions. They're running the session. You need to nip that in the bud. Demonstrate that your approach is different and teach the client how to behave in your sessions.

Now, I always treat it like it's no big deal. I'll say, "Wait! Don't start without me!" Right away, they'll open their eyes. I'll laugh. Then we start the process over again. Why? Because I want to make sure the client follows my instructions right from the start.

Induction Set Up

1. Look at my hand.
2. Take a nice deep breath in, fill up your lungs . . .
3. Hold it, hold it, hold it . . .
4. Now exhale, relax, and close your eyes . . .
5. And let the body begin to relax.

---

1. "Look at my hand."

Every suggestion serves a purpose. The first suggestion tells the client to do something specific. "Look at my hand."

This teaches the client to pay attention to the things you want them to pay attention to. Throughout the process you'll be asking the client to notice things that they don't normally pay attention to – like feelings. You're setting up for that to happen.

2. "Fill up your lungs."

Filling up the lungs has a purpose. It creates a little physical tension in the body. The shoulders will lift a little. The chest will expand a little.

3. **"Hold it."**

Holding the breath a few moments will help make the client more aware of the physical sensations of tension in the body.

4. **"Exhale, relax, close the eyes."**

When the breath is released, a feeling of relief will come over the body immediately because the client has *let go* of some of the tension they were holding onto. As a result, the body will start to relax. This is congruent with the suggestion to *let* the body relax. It's also a non-verbal suggestion that says, "Let it go, you'll feel better." This is a suggestion we're going to reinforce when it comes time to do the emotional release work.

5. **"Let the body relax."**

In a relaxation hypnosis session, the suggestion to "let the body relax" is going to get repeated a lot as part of the deepening process. This can help to release a lot of pent-up stress. The client may not even be aware they're holding onto all that stress and tension. As a result, when they emerge from hypnosis, they'll be feeling much better than when they began. That's what we want.

Make sure that your clients know when the hypnosis begins and when it ends by using a formal count-up to emerge the client. Don't just say, "Whenever you're ready, you can open your eyes." You need to take charge of your session from beginning to end. A formal count-up also gives the client time to emerge more fully. If the client is deeply relaxed, they'll need more time to notice the change as they emerge from hypnosis. A formal count-up can help to ensure that they don't feel groggy or develop a headache when they open their eyes.

If you begin every session with the five-step set up and end each session with a five-step emerging count, your client will experience the sense that their hypnosis session was the full-meal-deal. Remember, there should be no doubt that the hypnosis happened.

Permission to Relax Patter

Just let the body relax because ... many things have happened or are about to occur ... But for the next few moments ... you can allow yourself to become much more comfortable. So just give *your*self *permission* ... to relax.

And perhaps you can find a shelf ... somewhere off to the side, in your mind, where you can just ... set aside those thoughts or concerns. And just rest for a few minutes because there's nobody wanting anything, nobody needing anything ...

And you'll find that ... you can allow yourself to relax deeper with each and every passing breath. Enjoying this time for *you*. Just allowing the sound of *my* voice to guide you to become healthier in *all* ways – physically, mentally, and emotionally.

Utilize Sounds

There are things going on around you that your client may not have noticed during the pre-hypnosis conversation. But once you get them into hypnosis, they'll be more aware of environmental sounds. For example, the sound of traffic outside, the heating system coming on and off, or phone ringing in another room.

The problem is that hypnosis requires focused attention. If you're working in an environment where there's lots of noise, either inside or outside the session room, these things can become distractions. You want the client's full attention to be on you.

You can help the client to pay attention to your suggestions by utilizing those sounds as part of the induction process. For example, after the client closes their eyes, offer the suggestion, ". . . give yourself permission to set aside any worries or concerns, and just allow the sound of *my* voice to guide you." Then instruct the client to take a moment to *familiarize* themselves with the sounds of "this environment".

Remember, this is their first time with you. They don't know what to expect. Familiarizing the client with the sounds around them can provide safety. So, bring them to mind. Then, normalize them by informing the client that these are "just an ordinary part of this environment."

Give the client a moment to notice that those sounds are there, then give the suggestion to let them fade into the background. For example, I had a commercial office right downtown for a while. Across the street there was the ambulance garage. A block up the street there was a fire hall. There was a print shop right next door to my session room and the building backed onto the railway tracks. Every day the train would come rumbling by at 3 o'clock in the afternoon. It was never a problem.

I would just incorporate those things into the session as some of the things that might happen. For example, "During the session you might notice the sound of the train passing by . . . or the sound of a siren . . . or a phone ringing in another room . . . realizing … these are just the ordinary sounds of this environment. So, you can let those things fade into the background … as you go deeper into hypnosis."

An effective way to utilize sounds is to begin with the broadest field of perception. You can then incrementally narrow the client's field of attention down. This will make it easier for the client to enter a state of hypnosis. The idea is to gradually narrow the focus of attention from outer things to inside the body.

Start with sounds *outside* the room or the building. What obvious sounds are arising outside the room? Traffic sounds? Dogs barking? Lawn mowers? Bring the client's attention to them so they can set them aside. Then, let the client know what might happen.

What sounds *might* arise during the session? For example, if you're in an office building, there may be phones ringing, or doors closing, or people talking, in another room. Bring awareness to the things that *might* arise. Then, give the suggestion that those things are not important, they're the ordinary, everyday part of "this environment", so the client can let them fade into the background.

Next, bring the focus of attention *inside* the room. What sounds are in the room right now? For example, if there's music playing, bring the client's attention to that. Then, give a brief pause to allow the client to notice it. I have a clock in the room that ticks. I'll say, "You might notice the sound of the clock ticking …." Then I'll wait. (Tick-tock. Tick-tock.) The clock ticking is quite hypnotic, so I'll add, "And that takes you deeper into hypnosis."

Mention any other sounds the client might become aware of during the session. For example, the sound of paper shuffling. Shuffle some papers so they know what that sounds like. I have a squeaky chair so I'll say, "You might notice the sound of my chair creaking …." Then, I'll move around to make it squeak. I then add, "You might even come to *love* the sound of my squeaky chair." Or "You can use that sound as a reminder that *you're safe with me* here in my office." Whatever fits for you and the client. Finally, bring attention to the client's body resting comfortably in the chair and invite the client to, "relax e-v-e-n more … and notice how good it feels to simply … rest." That's it.

Sounds Utilization Patter[9]

And as you continue to relax … you'll be aware of everything during the session. So just take a moment, right now, to familiarize yourself with the sounds of *this* environment. You might notice sounds coming from outside the building. *(pause)* Or inside the building. *(pause)* Might be the sounds of traffic passing by or *(mention any other predictable sounds)* … The phone might ring in the other room, or *(any other predicable sounds)* … Or sounds inside the room such as the sound of the music playing *(pause)* … or the ticking of the clock *(pause)* … or the shuffling of papers … And as these are just the ordinary, everyday sounds of *this* environment … you can allow those things to just …. fade into the background … and just focus on the sound of my voice. Just let my voice guide you … to relax.

You only need to do this once. In future sessions, all you'll need to do is *remind* the client to take a moment to notice the sounds of the environment. Beginning with the broadest field of perception, noticing any sounds that might be occurring outside the room. Then incrementally narrow the focus of attention from outside … to inside … to the chair … and finally, to inside the body. And you'll have the client right where you need them to be – going deeper.

Remember, you can use anything that arises during a session as a deepener. Even a train rumbling by fifty feet away from the room can be used to take the client deeper. If sounds arise during the session,

---

[9] Inspired by Cal Banyan, Banyan Hypnosis Center

don't ignore them. Instead, invite the client to notice them, then let them fade into the background. Making it normal for those things to be there will make it safe for the client to dismiss them.

Use Physical Relaxation

Hypnosis is not relaxation. But I like to use relaxation in the client's first session for three reasons. First, it's slow. This gives the client time to notice changes as they're happening. This provides a sense of safety, making it safe for the client to follow your instructions. If the client follows your instructions to relax, they're going to start feeling more comfortable and secure.

Second, it's slow. This gives you time to assess and adjust to the needs of the client. As you observe the client's responses to your suggestions, incorporate whatever you're observing into your suggestions. This will help the client to relax more deeply because your suggestions will be congruent with what they're experiencing.

Third, it's empowering. Before emerging the client, bringing their attention to feelings and sensations of deepening relaxation they are experiencing can be used as *evidence* of the power of their own mind. After all, all *you* have done is offer a few suggestions and *they* have relaxed themselves. How cool is that?

Offer the suggestion, "It's by following my instructions that *you* have created these wonderful feelings of ongoing, deepening relaxation." This helps the client to realize that *they* have the power. You're not controlling them. You're simply guiding them to feel better. Then, add the suggestion, "This is an ability you *have*, and you can use it anytime you want or need to feel better." (Teaching them self-hypnosis will allow them to do just that.)

Mind and body work together. As the body relaxes, the mind will relax, and the client will naturally begin to drift into a state of hypnosis. But if you're not sure that the client is following your instructions, you can always test. What you want to know is … are they relaxing *physically*?

To test for physical relaxation, say, "In a moment I'm going to lift this hand a couple of inches." Touch the client lightly on the wrist so they'll know what to expect. Then say, "If you have followed my instructions, this arm and shoulder and wrist should be very relaxed." The suggestion that follows is, "This arm and the wrist should be very relaxed. It should feel loose and limp and very relaxed. And heavy … like wet spaghetti. Or a sopping wet dishrag. Understand?"

Make sure the client understands the instructions. Then, take their wrist and lift the hand a couple of inches above the arm of the chair. You don't have to lift it much, just enough to give it a little wiggle. The wrist and the arm should feel heavy and kind of wobbly.

Most of the time, the arm will be very limp. You can then reinforce the response by saying, "That's good" or "Wonderful …" Then, stack another deepener on top of it. For example, "The deeper you go, the better you feel…"

One of the things you can do, after conducting the test for physical relaxation, that feels really good, is to gently drop the client's hand onto the arm of the chair. Give the suggestion, "As I drop your hand back onto the arm of the chair, double the relaxation. It feels so good."

There's a little shock that accompanies the hand drop that will cause the client to deepen. You may even notice the client grin a little when you do this.

Ready For Regression

A more maternal approach is to place the client's hand on their leg, then gently press down on the back of their hand while delivering another deepening suggestion. This feels very comforting and reassuring.

Some people hold a lot of tension in their shoulders so, after testing the wrist, check their shoulder. If both wrist and shoulder are loose and rubbery you'll know that the client is following instructions.

However, if the client suffers from arthritis of bursitis, they may not be able to relax the shoulder. In this case, just test the other wrist. If both wrists are loose and limp, the client is following instructions to relax. That's what we want. Reinforce that response with a little praise. You know, "That's good!" Or "You're doing great!"

Some clients will try to help. When that happens, you'll feel it. When you lift their wrist, the arm will feel light and floaty. It will drift up on its own. If the client is trying to help, they're not following your instructions. Don't let them get away with that! Take charge and say, "Don't help! Let me do all the lifting."

Remember, you're teaching the client how to respond to your suggestions. This is the key to your success - make sure that the client follows instructions before moving onto the next step. If the client needs to practice this a few times, that's fine. You can always start over.

There's no need for the client to open their eyes. Just repeat the pre-induction instructions.

1. Take a nice deep breath,
2. Fill up the lungs,
3. Hold it . . . hold it . . . hold it . . .

4. And now exhale and *melt down* . . . from the top of the head to the bottoms of the feet, sending a warm wave or relaxation throughout the body.
5. And notice how good that feels.

Remember, holding the breath builds up a little tension in the upper part of the body. When the client releases the breath, it brings a feeling of relief which brings on the relaxation response. If you repeat this several times, it will help to release tension from the body and the client should start to feel more relaxed. If that doesn't work, change your induction.

Release Tension with the Breath[10]

Now, take a nice, deep, relaxing breath in. Really fill up your lungs. And now hold it, hold it, hold it …. (*build the tension*)

And now exhale, relax, and MELT DOWN from the top of your head to the bottom of your feet. That's good.

Take another deep, relaxing breath in. All the way to the top. Hold it, hold it, hold it …. And now exhale and MELT DOWN. Relaxing even deeper.

Third time's the charm. Take a nice, relaxing breath in. Hold it, hold it, hold it. … And now exhale and MELT DOWN, relaxing much more deeply relaxed.

Most people do just fine with a relaxation induction the first time. After all, there's nothing threatening about relaxing. Relaxation feels good. But relaxation hypnosis isn't for everybody. For example, someone who is very analytical, or in their head a lot, may find a slow

---

[10] Source: Raveen, Stage Hypnotist and Illusionist, BC

induction irritating. This is because a slow induction gives them too much time to think. They get frustrated because they're thinking, "It's not working!" Which is true.

If what you're doing isn't working, change it! The best induction for an analytical client is a rapid induction! Get them into hypnosis quickly. *Then* you can offer some suggestions for relaxation, and they'll accept them. Your ideal client isn't thinking or analyzing or trying to anticipate what's going to happen next. They're just following your instructions without thinking. What we want to do is get them out of their head and into their body.

So far, you have taught the client to follow your instructions by formalizing the induction. You have utilized sounds to get rid of distractions by incrementally narrowing the client's awareness from the broadest field of perception down into the body. That's where we need the focus to be.

We haven't even started the induction process, yet. This is just a pre-induction setup where you're teaching the client and observing responses. This will make it easier for you to get the client into hypnosis. It will also give you a better client to work with when it comes time to do the regression work because, to access a Bridge to the past, the client must be willing to follow instructions to feel their feelings. This is what we are setting up for in the first session.

Body Awareness Exercise

Where do we feel our feelings? In the body, right? That's where we want the focus of attention to be because the subconscious mind is the feeling part of the mind. It communicates through emotions and sensations in the body[11]. The Body Awareness Exercise is a way to incrementally guide the client into the body. That's where you need them to be – not in their head.

Begin by bringing the client's awareness back to the breath and have them notice what it feels like to "just breathe". Give them a few moments to notice the feelings and sensations of the breath. Bring their awareness to how the breath comes into the body through the nose.

Then, have them notice what it's like, as the breath comes down into the chest, and how it fills the lungs, and what it feels like in the chest, and the stomach, and the diaphragm. And how deeply the breath comes into the body. Just noticing what that's like. Then, have them notice any feelings or sensations in the body as the breath goes in … and out.

Use a lulling tone as you say these words and watch the client's breath so that you can pace their breathing as you give the suggestion, "In and out … in and out." It's a great deepening technique.

When a person is holding onto stress or tension their breathing gets shallow. Deepening the breath will help the client to let go of some of that tension so they can relax more deeply. You can then invite the client to bring their awareness more fully into the body and have them notice how the body feels from the inside.

---

[11] Candace Pert, author of Molecules of Emotion, gave a talk called, 'Your Body is Your Subconscious Mind.' Highly recommended!

Ask the client to do a little scan and notice how it feels – in the throat, the chest, the stomach - any comfort or discomfort there. Then ask, "What did you notice?"

Body Awareness Exercise[12]

That's good. Now, just bring your awareness to your breathing. And just notice what it feels like ... to just breathe. Realizing, there's no need to do or try because ... your body knows how to breathe. It's been doing *that* since the day you were born. So just relax and *let* the body breathe. And just notice what that feels like.

Notice the feeling of sensation of the air coming in through the nostrils. (*pause*) You might notice how the air seems to come in more through one nostril than the other ... That's fine. That's normal. Notice the sensations in your body ... as the air comes down into the chest. (pause)

How it fills the lungs ... the chest ... the stomach ... the diaphragm. Just noticing any sensations there as the breath goes in and out ... in and out ... in and out. (*pace the breath*)

And as you continue to breathe ... naturally ... much more comfortable now... See if you can bring your awareness *more fully* into the body. And just notice how the body feels from the *inside*.

Just do a little scan and notice how the body feels on the *inside* ... in the throat, in the chest, in the stomach. Any comfort or discomfort there or anywhere else. And tell me what do you notice?

The reason for asking this is because hypnotherapy is an interactive process. We're getting the client participating a little by giving you feedback. That's a part of the healing process. But there's also another

---

[12] Inspired by Randy Shaw, Results Beyond Expectation, Utah

reason for doing this. These are the primary areas where emotions express in the body. We feel our emotions in the torso – primarily in the throat, the chest, and the gut. When it comes time to do the regression work, you're going to need a strong emotion to access a bridge to the past. You're setting up for that now by teaching the client what to pay attention to in the body.

Body Awareness Deepener[13]

Bring the client's attention to their feet and have them notice the feeling of any sensation in their feet. Notice any comfort or discomfort there. Any warmth or coolness. Anything that might be touching the feet. Then give the suggestion that the awareness of those feelings and sensations takes them deeper.

Next, bring their attention to the feeling of their pants touching their legs.

Then, bring awareness to their sleeves touching their arms.

Finally, bring awareness to their back pressing into the chair.

Anchor safety to the feelings and sensations of the back pressing into the chair. This creates a "safe place" without the need for guided imagery.

Most of the time, the client will say that they feel relaxed, or comfortable, or "really good." Affirm this by saying, "That's good." If they notice some discomfort there, that's okay, too. You want the client to be willing to allow uncomfortable feelings to come to awareness.

---

[13] Inspired by Cal Banyan, Three Important Things

In this case, point out that "that feeling" is their subconscious mind speaking. For example, I would just say something like, "That's okay. That's *your* feeling." Which is true! I would then validate the feeling by saying, "That feeling is allowed to be there."

Validating a feeling validates the subconscious mind. This increases rapport. This would be a good time to remind the client, "This is how the subconscious mind communicates; it speaks through feelings, and emotions, and sensations in the body, as well as pictures and memories." These are the things we want to pay attention to because, in regression sessions, we focus on feelings and emotions.

If the client is dealing with a physical issue, insert a few suggestions about the wisdom of the body. For example, how the body knows how to breathe, and how the body is the subconscious mind, and how that's where we feel our feelings, and that the body knows how to heal.

You could include suggestions about how the subconscious mind is responsible for all the body functions such as breathing, circulation, perspiration, salivation, and so on.

Remind the client that their subconscious mind has been taking care of them since the day they were born. This makes the subconscious friendly. When the body becomes the enemy, the subconscious mind becomes the enemy. That's a problem you need to address. You can do that by educating the client about how the mind and body work together.

Remember, the body is the subconscious mind. Expand that idea a little by suggesting the body already knows how to heal. The subconscious mind already knows how to heal. All it needs is a little help. That's why they're seeing you.

> **Body Wisdom**
>
> Healing happens – given the right conditions. For example, if you cut your finger, the body knows how to heal that. All you need to do is make sure that the wound is clean, and the healing will happen. Same thing if you break a bone. All you need to do is set the bone in place, and it will heal - naturally.
>
> This is one of Nature's little miracles that science doesn't really understand how it works, yet. But the Mind and Body work together. So, the body-mind already knows how to heal. And healing happens – when we allow it to happen. But right now, there's nothing you need to do except … notice.
>
> Just let the breath come and go. Let the body breathe. And notice what it feels like… Notice what it's like …. as the breath comes in through the nostrils. You might even notice that the air seems to flow more easily through one nostril more than the other. That's normal. And now, to relax even more, I'd like you to bring your awareness to your eyelids, and the area around the eyelids . . .

The key is to make your instructions relevant to the client's issue and use them to set up positive expectations for the healing process. Healing is natural. Healing happens under the right conditions. This is an observable fact. If you cut your finger, the body knows how to heal that. All you need to do is make sure that the wound is clean, and healing will happen. The same is true if you break a bone. All you need to do is set the bone in place the body will heal it naturally.

This is one of Nature's little miracles. Science doesn't fully understand how it works, yet, but the mind and body work together. "The body-mind already knows how to heal. And healing happens when we allow it to happen. But right now, there's nothing you need to do except notice. Just let the breath come and go. Let the body breathe and notice what it feels like."

Invite the client to notice what it's like as the breath comes in through the nostrils. They might even notice that the air seems to flow more easily through one nostril more than the other. Tell them, "That's normal."

In fact, Ernest Rossi did some research into this. It has to do with Ultradian Rhythms. Brain activity goes from left brain to right brain, and then whole brain, in predictable cycles. You can tell which hemisphere of the brain is active based on which nostril the breath is coming through into the body! Something else that Rossi discovered is that Nature's cycle is roughly 90 minutes. He commented that this might be the ideal time frame for a therapy session because *hypnosis happens*.

Rossi was adhering to the standard counseling session which is usually 55 minutes. What he discovered is that if you allow 90 minutes for the session, the client is naturally going to naturally cycle into hypnosis during that time. As a result, they'll become more suggestible.

Cool, right?

Hypnosis happens. All you need to do is watch for it to happen. Watch the client during the intake process because, often, they'll be in hypnosis long before you even start the induction. As a result, you don't always need to use an induction. However, for the first session, it's always best to use a formal induction because you need to provide proof that hypnosis happened.

Remember, the client needs to know when it begins and when it ends. That's why we start with, "Look at my hand." This teaches the client to recognize when you're beginning the hypnosis.

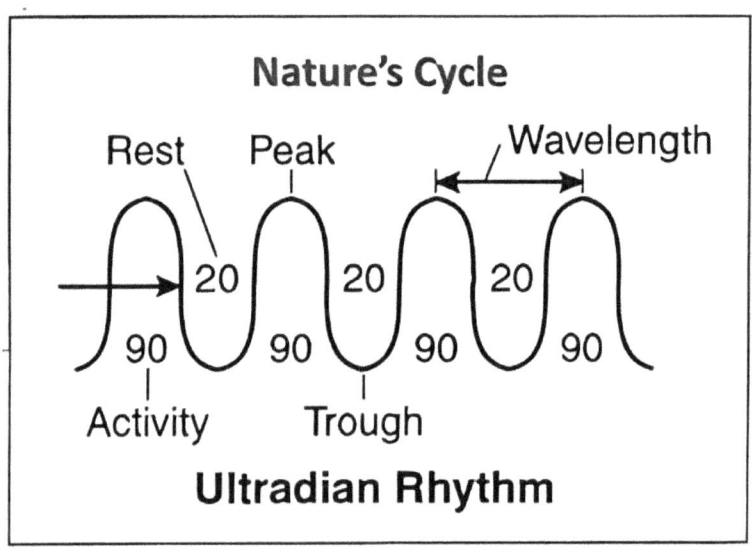

Autosuggestion

Autosuggestion is a technique that was developed by Emile Coué at the beginning of the 20th Century. (Coué created the famous affirmation, "Every day, in every way, I'm getting better and better.") He recognized that suggestions don't last unless you reinforce them repeatedly.

To get a lasting result you need to get that suggestion into the subconscious mind powerfully. Autosuggestion gives you a way to do that. Autosuggestion is where the client gives *themselves* a suggestion. Coué recognized that this is something we're already doing. It's called "self-talk".

Unfortunately, many of the things we say to ourselves, in the privacy of our own minds, aren't that nice. Some of those things can be downright nasty! We need to change that.

Autosuggestion is a powerfully effective technique that you can use in your regression sessions. The way to use autosuggestion in your sessions is to have the client say the suggestion out loud. This is much more powerful than direct suggestion because anything the client might say to themselves is going to carry more weight than anything you might say.

You can use autosuggestion instead of direct suggestion to reinforce positive changes, validate a perception, choice, or shift toward a better feeling. This teaches the client to trust their perceptions. You can use autosuggestion both as an uncovering technique and as a compounding technique. This teaches the client to work with you in an interactive way. You can also use it to test the acceptability of a suggestion.

This helps to put you in the driver's seat in your sessions by allowing you to find out whether it's okay to suggest a particular concept or idea. When there's a block, you know not to use that suggestion until you clear the block.

That's a lot of mileage for a simple technique.

Whenever something happens, there's going to be a response. For example, when you offer a suggestion, the subconscious mind will respond by sending a signal through the body. The client will feel the subconscious response physically. Either it will feel good or not-so-good. That's what you want.

But you don't know what the response will be. Not really. The suggestion may sound good to you, but the client's subconscious mind may have other ideas. If a suggestion is acceptable, the body will relax. The client will feel this relaxation response physically – in the body – as sensations of comfort. But if a suggestion isn't acceptable, it's going to generate resistance which the client will feel as physical sensations of tension. It will feel uncomfortable. That's good. That's the subconscious mind communicating.

But that's *not* a suggestion you want to keep repeating because it can make the problem worse. When a suggestion generates internal resistance, that's the subconscious mind saying, "Nuh-uh. Not okay. Not true." And now you know. That suggestion is not acceptable. There's a block. Removing that block might just be the next step in the client's healing process. This makes autosuggestion a useful technique because it gives you a way to get direct feedback from their subconscious mind before you ever offer a suggestion.

Autosuggestion gets the client participating in their own healing by getting them to pay attention to their built-in, Biological Feedback System. Sure, you could set up ideomotor signals to communicate with the subconscious mind. But it is already communicating through feelings and sensations in the body. Why not just pay attention to that?

You're already set up for autosuggestion because the Body Awareness Exercise gets the client paying attention to how the subconscious mind communicates through the body. And regression hypnosis is an interactive process. This invites the client to be an active participant in the process by getting them to focus on the body to discover how something feels.

This gives you a way to test. It's also a great way to prove to your client that their subconscious is trying to communicate with them, and that it's meant to be helpful. The subconscious mind wants the client to feel better. When something doesn't feel good, that's the subconscious mind letting them know, "Hey! There's a problem here!"

The Autosuggestion Technique is one simple technique that's easy to incorporate into healing sessions. It teaches the client how to work with their subconscious mind and it can seriously jack up the results you're getting in your regression sessions.

1. Establish a Baseline

First, you need to establish a baseline. Try this yourself. Say something that you know is true. For example, "My name is … and say your name." Say it out loud. As you give yourself that suggestion, notice how it feels. Most people will say it feels normal or true. It feels comfortable to say those words.

Now try saying this. "My name is … Marilyn Monroe … or Barney Rubble … or Fritz the Cat." Notice how it feels as you say that. Most people will say it feels a little funny. Or it feels off. Or it doesn't feel true. Now try saying these words … "I am rich" … and notice how that feels.

If you felt a little uncomfortable, welcome to Planet Earth. If you didn't feel a little tension as you said those words, congratulations! But most people are going to notice there's a little glitch in the system. That's the subconscious mind saying, "Nuh-uh … not true …" … which means that *that* suggestion is not acceptable. That's your Biological Feedback System kicking in.

This is why affirmations can make a problem worse. If it's not true, your subconscious mind is going to kick up a stink. Your subconscious mind is there to protect you by keeping you consistent with your beliefs. That's its Prime Directive. As a result, it's going to generate internal resistance to any suggestion that doesn't match your existing beliefs.

The problem is that not all our beliefs are true. But the subconscious is duty-bound to protect them *as if* they were true. It does that by putting up resistance. Resistance doesn't feel good. So, any suggestion that doesn't fit with a client's existing beliefs can make them feel worse.

Autosuggestion is a technique that you can use to test the acceptability of a suggestion. You'll know, right away, whether to use a suggestion. This can help you to get rid of the resistance and get better results. If a suggestion is not acceptable to the client's subconscious mind, it's going to generate resistance. Resistance feels uncomfortable. This tells you that there's a block to the client's ability to accept it. If the client feels comfortable, or relaxed, or good, that's a suggestion that's going to go in and be accepted because, subconsciously, it's true. It's a match for their beliefs or what they're experiencing internally.

The client's Biological Feedback System can tell you when a change has occurred. That's something you would want to compound powerfully through repetition. But in the first session, you're just teaching the client how to work with you.

2. Validate the Feeling

When you have the client do a little scan of the body, instruct them to give you a report and tell you how they're feeling physically. Whatever they're experiencing, that's their truth. Validate it using autosuggestion.

Most of the time the client will report feeling pretty good, or relaxed, or comfortable. In this case, affirm that awareness by having the client say it out loud. "I feel good." Or "I feel relaxed." Then, add something to it.

The suggestion I like to add is, "I'm *allowed* to feel good," or "I'm *allowed* to feel relaxed," because I want to encourage the client to allow feelings to come to awareness. I want them to give their feelings permission to be there, even when they don't feel good.

If they did a scan of the body, and they noticed some tension, or discomfort, or some pain there, that's okay, too. Your response is still the same. "That's good. That's *your* feeling. That feeling is *allowed* to be there."

Good or bad, comfortable or uncomfortable - validate the feeling. Validating a feeling is validating the subconscious mind and what it has to say. This makes it safe for the client to feel their feelings. It will also get you powerful rapport with their subconscious.

Remember, feelings are how the subconscious communicates. That feeling is their subconscious mind speaking. That's the subconscious mind's truth. Making it okay for the client to feel their feelings is going to make your job easier by allowing you to access a path to the causal event. Make it okay for those feelings to be there. They're allowed to be there.

3. **Affirm the Truth**

You can even thank their subconscious mind for being willing to communicate. Then invite the client to speak the truth out loud by saying, "I feel …" tense, or pressure, or whatever they happen to be noticing because that's the truth of their experience. Then have the client say the following statement, out loud, and notice how it feels. "This is my feeling. I'm allowed to feel my feelings."

Most of the time the client will tell you that it feels good to say those words. It feels empowering because it's true. They're no longer trying to get away from their feelings – which never works. Putting a lid on your bad feelings puts a lid on your good feelings, too. Ask anyone who is taking anti-depressants. Pushing against a feeling that doesn't feel good just increases the internal pressure. We want to put an end to that avoidance strategy so the client can heal.

Teach your clients to pay attention to feelings in the body. Teach them that the body is the subconscious mind and that they can trust it. Teach them to honor their subconscious mind by honoring their feelings. And give the body permission to speak. Not only can this get you incredible rapport with the client's subconscious mind, but you'll be also creating your ideal client for working with emotional issues.

CHAPTER 4:
Modify the Elman Induction

My preferred induction is the Elman Induction[14] because it's elegant. It provides a very step-by-step procedure for guiding a client into a state of somnambulism in less than five minutes, has built-in tests and Convincers, and can easily be adapted to any client. Technically, this is a rapid induction, but you can easily convert it into a relaxation induction which is how I utilize it in the first session.

Eye Lock Test

The Elman Induction begins with an eye lock test. This is where you give the suggestion, "Relax the eyelids to the point they won't work. And when you're convinced that they won't work, give them a test, and *satisfy yourself* that they won't work."

The eye lock test is not a test for hypnosis. It's too soon for that. The eye lock test is a test for *compliance*. Some people think that compliance means control. But all that compliance means is cooperation. The eye lock test tells you whether the client is willing to cooperate by following

---

[14] You'll find this induction in Dave Elman's classic book, Hypnotherapy.

your instructions. That's useful feedback. But it's also a test that the client can fail. For example, you give instructions to relax the eyelids to the point they won't work. Then, when you conduct the test, the client opens their eyes and looks at you. It happens. But when it happens, you have a problem. For some reason, the client is not cooperating. The question is *why*?

Sometimes it's because you weren't clear enough when delivering the instructions. Sometimes the client wasn't paying attention. Sometimes they're flat-out challenging you. They're thinking, "make me!"

For whatever reason, the client is not willing to follow your instructions. They're not cooperating. When a client fails the eye lock test, they're going to start thinking, "This isn't working …" Now they're back up in their head.

Before you can proceed, you need to resolve the problem which burns up session time. But what if there was a way to make sure the client was going to pass the test, every time? What if you could make the test fail safe?

Make the Test Fail-Safe

I discovered a simple solution that works every time. You can use it in individual sessions. You can use it in group sessions. And it works with everyone. What it does is, it makes the client responsible for the result. If they fail the test, it's not that it didn't work. It's that the client didn't do it right. That's okay because they're just learning, right?

We have already utilized physical awareness and tested for physical relaxation. You have already established that there is *some* relaxation present. All you need to do is instruct the client to bring their attention to their eyelids and *double* the relaxation there. Then tell them to keep doubling the relaxation in the eyelids until *they're sure* they won't work. Add this with emphasis, "*I can't do this for you!* Keep doubling the relaxation until you're *sure* they won't work."

> **Eye Lock Test #1**
>
> The easiest muscles in the body to relax are the eyelid muscles. That's how we close our eyes. We do it by relaxing the muscles that were holding the eyelids open. You can relax your eyelids to the point that they just won't work. And so long as you allow that relaxation to remain there, those eyelids will remain relaxed and remain close. And they just won't work.
>
> I'd like you to do that now. Allow those eyelids to relax so much that they just won't work. And when you're satisfied that you've done that, that they're that relaxed that they just won't work, take a nice, deep, relaxing breath in, and relax even deeper. (Wait for the breath)
>
> That's good. Now, in a moment, I'm going to ask you to check to make sure that they won't work. And if you have followed my instructions, you'll find that your eyebrows will go up and down, but the eyelids remain closed.
>
> Now, let's be clear. I'm not asking you to check to see if you can open the eyes. I'm asking you to allow those eyelids to relax so much that they just won't work. Understand?
>
> That's good. Go ahead, now. Give them a little check and *satisfy yourself that they just won't work*. (Watch for movement in the eyebrows.)
>
> Stop testing and go deeper relaxed.

Here's the fail-safe. "If those eyelids were to open, it would simply mean that you need to double the relaxation a few more times. So, keep doubling that relaxation until you're *sure* they won't work." Do you see how this makes the client responsible for the result? Now, all you have to say is, "*When* you feel that those eyelids are that relaxed … that they just won't work …. take a nice, deep relaxing breath in … and as you release the breath, go deeper."

Now all you need to do is sit back and watch for the breath. As soon as you see the in-breath, give the suggestion, "As you exhale, *melt down*, and go deeper relaxed." And you're all set to go.

The next step is to conduct the test. The way to do this is to tell the client, "In a moment I'm going to ask you to check to *make sure* that they won't work. And *if you have followed my instructions* the eyebrows will go up and down. But the eyelids will stay relaxed and remain closed."

This is a reminder that the client is responsible for the result. The suggestion for eyebrows to go up and down gives you a visual cue. You'll know when the client is performing the test because the eyebrows will tell you but watch carefully. Some will give you the Groucho Marx eyebrow lift. With others it will just be a twitch or a flicker. Every client is different.

When the client passes the eye lock test, it doubles as a convincer. The instruction to *satisfy yourself* tells the client that they're not trying to prove anything to you. They're just satisfying their need to know that the eyelids won't work. Some clients will be really surprised by this. Complete the test by saying, "That's good. Stop testing and go deeper relaxed."

You are now set up for the next step, which is to transfer the relaxation from the eyelids to the rest of the body.

> **Fail-Safe Eye Lock Test**
>
> I'd like to help you relax more. Would that be all right?
>
> Okay. Now, to help you, I'd like you to take your attention to the eyelids ... and the area *around* the eyelids... And double the relaxation there. Now double it again. And again. And again. Keep doubling the relaxation over and over again, until they feel *so heavy that they just won't work*.
>
> Now, *I can't do that for you*. When you feel that your eyelids have reached the point that they're that relaxed, that they just won't work ... take a nice relaxing breath in (*watch for the breath*).
>
> And on the next exhale ... MELT DOWN. Very good.
>
> Now, in a moment ... I'm going to ask you to *check* ... *to make sure* that they're that relaxed ... that they just won't work. And if you have followed my instructions, you'll find that *the eyebrows go up and down*, but the eyelids remain relaxed and remain closed.
>
> Now, if the eyelids were to open, that would simply mean that you need to double the relaxation a few more times. So keep doubling the relaxation until *you're sure* they won't work. And when you're sure they just won't work, go ahead and give them a little tug. Satisfy yourself that they won't work. (*watch that they test*)
>
> That's good. Stop testing and go deeper relaxed. You're doing great because now we have a wonderful model for the relaxation you're *going* to create in your body.

Increase Physical Relaxation

Instruct the client to take a nice deep breath in and, as they breathe in, to take the relaxation up to the top of their head. Then, on the outbreath, have them send that relaxation down and throughout the body. This deepens the *physical* relaxation which will help to ensure the client has a positive first experience with you.

> **Physical Relaxation**
>
> You're doing great, because now we have a wonderful *model* for the relaxation you're going to create in your body. Now, take a nice, relaxing breath in. And send that relaxation up to the top of your head. And just let the top of the head begin to *feel* relaxed … just like those eyelids are relaxed. (pause)
>
> And now, MELT DOWN. Just imagine what it would be like to be warm, soft chocolate … and MELT DOWN … relaxing the front and the back of the head … And the forehead, and the cheeks, and the jaw …
>
> And all the way *down* the neck …and across the shoulders … and *down* beneath the shoulder blades … *Down* the arms … *down* to the elbows … *down* to the wrists …*down* to the fingertips.
>
> And from the shoulders … *down* to the chest…. *dow*n to waist and into the pelvis. *Down* to the hips … and the thighs … *down* to knees … ankle… all the way *down* to the tips of the toes … deeper and deeper relaxed. (*pause*)
>
> And just notice how that feels. Feels good, doesn't it?

In the traditional Elman Induction, you have the client open their eyes and then close their eyes. This is called Fractionating. I don't use Fractionating here, however. I figure that, if the subconscious mind makes no distinction between real and imagined, why not just have the client just imagine relaxing the eyelids?

Engage the client's imagination by using suggestions to increase awareness of what it is like to go much more deeply relaxed. We will be using fractionating later for a more specific purpose. But for now, all you need to do after the eye lock test is instruct the client to transfer the relaxation from the eyelids throughout the body. Then repeat the process two more times.

1. Relax the eyelids.
2. Eye lock test.
3. Relax the body.

The second time through, you follow the same steps. Only this time the suggestion is to relax the eyelids *ten times deeper*. Conduct the eye lock test again. Then, take *that* quality of relaxation up to the top of the head and send it down throughout the body – just like the first time. Only this time, the *body* is going ten times deeper relaxed.

1. Relax the eyelids X 10
2. Eye lock test #2
3. Relax the body X 10

I like to ask, "Do you feel that relaxation coming on, now?" This brings the client's attention to the fact that something is happening.

Usually, they'll nod or smile or hum blissfully. This gives you confirmation that they're experiencing what you're suggesting. You can then offer the suggestion, "The deeper you go the better you feel. And the better you feel the deeper you can go."

Repeat the sequence a third time. Only this time, instead of the suggestion "ten times deeper", give the suggestion to double the relaxation.

Eye Lock Test #2

Now, in a moment we're going to do this again. And *this* time you'll find that you're able to relax ten times deeper relaxed. Just imagine what it would be like to be ten times more deeply relaxed. Want that and you can have it very easily.

Once again, bring your attention to the eyelids and allow them to relax ten times deeper relaxed. And when you've done that . . . satisfy yourself. Give them a good test. (Good, stop testing and go deeper.)

Now, take another deep, relaxing breath in and send *that* feeling of relaxation up to the top of your head. Only *this time*, allow the top of your head to go ten times deeper relaxed.

And on the next exhale MELT DOWN, send that relaxation *down* ... let it be as if you *meant* to **go ten times deeper relaxed...** That's right. *Ten times deeper relaxed* ... Just as if you were a rag doll ... loose, limp, and relaxed... from the top of your head to the bottoms of your feet. Every muscle, every nerve, every fiber going deeper and deeper relaxed. And notice how good that feels. That's right. *Do you feel that relaxation coming on?*

That's good, because the only thing you care about today is how deeply relaxed you *can* go. The deeper you go, the better you feel. And the better you feel, the deeper you *can* go.

You established a degree of relaxation and tested it in the first round. You then compounded that relaxation by a magnitude of ten. And now you double that magnitude.

1. Relax the eyelids X 2
2. Eye lock test #3
3. Relax the body X 2

> **Eye Lock Test #3**
>
> One last time. Take your attention to those eyelids. Now double the relaxation. Now double it again. And again. And again.
>
> Now, send *that* feeling of relaxation up to the top of your head. And on the next exhale, MELT DOWN, sending a warm wave of relaxation down and across your entire body. Really allowing this physical Part of you (*touch arm*) to go many, many times more deeply relaxed. Just let yourself go loose, limp and relaxed... like a wet dishrag.

Hand Drop Test

This sequence is then followed by the hand-drop test. The hand-drop test is another test for compliance. This time, you're checking to see if the client has followed your instructions to deeply relax the body.

> **Hand Drop Test**
>
> In a moment, *I'm* going to check the relaxation. All I'm going to do is just lift this arm a little (*touch arm*). So, you let me do all the lifting, okay? We want this arm to be loose and limp like a rag doll. So, when I lift this arm, it should feel *heavy* to me. But it should be *loose and limp* like a rag doll or wet spaghetti. Understand? (*test*)
>
> That's good. Because the only thing you care about today ... is how deeply relaxed you *can* go. The deeper you go the better you feel. And the better you feel the deeper you *can* go.

Test for State

Too many novices assume that if the client looks relaxed, they must be hypnotized. That's just not true. Even if they are in a state of hypnosis the client may not realize it. And *you* won't know for sure unless you test. *You need to test.*

First, convince yourself. Verify that the client is in a state of hypnosis by using a covert test. (Eye lock is a test for a light state of hypnosis.) Then, prove to the client that hypnosis is happening by using an overt test.

Remember, the client needs to be convinced that something more than relaxation is happening.

Arons Hypnotic Depth Scale

Stage	Level	Test
1	Hypnoidal; very light state (Hypnogogic)	Eye lock
2	Light hypnosis	Catalepsy in large muscle groups
3	Medium hypnosis	Aphasia Inability to walk Partial analgesia
4	Threshold of Somnambulism	Glove analgesia Amnesia
5	Somnambulism	Anesthesia Positive hallucinations Real age regression
6	Profound somnambulism	Negative hallucinations

1. Covert Test

First, use a *covert* test to verify that the client is in a state of hypnosis and not merely relaxed. Different schools use different depth scales. What matters in your sessions with paying clients is that you're able to recognize when hypnosis is happening, then establish the appropriate depth for the client's issue.

Some issues only require a light state. Some issues require a deeper state. Deeper states are more healing states. For example, if you were just doing a past life excursion, all you would need is a light state. People will go to a past life spontaneously while tapping, particularly when it fits with their beliefs. But even when you're doing the deeper work, clients will occasionally bounce back into a past life. You can get surprising results working in a past life. The key is to help the client connect their previous life experience to their current life issue. Otherwise, it's just a recreational trip. And if you don't convince the client that they're hypnotized, they'll be tempted to think they just made it all up. Or worse, take it all literally.

The subconscious mind makes no distinction between real and imagined. As a result, anything that comes to mind is always going to be a blending of reality and imagination. That's okay. You can create real change working with an imagined event. For example, you can get real results working in a dream. This is because the images, real or imagined, are all coming from the same place – the client's mind. What makes an event "real" is how it feels. But if the client doesn't believe they were hypnotized, they won't be convinced that change will happen.

The Numbers Challenge

Real regression requires somnambulism. This is because you need access to emotional states to facilitate regression-to-cause. Somnambulism is an ideal working state for pretty much any issue. If you can get a person into somnambulism in less than five minutes, why not just go there? It's not about going uber-deep or getting the client Gozo'd. It's about guiding the client to the depth necessary to do the healing work.

The traditional Elman Induction uses the Numbers Challenge to test for somnambulism. This is also known as the Losing the Numbers Test. To conduct the test, you give the suggestion to begin counting back from 100. The client is to say each number out loud followed by the words, "deeper relaxed", and with each number they say to relax the numbers out or imagine them dissolving and fading away.

Numbers Challenge

Now, you have relaxed *the body*. You can relax the mind to the same beautiful depth that you have relaxed the body. Here's how you'll do it. In a moment, when I tell you, you'll begin counting out loud ... starting with the number one ... You'll say the number s-l-o-w-l-y and then say the words "deeper relaxed."

Here's the secret to your success. As the body relaxes, the mind relaxes. That's what we want. So, as you hear the words, "deeper relaxed" just imagine ... what it would be like ... to be *so relaxed* ... that all the numbers have relaxed right out of your mind. Okay?

Now, you can have them back later if you wish, but for now, I'd like you to just *let them* disappear and be gone so that you can begin to enjoy that wonderful, deep *mental relaxation* that feels so good. Okay?

Okay, here's how you'll do it.... *(pace client's breathing)*.

One – d-e-e-p-e-r r-e-l-a-x-e-d *(pause)*,

Two – d-e-e-p-e-r r-e-l-a-x-e-d *(pause)*,

Three – *d-e-e-p-e-r r-e-l-a-x-e-d (pause)*. You'll find that it doesn't take very long. You'll find that after only a few numbers you will have relaxed *so much* that all the rest of the numbers will have faded away completely. There just won't be any more numbers and you'll find yourself enjoying that beautiful, wonderful state of *mental* relaxation. And *when they're all gone* ...you can let *me* know by saying "All gone." Okay?

Okay, now ... begin ... ("One, deeper relaxed") S-l-o-w-l-y now ... begin relaxing the mind ...

("Two, deeper relaxed")*(softly)* G-o-o-d ... just let them f-a-d-e a-w-a-y ...

("Three, deeper relaxed") Gently now ... drifting farther and farther away, as if they were birds or clouds, just floating away. ("Four, deeper relaxed") Just fading away now ... going dim and distance, like little boats sailing off into the horizon.... Going ... going ... Let me know when they're all gone ... going ... (gone).

(Client still counting?) Gently now ... *(forehead tap)* Push them out! You don't need them! .... Going, going, going . . . All gone?

Good. As the mind relaxes the body relaxes. As the body relaxes the mind relaxes. And you just keep going deeper, and deeper, and deeper ... relaxed.

Alternatively, you can instruct the client to begin counting from one. This works better for competitive types. As there are potentially endless numbers, they're more likely to give up rather than "go for the gold." With analytical types, you can add a confusional element by having them count back in threes.

Repeat the instructions. Then, instruct the client to begin and to let you know when they're all gone.

Fractionation Test/Deepener (Covert Test)

The Numbers Challenge is supposed to be a test for the threshold of Somnambulism. But there's a problem. The client can just *tell* you that the numbers are gone when, in fact, they're not. Because you have no way of knowing, for sure, whether the client let the numbers go, this is a good test for compliance. But for somnambulism? Not so much.

For this reason, I modified The Elman by swapping out the Numbers Challenge for the following Fractionation Test/Deepener. There are several benefits to using this modification.

First, if the client isn't already in hypnosis, they soon will be. You can always Fractionate them into Somnambulism.

Second, it's a covert test. If the client fails the test, you simply continue to fractionate until they do pass it.

Third, as soon as the client's responses become automatic, you'll know they're in Gonzo Land. They're no longer anticipating the next count, which means they're right where you need them to be.

Eye Fractionation with Test[15]

Now, just let this arm *(touch arm)* be *very* loose and limp because ... in a moment, I'm going to lift this arm. I'm only going to lift it a little, but this is important. When I do, you let me do all the lifting. Okay?

So, when I lift this arm, it should feel *heavy* to me, like a piece of marble or stone.... but *loose and limp* and very relaxed. Understand? *(lift and test)*

Next, I'm going to count to three. On the count of three, let those eyes open. I'll say the word "sleep" and snap my fingers like this *(snap!)*.

The moment you hear the snap, let those eyes close. And you will go even deeper. And feel better each time. *(Repeat instructions)*

1, 2, 3 ... *(Wait for eyes to open.)* Sleep! *(snap fingers!)* And go deeper.

(Immediately deepen. Place hand on forehead and roll gently from side to side.) As I gently rock your head just allow yourself to go loose, limp and relaxed.

Once again, I'm going to count to 3. On the count of three, those eyes will open. When you hear the snap *(snap fingers!)* ... Instantly, automatically, spontaneously eyes close down. And go even deeper.

1, 2, 3 ... *(Wait for eyes to open)* Sleep! *(snap!)* ... And go deeper. *(Immediately place hand on forehead and roll gently from side to side.)*

Let yourself melt down even deeper now. Drifting down deeper with each and every breath you exhale. Every word takes you deeper. Every thought takes you deeper. Every sensation. Deeper and deeper. You'll find that every time I do that you will go deeper and deeper into hypnosis. So let's do that again. 1 – 2 – 3 – "Sleep!" *(snap!)* ... and go deeper. *(repeat and develop a rhythm, compounding the respond so it becomes automatic)*

Immediately conduct test.

> **Test:**
>
> 1, 2, (pause)… (There should be no anticipation of the next count.)
>
> 3, (eyes should open with some difficulty)
>
> Sleep! (snap!) … And go deeper.
>
> (head roll) Every part of you is responding beautifully. Perfectly now, as you are learning how to allow that part of you that makes all changes … to respond effortlessly to all of my suggestions.
>
> And you'll find that, as I continue to talk to you all of these suggestions are working at a very deep, deep level. And all changes will occur automatically … because this is what you desire now.

2. Overt Test

Once you have verified that the client is in hypnosis, use an *overt* test to convince the client that something amazing is happening. That's the best way to turn a skeptic into a believer. Show them that they are in an altered state of mind, and you'll surprise them. For example, you can use a simple catalepsy test. Arm catalepsy is pretty impressive!

Eye Catalepsy Test

The Eye Catalepsy Test is a test for Somnambulism. Here, it doubles as an overt test or Convincer. I prefer this test because it's quick and is a more accurate test for Somnambulism than the Numbers Challenge. With the eye catalepsy test, you can see that the eyelids are locking down tightly.

---

[15] Inspired by Gerald Kein, Omni-Hypnosis Center

The suggestion, "They twitch and tighten, twitch and tighten, twitch and tighten ..." is a covert test. When you see the eyelids twitching or fluttering, you'll know that the client is accepting those suggestions. This makes the overt test fail-safe. When the client tests, you want them to *test hard*. Make sure the eyes won't open. Don't be shy. Make the client convince *you* that the eyelids won't work.

> ### Eye Catalepsy Test/Convincer[16]
>
> As I touch you on the forehead, those eyelids lock tightly together. As I count from one to five, they *lock and seal* in the down position. With every number I say that feeling grows more real. By the time I reach the count of five they're locked tightly together and sealed in the down position. ....
>
> One – those eyelids grow heavy like lead. They lock and seal in the down position. Two – more powerfully now, like they're one solid sheet of skin, no seam, no separation. Three – *welded* shut, so much so that the more you try to open them the tighter locked down they become. Four – On the next count they're locked and sealed. The more you try to open them, the tighter locked down they become. Five – Locked and sealed.
>
> *Satisfy yourself now and give them a good test.*
>
> (Stop testing, relax and go deeper)

Induce the Wow Factor

The Eye Catalepsy test can double as a Convincer because, at the end of the session, you can ask the client, "What was it like when you couldn't open your eyes?" This induces the Wow Factor.

---

[16] Inspired by Stephen Parkhill, author of Answer Cancer

Glove anesthesia makes a great convincer. This is the one to use with clients who are dealing with chronic pain. They need real proof that you can help to get them some relief. Analgesia or anesthesia is tangible proof. Now you feel it, now you don't. If you get a client who's a real skeptic, this is the Convincer to use to dispel their doubt. It's also good for smokers. You can numb their lips or their tongue or fingertips. Then anchor it to cigarettes[17]. (Mwah-hah-hah ….)

The goal is to show the client that something interesting is happening. And it's happening simply because they have chosen to follow your instructions. Anything you can do to show the client that something more than just relaxation is happening can be used as proof, not only that they're hypnotized, but that they have the power within themselves to create change. You'll blow their socks off.

That's the Wow Factor. So, be sure to tell them, "You did that!" Encourage the client to own it. This is evidence of the power of their subconscious mind. When they get that realization, you'll have made a believer of them. Not only will this get you stellar results. It will get you referrals. That's the Power of Wow.

Deepen Immediately

Once you've conducted the test for Somnambulism, you always need to deepen the client to get them below the threshold of Somnambulism. A quick mini-progressive relaxation can be very effective at this point in the induction process.

---

[17] Smoking trick from Ines Simpson, Simpson Protocol.

I like to have the client imagine what it would be like to be warm, soft chocolate melting down. This makes it a yummy experience for the client. And it's a quick deepening technique.

> **Mini Progressive Relaxation Deepener**
>
> Now we just do one, last, little scan … From the top of the head down to the forehead … everything relaxed . . .And we scan down to the cheeks and the jaw, everything relaxed.… Down further now to the shoulders and chest… down the back, and beneath the shoulder blades … Down the spine, and all the way down to waist …. And down to the fingertips … everything is deeply relaxed … And now, all the way down to knees, down to the ankles, down to the toes … deeper and deeper relaxed. Feels good, doesn't it?

Body Tour

If you've done lots of deepening, the client should be feeling much better than when they began. They may not realize it, though. You need to make them aware of this change. Then, help them to claim ownership for having created that change.

First, bring the client's awareness back to the body. Ask them to do a tour of the body and notice how they feel. Then ask them to give you a report. How do they feel *now?* I like to use Sentence Stems Completion in sessions. This is where you offer the client the beginning of a sentence and ask them to complete it. For example, here I would say, "Say 'I feel" and put an ending on it."

Take a Tour Script

From this point on, every gentle breath that you exhale can take you deeper.... Sounds around you will not bother or disturb you. The only sound that interests you is the sound of my voice. Every word *guides* you deeper and deeper relaxed. Any sounds that do arise will only help and guide you to go deeper.... relaxed.

Take a tour of your body. Notice how you feel. Say, "I feel ... and put an ending on it.

(If the client is feeling good/relaxed) Realize this state of relaxation and *utter calmness* ... has been completely achieved by *you* - and no one else. No one can ever *make* you relax. I have simply delivered a few suggestions, and *you* have relaxed *yourself*.

This is the power of *your* subconscious mind! And your subconscious mind has the power to make you into the kind of person you *want t*o be. (A thinner person. A healthier person. A happier person.)

So I want you to realize just how *powerful* you are!

(If the client reports some discomfort) That's okay. That's your subconscious mind talking. It knows why you're here. *(tie to presenting issue)*

The subconscious mind is the *feeling m*ind. It speaks through images and feelings. So, *all* your feelings are good – even the uncomfortable ones. They're there to help and guide you so you can feel better.

(Optional: teach tapping here to get some relief. Then validate the change.) Realize ... *this* is the power of *your* Subconscious Mind! It has the power to make you into the kind of person you *want t*o be. And if you can feel it you can heal it.

If the client reports feeling better ask, "What's changed?" Let them tell *you*. For example, if the client says that they're feeling more calm and relaxed, validate the change by saying, "You did that!"

Remember, the client has the power, not you. Help the client to realize this by turning it into a revelation. If the client is feeling awed and inspired, you could even invite them to transmit a feeling of "thank you" to their subconscious mind for giving them this experience.

Focus on Feelings Patter

Hypnosis is not what most people think. It's not being unconscious, or unaware, or losing control. It's taking back control by becoming *more* aware of how you *feel*... so you can take back control of your life.

From now on, whenever we do hypnosis together, the moment you close your eyes, you focus your attention *inside*, on the *feeling*, in the *body*. Okay?

And you'll *be very aware of your feelings* because this brings you the benefits you want, the benefits of change. (*Benefits List*)

What if the client doesn't feel better? Validate the client's experience. The reason the client has a problem is because they've been at war with themselves. You want to bring them back into alignment by ending the conflict between their conscious and subconscious mind. The fact that they're noticing some discomfort is actually good news indicating that emotional stuff is bubbling up to the surface. Don't try to suggest it away. Validate it! Give it permission to be there. You'll be using it, soon enough.

Most of the time, the client is going to be feeling pretty good. They'll be purring like a kitten. Even a little relaxation is an improvement that can be validated. But if they're aware of some discomfort, that's okay, too. This is how it is for them. Remind the client (and yourself) that Rome wasn't built in a day and neither was the problem. It may take a little time to get the client out of it.

Teach the client that it's okay to allow the feeling to be there. If you use tapping, this would be the perfect time to guide the client to release some of that discomfort. You don't have to resolve it all. Just show the client that it's possible to get some relief. They don't have to hold onto the feeling. They can release it.

Regression hypnotherapy isn't a single-session approach. It's unreasonable to think you're going to transform a lifetime of pain with a single session. What you *can* do is validate where they're at and make it okay to be there. This will allow you to make whatever their experience happens to be *relevant* to the healing process.

If they're still feeling tension or pressure or fear or discomfort, that's okay. Let them know that *"that feeling"* is their subconscious mind communicating. Uncomfortable feelings and emotions are signals coming from the subconscious level of mind. "That feeling" is coming out of the event that caused it!

Realize their subconscious mind knows why they're seeing you. And it wants what the client wants – to feel better. Make the feeling acceptable because "that feeling" is a Bridge to the past.

Any shift toward the better is something you can build on. So, validate it. The subconscious mind is *qualitative*, not quantitative. If you can prove that they can feel better, it will create space to allow more feelings to come to the surface to be released. This will help you to get to the underlying problem.

Once you get a shift, come back to the realization that *this is the power of the subconscious mind.* Then, connect the dots between the hypnosis and how much better they're feeling.

Any shift can be used as *evidence* of the power of their subconscious mind. This is a power they already *have*. With your help, they can *use* it to create the change they want.

The client wants to believe this is true. If they didn't, they wouldn't be in your chair. There's a Part of them that already believes it's possible. You can foster this belief by giving them *evidence* that it's true.

Whether it's a small shift toward the better, or a ginormous sense of relief, find a way to make the client's first experience with you a revelation. That way, even if they've experienced hypnosis before, they'll *know* what *you* do is different. And they'll be looking forward to their next session with you.

There's no need for a long, drawn-out induction in every session. It's boring and burns up precious session time. Once you have taught the client how to enter the state of Somnambulism, they already know how to get there. All you need to do is install a trigger for re-induction and your client will be push-button in subsequent sessions.

Guess what? It's already done. You've already installed the trigger for re-induction! You just need to test to make sure that it will work in subsequent sessions.

Hypnosis is hypnosis. The only difference is how you use it. ~ **Alex Smith**

CHAPTER 5:
Emerge (Not Really)

When you emerge the client, they should be very impressed with themselves. You want to encourage that. But *before* you emerge the client, you need to test the trigger. Make sure that it's going to work! This is really easy to do. All you need to do is count the client up as *if you* were emerging them. You're not actually going to emerge them. You're just going to do a count from one to three and have the client open their eyes. When they open their eyes, they'll *think* they've emerged. The re-induction will then act as a deepening technique because what you're really doing is stacking one deepener on top of another. (This will get you uber deep hypnosis.)

Begin by setting up for the emerging count. "In a moment, I'm going to count from one to three to bring you back up. On the count of three, those eyes will open. You'll feel relaxed and refreshed - just like you've had a good night's rest - really feeling good." Coach to the positive by adding a few suggestions for how well they've done, and how proud they can feel for having given themselves this gift. That sort of thing.

Give the client the impression that they're going to emerge. Remember, you're not emerging them. You're just having them open their eyes on the count of three. Immediately, when the client opens their eyes, tell them to look at you. Say, "look right here" while pointing to the spot between your eyebrows. Then, give them the hypnotic stare as you nod and say, *"Feel good?"*

Hypnotic Stare

The first suggestion is, "Look right here" as you point to the spot between your eyebrows. Direct *your* gaze to the space *between* the client's eyes. To the client it will feel like you're looking them in the eye. It feels a little creepy. But it has a deepening effect.

I think what's happening is that it triggers a little flight response. That's an old-brain response. The client won't notice it but it's an automatic response. If you stare a dog in the eye, the dog will read that as a sign of aggression. The natural response to a perceived threat is to retreat. Because there's no place to go, the escape route is to go within. And because the client is already in hypnosis, this mini retreat has a deepening effect.

Remember, the client is still in hypnosis. Don't start a conversation. Don't engage the client's conscious mind. Just keep talking to their subconscious mind by delivering suggestions. If you use a soft, lulling tone as you conduct the emerging count, it will have a deepening effect. As a result, when they open their eyes, they may feel a little disoriented. This can be used as another Convincer. You can just say, "(Look right here.) Wow! You really went deep *into hypnosis*, didn't you?"

If the client is obviously Gozo'd, you won't really need to do any more convincing. But for the obvious skeptics, even when they're totally Gozo'd, I'll use the Time Distortion Test.

Time Distortion Test

I used to do a time-distortion test with every client, mostly because I wanted to develop my skill by facilitating it. Plus, it's easy to forget to set up for it if it's not part of your routine. But I found that, most of the time, it just wasn't necessary.

You only really need to do a formal time distortion test with obvious skeptics. Seriously, you just can't argue with a personal experience of losing time. But you do have to remember to set up for it beforehand. If you forget to set up for the Time Distortion Test, you can still check for time distortion without. Just make sure the hypnosis session is at least twenty minutes long to ensure you have some depth. Then ask the client, "Give me your first sense . . . how long do you think you were in hypnosis?"

Remember, when the client opens their eyes, they will *think* they've emerged. They're still in hypnosis and, therefore, still suggestible. You've just given them the suggestion, "You were in hypnosis."

Most people will estimate that the hypnosis session took ten or fifteen minutes. They'll be surprised when they look at the clock and realize it's been thirty minutes. That's when you can point out that they just experienced 40%- or 50%-time distortion. Let them know that's evidence of deep hypnosis. If that's too much math for you, you can say, "Time flies when you're in Lah-Lah Land!"

Time Distortion Test[18]

(use a deepening tone!) "In a moment, I'm going to count from 1 to 3 to bring you back up. On the count of three, and not before, those eyes will open. And like I said, it wouldn't take very long to do this first session, so when those eyes open it will feel as if they have just closed for a few minutes.

"I want you to know how well you've done today! From now on, you'll be able to enter a state of hypnosis quickly and easily. And this ability is going to be so helpful for you. So, you can feel proud because next time it will be much more powerful.

"Even though we've only spent a few minutes doing hypnosis today, you're going to be surprised at how well you did. When those eyes open, you'll feel really good, really proud, and wonderful in every way.

Get ready ... ONE – even though we just spent a few minutes today doing hypnosis, you did wonderfully. You'll be able to enjoy all the good and beneficial effects. And next time it will be much more powerful.

TWO – preparing to open your eyes, and ...

THREE - Eyes open, notice how good you feel. Feeling better?

First impression – How long would you say you were in hypnosis. *Say this as a statement, not question. Any time distortion at all, say,* "Look at the clock!" *Emphasize this as "proof" of their ability to be successful.*

No time distortion? Emphasize subconscious mind's ability to keep time. For example, we can use this ability to program ourselves to wake up at a certain time in the morning or to spend a few minutes in self-hypnosis. Then proceed to install the trigger.

Once the client has passed the Time Distortion Test, don't allow any chit chat. Hold your hypnotic stare and ask, **"Would you like to see how quickly and easily you can go back into hypnosis?"** Slightly nod your head as you say this. It acts as a non-verbal suggestion. The client will nod in response because, of course, they want to go back into hypnosis! Who wouldn't?

Test the Trigger

When the client nods, that's their subconscious mind telling you that your suggestion is acceptable. It's now safe for you to proceed. Once you have the client's permission to guide them back into hypnosis, all you need to do is repeat the same steps you used to install the trigger. Compounding the response will teach the client how to go *back* into hypnosis very quickly in subsequent sessions using a simple hand drop.

The instructions for the hand drop are, "In a moment, I'm going to lift your arm and drop it back down onto the arm of the chair." What we're going to do is piggy-back off those instructions.

Step 1: Establish permission. Ask, "Would you like to see how quickly and easily you can go back into hypnosis?"

Remember, you're speaking to the client's subconscious mind. With the client's permission, you can now proceed to the re-induction process.

Step 2: Set up for the hand drop. Tell the client that you're going to lift their hand a couple of inches. Remind them to let you do the lifting and that the arm should be very relaxed.

---

[18] Inspired by Cal Banyan, Banyan Hypnosis Center

Step 3: Set up for the finger snap. Position your other hand in front of the client's face. Tell them to look at your hand. I'm right-handed so I lift the client's wrist with my left hand while positioning my right hand in front of their face.

Step 4: Formalize the induction. Tell the client to take a nice, deep breath in. As they inhale, use your hand to direct their gaze upward. At the same time, gently lift the client's wrist up and move it over so that it's positioned a few inches above their lap. That way, when you drop the hand, it will send a little shock through the body. This acts as a deepener. (It feels really good.)

Step 5: Fire off the trigger. The final step is to execute the following three actions at the same time.

1. Snap your fingers.
2. Give the command, "Sleep!"
3. Drop the hand into the client's lap.

As you drop the hand, fire off a deepening suggestion such as, "And go deeper."

The hand drop takes a little practice because it needs to be one seamless movement. It's all one action. "1,2,3 (snap!) And go deeper." If you've never done this before, grab a friend and practice it a few times. This will help you to get the timing down and your friend will love it. Go for Gozo'd!

Tweak Your Technique

When you direct their gaze upward, the client's eyes should follow your hand. As a result, they'll be looking upward a little. Your hand should be just about mid-forehead. This causes a little eyestrain which tires the eyes and creates a bit of tension.

As the client inhales, lift the wrist and move it over their lap. When the inhale reaches the top of the breath, say, "Hold it, hold it, hold it!! Build up that feeling of tension in the body. That way, when you execute the hand-drop, the client will get a "whoosh!" of relief. It feels really yummy, and the client will automatically drop right back down into hypnosis.

This is important. If you're working with a man, make sure you're positioning their hand to drop onto their leg and not their crotch. I learned this the hard way. If you drop their hand into the crotch, they're going to get a shock, all right! But it won't have a deepening effect. It'll emerge them. And they won't be too happy with you, either.

It's not that you'll hurt them. But the crotch is an area of vulnerability for a guy and they're very protective of the equipment. If something were to happen that is perceived as a threat to their manhood, their subconscious mind is going to emerge them. You do not want that to happen because they'll associate that negative experience with hypnosis. So, just a word to the wise – make sure the hand drops onto the leg, not the crotch. And only just a couple of inches, okay?

As soon as you drop the hand, the client will automatically release the breath as they close their eyes. When the hand plops into the lap, the client will get that little shock which naturally has a deepening effect. As soon as you say, "Sleep!" deliver the next suggestion. Don't give their conscious mind time to think. Immediately, offer deepening suggestions. In the first session, add the suggestion, "And you go right back down to that same beautiful state. And every time we do this you will go deeper than the time before."

The post-hypnotic suggestion for re-induction is: "From now on, whenever we do hypnosis together, the moment you close your eyes, instantly and spontaneously, you drop right down into hypnosis. And each time you will go deeper than the time before." And that's it. You have just installed a trigger for re-induction.

Continue to deep a little more, then bring the client's attention to how good it feels. Most of the time the client will experience is a kind of "Whoosh!" down into a deeper state. It's like sliding into a warm and fuzzy place. It's really yummy. So don't be surprised if the client has a big grin on their face. You can reinforce those good feelings by placing your hand on their shoulder and whisper, "Feels good, doesn't it?"

Often the client will just grin and nod. What this tells you is that they're really enjoying the experience. That's something you want to acknowledge and reinforce because the client is realizing something very important. They're realizing that following your instructions feels good.

Most of the time you only need to do it once. But if you don't get it right the first time, if you flub the timing, or the client doesn't respond instantly, repeat the re-induction sequence until you get the desired result. Remember, you are teaching the client while they are in a state of hypnosis. If they need to practice it a few times to get it right, that's okay. Just keep firing off the trigger until the response becomes instantaneous. This will give you a client who can get into hypnosis in a snap!

I have never had a client fail the test for the re-induction trigger. This is because they had already learned the steps at the beginning of the session. This made installing the trigger fail-safe.

> **Hand-Drop Re-Induction**
>
> "As I lift this hand, let it be loose, limp, and relaxed. Really heavy, okay?" *Lift arm to test for compliance.*
>
> *Place your hand just above client's eye level.* "Look at my hand. Take a deep breath, fill up your lungs . . ."
>
> *As they inhale, (optional: count from one to three), lift the arm a few inches and position it over their lap. Then, snap your fingers, drop their hand into their lap and utter the command,* "Sleep!"
>
> *Immediately place your hand on their forehead and gently rock from side to side using irregular movements.* "As I gently roll your head, you go right back down to the same beautiful state of hypnosis. And each time you go deeper."
>
> *Press down gently on shoulder, while pacing breathing.* "And deeper."
>
> "From now on, whenever we do hypnosis together, the moment you close your eyes, instantly and spontaneously, you drop right down into hypnosis. And each time you will go deeper than the time before."
>
> "As I lift and drop your hand, you will go twice as deep." (*Lift and drop the other hand.*) "Deeper down."

When you test the trigger it's *as if* you are re-inducing hypnosis - which you're not - but this acts as a powerful convincer. Practice the sequence a couple of times to compound the response. Then, give the client the suggestion, "From now on, whenever you want to go into hypnosis, I'll count to three, snap my fingers, and say the word sleep, and you'll return to this same beautiful state. And each time you'll go deeper than the time before."

Deepen Immediately

With a rapid induction, you always need to deepen immediately. If you give the client time to think they'll emerge themselves. Don't let that happen. Remember, the induction bypasses the Critical Faculty of the mind. That's hypnosis. But there's no depth. You need to deepen immediately to keep the client in hypnosis. Continue guiding the client to go deeper.

Because the hand-drop is so physical, I like to follow it with a kinesthetic deepener. For example, I'll either put my hand on the client's forehead or on their shoulder and do a physical deepening technique. If you don't have permission to touch the client then, obviously, you'll have to use a different deepening technique. Just match your technique to the client and you'll get good results.

Head Roll

I like to go for the forehead because my hand is already there for the snap. After you say, "Sleep!", all you need to do is place your hand on the forehead and rock it gently back and forth as you give the suggestion, "As I gently rock your head, let your body go loose and limp and relaxed."

This is a nice, gentle, maternal deepening technique. It also has a slightly disorienting effect which has a deepening effect. The head roll also gives you a way to test to see whether the client is following your instructions. If you're giving suggestions to relax and go deeper, then the neck muscles should be relaxing. As a result, the head will move freely.

Head Roll Deepener[19]

Immediately after you perform the hand-drop induction, place hand on forehead and gently rock from side to side using irregular movements.

Say - "As I gently roll your head, you go right back down to the same beautiful state of hypnosis.

"And each time you go deeper." Press down gently on shoulder while pacing breathing. "And deeper.... And deeper.

"From now on, whenever we do hypnosis together, the moment you close your eyes, instantly and spontaneously, you drop right down into hypnosis. And each time you will go deeper than the time before." (repeat)

"When I lift and drop your hand you will go twice as deep."

Lift and drop other hand as a deepening technique. "Deeper down."

(Optional: elicit and amplify feeling to regress)

The way to test is to make your movements erratic. Instead of rocking the head back and forth rhythmically, do it randomly so the client can't anticipate which way you're going to go. This makes it a test for compliance.

If the client follows instructions, the neck muscles will relax, and the head will go wherever you move it. And if there's any resistance, you'll feel it. If it feels sticky or like the head is moving on its own, they're not letting it happen. You need them to let it happen.

---

[19] Inspired by Gerald Kein, Omni-Hypnosis Center

In this case you would need to repeat the suggestion to relax. Make sure the client follows your instructions before moving onto the next step.

This is the key to your success. Always make sure that the client completes the step you're on before moving onto the next step. You need compliance. If it feels like there's some resistance there, give suggestions for letting go. If it feels like they're trying to help, tell them to stop. Say, "Don't help. Let me do all the work."

Shoulder Press

Another kinesthetic deepening technique that you can use is a gentle shoulder press. Just press gently down on the client's shoulder. It's not a push. It's a gentle pressure with a slightly downward motion.

The trick to the shoulder press deepener is to pace the client's breathing. When they inhale, the shoulder will lift a little. When they exhale, the shoulder will naturally drop. That's when you press down – on the exhale. This makes your suggestion to go deeper congruent with what the client is experiencing physically. As they exhale, they'll tend to drop down a little. This is a very effective deepener. And it feels really comforting to have a gentle hand on your shoulder.

You can also pair the shoulder press with a deepening count. Just watch the client's breathing. When you see it start to slow down you can switch from pacing to leading. Start to stretch out the interval between breaths and the client will follow. This will help to slow them down even more and they'll go deeper.

Congratulations! You have just successfully installed and tested the re-induction trigger. In the next session, all you'll have to do is

1. Conduct a preliminary check-in.
2. Ask permission to begin the hypnosis.
3. Get out your blanket.
4. Set up for the induction using the first four steps in this protocol.
5. Fire off the trigger and . . .
6. Deepen immediately.
7. Conduct a quick test for state and go to work on the client's issue.

As you can see, conditioning your clients for a rapid induction can save you a lot of time in your healing sessions, which will make you a more efficient healer in your sessions. Just a quick hand drop, and you'll be ready to go to work. The more time you can save on the induction process, the more time you'll have to devote to the healing process. Install the trigger in the first session and your client will go from zero to Somnambulism in a snap!

What next?

The purpose of the first session is to create your ideal client for regression hypnotherapy. This involves two distinct phases.

The first phase is the Conditioning process.

Optional Hand Drop/Kinesthetic Deepener[20]

Now as I touch your jaw (*gently position hands along the jaw line*) .... just let the jaw relax ...relax, relax ... (*you should feel the jaw let go*)

Touching your shoulders now (*gently press down on shoulders*) ... letting them relax completely ...

Touching your hands (*press down on hands*) ... deeper down, deeper relaxed ...

(*Lift arm*) Now, as I lift this arm, (*gently lift arm up*) just let the arm be very loose and limp, like a rag doll ... (*gently move arm around*) MELT DOWN into a state of *profound* relaxation.

(*lift and drop opposite arm*) Doubling the relaxation.

Do you feel that relaxation coming on?

Good. Now just wrap yourself in a warm blanket of relaxation. And let yourself go much deeper, because the only thing you care about today is how deeply relaxed you *can* go. The deeper you go the better you feel. And the better you feel the deeper you *can* go.

The second phase is where you train the client in readiness for regression hypnotherapy. Breaking the session up into two phases in this way gives you more time control because you can treat each phase as an individual session. This takes the pressure off you and allows you to be more client centered.

If the client needs more time to tell their story during the intake, that's okay.

---

[20] Inspired by Marilyn Gordon

If they need more time to understand things during the educational process, that's okay, too. Just allow at least thirty minutes for the hypnosis.

You need about twenty minutes to do the Conditioning Phase, and another ten minutes to debrief the client after emerging them. If you give yourself thirty minutes, you'll have enough time to take your client from "Ow" to "Wow!"

Ideally, your session would flow directly from the Conditioning phase into the Ready for Regression phase. But if you find that you're pressed for time, you can wrap things up once you have successfully tested the trigger for re-induction.

Once you have convinced the client that they experienced hypnosis, they'll be satisfied that they got what they paid for. They will emerge feeling better than when they first came in. They'll be amazed with how well they did. And they'll know that they've come to the right place.

If you need to wrap up the session following the re-induction process, allow a few minutes to deliver suggestions and celebrate the client's success.

Phase 1 Wrap Up

The purpose for the wrap up at the end of every session is to take whatever happened in the session and turn it into a revelation for the client. To do this you need to refer to the three key pieces of information you gathered onto your Session Worksheet:

1. Therapeutic Goal.
2. Conditions for Change.
3. Benefits of Change.

Begin with suggestions that reinforce this new ability the client now has. Help the client to realize that, like Dorothy in the Wizard of Oz, they've had this power all along, they just didn't realize it. And they can use this power to get where they want to go. How amazing is that? Then, tie this ability to the power to achieve their goal.

The way to do this is to use statements of recognition. For example, "Now you know ... you have this wonderful ability." "Now you know ... *this* is the Power of your subconscious mind." "Now you know ... you can use this power to create the kind of change you want."

If you're working on a behavioral change, you can deliver some suggestions based on the client's Conditions for Change list. These are the things the client believes will contribute to achieving their goal.

Finally, remind the client of all the rewards they hope to enjoy for having made all these changes. Get them to imagine what it will be like to be enjoying the benefits of having created this change.

Remember, the rewards of change are emotional. It's the feeling that makes it real. That's the motivating factor. Encourage the client to feeling the feelings that go with having accomplished their goal. Then, add a few suggestions for how the benefits continue to grow and expand as you continue working together, and emerge the client.

Emerging Suggestions

As you emerge the client, continue to pour in the suggestions. The goal is to emerge the client feeling *really good* about having made the decision to come to see you. That way, they'll be looking forward to their next session with you.

Suggestions for Wrapping Up

In a moment, I'm going to count from 1 to 5 to bring you back to your ordinary level of awareness. As I count from one to five, you become more and more alert to everything around you realizing that you are in the process of re-creating yourself. (tie to Therapeutic Goal)

Allowing yourself to finally become the person you were meant to be . . . by releasing everything that has been getting in the way of you feeling good about you. (tie to Conditions for Change list)

I want you to realize what a wonderful gift you have given yourself today. You gave yourself permission to feel better today. And you'll continue to enjoy all the benefits of having created this change because *now you know* ... (e.g. you have discovered within you this wonderful ability. And you can use it to create the kind of change you want.) This allows you to begin to feel healthier, happier, and more successful in every way.

As we continue to work together, releasing all remaining blocks, more and more you can discover what it's like to really be enjoying life free of the past. So, I'd like you now to take a moment to imagine what it's like to be moving forward with your life. Moving into your future, taking with you all these wonderful, positive changes that you have created for yourself. And as you do, experience what it is like to be doing things free of the past.

Let yourself experience it vividly, using all your senses, as if it's already true. Sense it, see it, hear it, feel it. Use all your senses. And experience what it's like to be enjoying all the benefits. (go through Benefits List)

Okay. The subconscious mind now has the information it needs. (pause). Just take a few moments, now, to just be in that place and relax. And notice how good you feel. Feel good?

Emerging Statements:

On the count of five, those eyes will open. You'll feel alert and energized, as if you've enjoyed a wonderful, restful night's sleep. Feeling comfortable and alert, with all your energy back. *Really feeling good.* Get ready …

ONE – Slowly, easily and gently, just feel yourself coming back up to your ordinary level of awareness, as the subconscious mind recedes to powerfully reinforce all the positive changes you created here today …

TWO – As all these changes go to the deepest Part of you, they make a permanent impression – physically, mentally, emotionally, and spiritually – allowing more and more positive change to occur, easily and effortlessly from now on …

THREE – Eyes clearing now as the *conscious* mind now steps forward to take over the ordinary activities of your daily life. Sensing within you a greater confidence. And feeling good. Able to use the insights, and awarenesses, in a way that is most beneficial to you.

FOUR – On the next count those eyes will open feeling alert, refreshed, relaxed, rejuvenated, feeling wonderful in every way. Get ready …

FIVE – Open your eyes, feeling great! Good job!

When the client opens their eyes, say, "Good job!" Give them a verbal pat on the back for a job well done. Then, give yourself a pat on the back because you have just successfully conditioned another client for hypnosis, and you're all set up for future sessions. Good job!

Conditioning Phase Checklist

Preliminary Set Up

1. Three Ps
2. Intake Process
3. Educational Pretalk
4. Potty Break
5. Session Worksheet
6. Three Permissions

The Induction

1. Formalize the Induction
2. Sounds Utilization
3. Physical Relaxation
4. Autosuggestion (optional)
5. Eye Lock Test
6. Hand Drop Test
7. Fractionate/Covert Test/Deepener
8. Overt Test/Convincer
9. Mini Progressive Relaxation Deepener
10. Body Tour
11. Emerge (not really) with Time Distortion Test

Install Trigger

1. Formalize the set up for hand drop.
2. Fire off the trigger.
3. Deepen immediately.

Every problem is the result of a life experience. –
Dr. Geerd Hamer

CHAPTER 6:
Preliminary Check In

Once you have installed the hand-drop for re-induction, you're all set up for the client's next session. When the client comes back in, the first thing you need to do is a preliminary check-in. This gives the client a few minutes to fully arrive while allowing you to get a better idea of how best to proceed with the session. The check-in is a strategy that allows you to uncover the information you need to guide the session. It's an important part of a multi-session system because it's all about testing the results.

The only way you can ensure a complete resolution of the problem is to test your results. And the only true test is in the client's daily life. That's where the rubber meets the road. So, you need to pay close attention to what happens between sessions.

Realize that clients don't always share everything with you right away. They can withhold information that might be relevant to their healing because they don't think it's important, or they're too embarrassed to tell you about it. They may not feel comfortable sharing it with you right away. As a result, it may take them several sessions before they're willing to fess up.

These are the folks who don't benefit from a one or two session approach. A multi-session program gives them the time they need to feel safe enough to allow change to happen.

The way to think about your preliminary check-in is as a continuation of the previous session because change doesn't happen in the session. It happens after the session. That's when post-hypnotic suggestions take effect. After the client leaves your office, their subconscious mind is going to continue to work on their issue. As a result, stuff can find its way to the surface between sessions.

Two Important Questions

It only takes about 10 or 15 minutes to conduct a preliminary check-in. But if it takes a little longer, that's okay, too. It's more important to be client centered. That will get you better results. Just don't turn it into chit-chat. Your check-in is a preliminary uncovering strategy that's meant to answer two important questions. The first question is, "What do you remember about the last session?" The purpose for asking this question is to pick up where you left off in the previous session.

Ask the client to mentally do a little rewind and go back to their last session. Then, ask them to tell you, "What do they remember about that session?" This will help to refresh your memory, but more importantly, it can be very revealing.

Hypnotherapy is a journey of self-discovery and self-healing. Often what you'll find is that the client will share more about their first session than they did the first time. The client may have had some realizations after they leave the session.

Giving the client a few moments to share in retrospect can result in more insights being brought to light. Insight is a precursor to understanding. It's the conscious mind making sense of things. That includes why the client is taking this journey with you.

The second question is, "Tell me what happened between sessions." This is because hypnotherapy naturally stirs things up at a subconscious level of mind. Following a session, the client's subconscious mind is going to go to work. It's going to be sorting through things and finding ways to integrate change. This can result in things bubbling up to the surface.

The client may remember situations that they haven't thought about in years. They may have interesting dreams. Emotions can start bubbling to the surface – sometimes unexpectedly. That's the subconscious mind speaking. And it knows why the client is seeing you.

During the check-in, these are the things to make note of because they are relevant to the client's issue. Maybe they felt great following the session, but it only lasted for a couple of days. Maybe they lost the better feeling they had when they left your office. Maybe something happened to trigger them.

If the client felt great following a session, but they couldn't hold onto the change, or they got triggered, this tells you what the next step in the healing process needs to be. That's an emotional issue. Now you know. Surface techniques are not going to get the job done. There's an unresolved emotional issue that keeps reinstalling itself. That's what's calling for resolution. The next step is to find out where "that feeling" is coming from.

Maybe the client slept well for the first time in ages. If so, this is good news because many people are sleep deprived. A person who isn't getting enough sleep can't think clearly. That's why sleep deprivation is the leading cause of motor-vehicle and job-related accidents. It impairs a person's cognitive abilities. Improving a person's sleep can make a significant difference in how they think, and feel, and behave. This can also improve your overall results.

Regression hypnosis is a process of revisiting and re-evaluating past events. Sleep deprivation can block your client's ability to think clearly enough to evaluate what was revealed to them during a session. That can block change from happening.

It takes consciousness to change consciousness. The client needs to see for themselves how experiences in the past have been creating their future. Then they can decide to allow change to happen. You can't just tell them. They must decide. But to do that they need to be able to think clearly. Helping your clients to sleep better can help clear the mental fog. This will give you a better client to work with.

When we sleep, the conscious mind goes into abeyance and the subconscious mind goes to work on emotional healing and memory reconsolidation. There's learning taking place. This is a process that will support the client in healing.

The client's first session is naturally going to stir things up. As a result, something is going to happen between sessions. You just need to find out - what? Use your pre-hypnosis check-in to ask the client, "What happened during the last session?" Then find out what happened between sessions. This will tell you how best to proceed in this session. You'll know what the next step needs to be. That's all you ever need to know.

What's the next step?

Once you have completed the preliminary check-in, the next step is to guide the client into hypnosis. This is where you pull out your blanket and say, "Ready?" Then, induce hypnosis using the hand-drop, deepen immediately, test for state, and you're ready to roll. And because it only takes a few minutes to get a client into Somnambulism, the rest of your session will be free to get to work on the client's issue. Nice, right?

If you're only doing direct suggestion work, using a rapid induction means your session time can be much shorter. But if you're planning on doing regression hypnosis, you're going to need roughly 90-minutes for the hypnotherapy session. A two-hour session worked best for me because I utilize a lot of testing and compounding in a session. And I don't like to rush a client. That's just my style. It's all about being thorough.

For the first session, if you give yourself a two-hour timeframe, you'll have plenty of time to do what you need to do without having to rush yourself or the client. If it takes less time to do what you need to do, that's fine. You can wrap things up and send the client off to test the result.

Remember, they're paying for the results, not the session time. But if you bump into a pocket of unresolved emotions, you'll have the time you need to process it and get the client some relief.

When the client emerges, you want the client to feel much better than when they began. Remember, you don't have to resolve the whole problem all at once. You just need to show the client that you can help them to feel better. They'll happily come back in for their next session.

Whatever happens between sessions will tell you what the next step needs to be. The steps are always going to be the same. It begins with your preliminary check-in. This will tell you what to focus on in the session. Test the results in between sessions and, when the problem is gone for good, you'll know.

Subsequent Session Checklist

1. Preliminary check-in/uncovering procedure.
    a. What happened in the last session?
    b. What happened between sessions?
2. Set up for hypnosis by providing a blanket. "Ready?"
3. Induce hypnosis using the trigger.
4. Deepen immediately.
5. Test for state
6. Proceed with the regression session.
7. Wrap up session powerfully by tying the session to the client's:
    a. Therapeutic Goal
    b. Conditions for Change
    c. Benefits of Change
8. Emerge the client.
9. Debriefing
10. Test the results

CHAPTER 7:
The Core Work

You'll find that clients will regress much more easily if you ease them into the process. The Ready for Regression Session focuses on preparing the client for the regression work by giving them a taste of how you will be working together in future sessions. Taking the time to make sure that the client is ready for regression will also help you to feel more confident guiding the process.

Human beings fear the unknown. This includes the territory of their own mind. You need to make it safe for the client to go there. Safety is the subconscious mind's primary concern. Your job is to work with that by proving that the client is in good hands, and that it's safe for them to follow your instructions.

The place to begin is by creating a safe environment in which you can introduce the client to all the processes you will be guiding them through. Instead of dumping the client into a painful event, right from the get-go, why not just use the first session to give them a positive experience of regression? There's no resistance to going back to happier times.

A positive regression gives you a way to satisfy the subconscious mind's primary need for safety by reducing the number of unknowns. This will give you a more hopeful client. It also provides the opportunity for you to assess where the client is at so that you can decide what the next best step might be for that client. For example, some clients require some resourcing to be ready for regression. This will give you a more willing and capable participant when the time comes to dive into painful events from the past.

Ideally, you want to make the client's first experience with you a positive one. Prove that nothing bad is going to happen, that you can be trusted to keep the client safe. Provide some relief. You don't have to resolve the whole problem. Just use the session to make sure your client is *ready* to go where you need them to go and do what you need them to do by teaching them how to work with you to get a result.

This will help to reduce fear and resistance to the overall process. As a result, their subconscious mind won't be throwing up blocks to protect the client. Instead, it will be working with you. Make no mistake, the subconscious mind will gladly show you where the bodies are buried, once it realizes that you can be trusted! A positive regression provides a safe environment in which you can introduce the client to the techniques and processes that you will be using in future sessions. This will make them familiar. (Remember, subconsciously, familiar is safe.)

The Ready for Regression Session allows you to introduce the tools of regression hypnosis within the context of a safe environment, assess the client's readiness for regression before you start asking them to dive into the pain of their past, and prepare the client for the interactive processes that you will be guiding them through as you work together to resolve the client's problem.

Regression-to-Cause Hypnotherapy Tools

The following six essential tools are all you need to get a real and lasting result working with even the most complex issues. Master the basics and your sessions will rock!

1. Age Regression

There are many different approaches to age regression. The focus of regression-to-cause is to locate the event responsible for generating symptoms and resolving the problem there.

2. Releasing Techniques

The two Rs in R2CH are regress and release. Regression gives access to the information trapped in the causal event. Releasing removes the subconscious requirement for symptoms. Releasing techniques that are very effective in regression therapy sessions include: Talking, tapping, moving the body, and pillow therapy.

3. Parts Work

Parts Work or Parts Therapy is central to regression hypnotherapy. Parts express through feelings and behaviors. They take the form of beliefs. Inner Child Work is Parts Work in a childhood event because the events responsible for forming core beliefs occurred in childhood. As a result, that's usually where we need to go to get the healing.

Parts Work allows you to identify core beliefs, unmet needs, and automatic responses that are contributing to a client's problem. The goal is not to try to get rid of them. The goal is to transform them into positive resources.

4. **Resourcing Techniques**

Resourcing techniques allow you to uncover and/or liberate internal resources and sources of empowerment that can help the client to heal. These things often come disguised as obstacles or blocks.

5. **Forgiveness Work**

Forgiveness is the final stage in the Devil's Therapy. Forgiveness simply means "letting go." When the client lets go of the problem, healing happens. In fact, forgiveness is the healing.

6. **Direct & Autosuggestion**

Suggestion is the basis of everything we do. Direct suggestions are employed to guide the healing process. Autosuggestion can be used to test the acceptability of a suggestion. It's also a powerful delivery system for acceptable suggestions.

Root Cause Theory

An analogy commonly used to describe the basic theory of regression-to-cause is the lowly dandelion. Dandelions are notoriously difficult to get rid of. When a dandelion shows up in your lawn, you've got a problem. If you ignore it, the problem tends to get worse over time, not unlike many of the problems clients come to you for help with.

If you cut the top off a dandelion, you'll get rid of the problem ... for a while ... That's a symptom management approach. The problem with symptom management is that it is only a matter of time before the problem comes back. Worse, it starts to invite a few of its friends over. That's when the party gets started.

This is what we find with hypnotherapy. If you fail to resolve what's *causing* the symptoms, the problem will tend to get worse over time. When surface approaches fail to resolve the problem, it is because what's visible on the surface isn't really the problem. What the client *thinks* is the problem is just a symptom of the *real* problem. That's coming out of their personal past.

It doesn't matter how many pills you throw at the problem, or how many techniques you apply, if all you're doing is treating the symptoms, the client will still have the problem. And the symptoms will persist. This is the problem with throwing a surface approach at a deeper issue. You might get a short-term result but, eventually, there will either be a recurrence of the symptoms or symptom conversion.

Symptom conversion is when the problem morphs into something else. Usually, it will be something that's harder to get rid of. The way to think of a symptom is that it is a messenger. When a client comes to you with a problem it has usually been around for a while. The symptoms might have started out as a whisper. But most people ignore the early signs. Bad idea.

When you don't pay attention to the whispers, they're going to become shouts. It's just how the subconscious mind works. Symptoms serve the subconscious directive. They're not the problem. They're a subconscious solution to the underlying problem. That's why, when you use a surface approach and it doesn't work, you need to use a deeper technique. Regression hypnotherapy is a deeper technique.

Too many hypnosis practitioners only deal with symptoms. They think that behavior is the problem, or the pain is the problem - whether it's physical or emotional - and the focus is on getting rid of the symptoms. That's like telling the subconscious mind to shut up. Not a good idea.

The problem is that, sometimes, the technique will work. Sometimes the symptoms will abate. But very few hypnotherapists track their results over time. They never really know whether the problem has been resolved for good. If there happens to be a recurrence of symptoms, sometime down the road, they'll never know. Worse, the client will just assume that the hypnosis didn't work.

The hypnosis *did* work – at least, for a while. The problem is that you can't use surface techniques on a deeper issue and expect to get a lasting result. For example, persistent problems that haven't responded to other treatments; chronic conditions that have a long history with the client; destructive/addictive behaviors that often have their roots in identity; issues involving complexity such as syndromes.

This is what makes regression hypnotherapy different from other approaches. The therapeutic goal is not to offer short-term relief. It is not to manage the symptoms. It is to resolve the client's issue – for good. The way we do this is by keeping the focus on whatever has been *generating* symptoms because symptoms are seldom the whole problem. To get a lasting result you need to find out what is *causing* those symptoms. That's the real problem. That's what's calling for resolution.

The symptom might be negative self-talk, an uncomfortable feeling like anxiety, unwanted habitual behaviors, or even physical symptoms - anything from eczema to cancer - but these things all have one thing in common; something happened to cause them.

Every problem is the result of a life experience. In the absence of an *organic* cause, the solution to the problem must lie in the client's personal history. Thoughts, feelings, and reactions don't just come out of the blue. These things are learned. They're based on past experiences.

Something happened. Whatever that "something" happens to be, it is in the client's history. That's where we must go to solve the problem. The problem is coming out of the client's subconscious mind. That's where all our feelings and memories are stored. While hypnosis gives us access to the subconscious level of mind, regression gives us access to life experiences that have been feeding into the client's problem.

Regression-to-cause allows you to identify and remove the underlying cause. Then there is nothing left to generate the symptoms. Remember, symptoms are not the problem. Symptoms are merely evidence that there *is* a problem. They're messengers coming from the subconscious mind, alerting the conscious mind that there *is* a problem. What the *real* problem is will be revealed through the healing process.

The *real* problem is the story. It's a life story that *begins* with the Initial Sensitizing Event (ISE). It *develops* through all the subsequent events. And it is all leading up to where the client is *now*, in their present life, where it takes the form of symptoms.

The problem is that the story isn't over yet. To give the client the ending they deserve, you need to go back to the beginning, find out what happened, find out how their whole tale-of-woe got started, and resolve it there.

Find the Roots

The ISE is the root of the problem. It is the causal event that sensitizes the client to a particular pattern. Once the pattern has been established in the ISE, situations in daily life can act as reminders of the unresolved, painful aspects that are still trapped in the ISE. These events will then re-stimulate the underlying pattern, making it stronger.

Any event that is related to the client's issue, but comes *after* the ISE, is called a Subsequent Sensitizing Event (SSE). An SSE acts as a *reminder* of the ISE. As a result, it *re-stimulates* the underlying pattern, which then reinforces the underlying, unresolved problem. This is why problems tend to get worse over time. Other issues can then get added to the mix as the pattern continues to grow and develop through these subsequent events. But these are *secondary* issues. As such, they're generally easy to clear up once you have resolved the ISE.

Some issues are relatively simple to deal with. They have a kind of linearity to them. There's a direct path from where the client is now back to the causal event. There might only be a few events feeding into the issue. And there's only one emotional layer to deal with. This is the basic regression model most of us were taught. But in *real* life, not every issue is going to fit the model. This is because problems tend to grow and develop over time. As they grow and develop, more stuff gets added to the mix, and this can create complexity.

This doesn't change your approach. The steps are always going to be the same. It just means that some clients are going to need more time to get a complete healing simply because there's more stuff inside calling for resolution. You need to dig down beneath the surface and pull out all the roots. If you're thorough, and you get everything, then there will be nothing left to generate the problem. That's when the problem is gone, for good.

This is why you need to be thorough. You need to make sure that you get everything. And the way to do that is to test. You need to test to make sure that you got everything that's been feeding into the problem because there can be multiple events, and multiple aspects, and layers of perception, and thought, and feeling. All these things are contributing to the problem.

Once a person has been "sensitized," repeated stimulation of this pattern will have a compounding effect. This is what SSEs do. They're not the *cause* of the problem, but they're reinforcing it, making it stronger. And every time a triggering event occurs the symptoms will get worse.

An SSE is like fertilizer to a dandelion. It's feeding the problem. Every time the client bumps into a situation that reminds them of the ISE – either consciously or unconsciously – it reinforces the underlying problem. Plus, more stuff can be added to the mix, which just adds to the overall problem.

The issue might have started out as something quite small. In fact, the ISE is often no big deal, at least, as far as the *Adult* consciousness of the client is concerned. But the subconscious mind has a talent for making a mountain out of a mole hill.

Kindling

Dr. Robert Scaer is an expert in trauma. He holds two degrees, one in psychology and one in neurology, which makes him a brain scientist with an understanding of how the mind works. He calls the ISE an event of "kindling."

Kindling is a process of setting up for a fire. If you've ever been camping, you know how this works. You scrunch up a bunch of paper. Then you add a layer of small bits of wood. Then some bigger pieces of wood. This gives you a base for starting a fire.

The ISE is a base for starting a problem. All it takes is a "match" and the whole works will burst into flames. That's when symptoms will appear.

The ISE is laying the *foundation* for those symptoms. Sometimes the symptoms will occur immediately following an ISE. But what is more common, for the average person, is that symptoms don't appear until much until later in life.

What determines when the symptoms show up has to do with repetition. Repetition is what reinforces the pattern. The more events there are, the more reinforcement there is, and the quicker symptoms will appear. For example, sexual abuse in childhood tends not to be a one-time experience for a child.

Not only is the child experiencing the same trauma over and over, again, these events happen over a short period of time. As a result, symptoms will show up sooner, typically in adolescence.

For the average person, symptoms show up in mid-life. It takes that long for the problem to reach a sort of "critical mass." This is because, most of the time, the ISE is relatively weak.

The causal event is the ISE. Then another, similar situation arises. That's an SSE. Then, what follows is often a whole series of SSEs leading up to symptoms coming to the surface of awareness at some point in the client's life. SSEs act to re-stimulate the pattern. It takes a while to reach the point where the problem has enough power to express as symptoms. That's what the conscious mind *thinks* is the problem. But it's merely a symptom of an undigested, painful experience trapped in the ISE.

Every SSE is, in some way, a *match* to the ISE. It's acting to reinforce the underlying pattern. Eventually, the whole thing reaches the point of ignition and POOF! – like a fire, symptoms appear, seemingly out of nowhere.

This can come as a shocking surprise to the client because the feeling or response will be irrational. This is because the feeling/response is not coming out of what's happening now. It's coming out of a past event. That event is stored in the subconscious mind. As a result, the client will feel out of control because the conscious mind doesn't have the power to control *that*.

The conscious mind then does what it does best; it tries to gain a sense of control by coming up with a reason to explain the symptoms. This is what clients will do. They'll tell you *why* they have the problem. Sometimes they're right. Sometimes the client will be able to identify a specific event where the symptoms first appeared. For example, an outbreak of eczema might have appeared after a stressful experience. This is useful information that can help you to guide the process.

This is why your intake process is so important. It can provide important clues as to when the problem got started. Just know that the reason the conscious mind hasn't been able to resolve the problem is because it doesn't have the whole story. Whatever the client *thinks* is the problem isn't the *real* problem. That's why they need you!

A consciously remembered event is more likely to be the Symptom Producing Event (SPE). For example, a person with a phobia can tell you when they had their first panic attack. That's the Symptom Producing Event. Most of the time the ISE will be earlier than that. The goal is to locate the *first* time and thoroughly clear everything. We want to pull out all the roots. This ensures that nothing can grow back.

Anything unresolved in the ISE needs to be neutralized. When the ISE is clear, all the changes will then ripple throughout the mind-body system. As this happens, it will have a weakening effect in all subsequent events. Nice, right?

This is a natural process that you can encourage through the process of growing the client up through the SSEs. Think of this as future pacing from the ISE. Growing the client up through the SSEs gives you a way to test the results during the session.

If the client returns to an SSE and bumps into the same problem that was in the ISE, you'll know that you missed something. This means that the client still has the problem. In this case, go back to the ISE and take care of it. Then, test again.

If something new arises in the SSE, that was *not* present in the ISE, it would be safe to assume that you've located an aspect that got added later. Because it is specifically associated with that SSE, it's a secondary issue. Most of the time, these are easy to clear. But if you bump into strong resistance, you may find that the SSE is pointing to an ISE for *that* specific perception, thought, or feeling.

I know. It sounds complicated. But this can happen when you're dealing with an issue that has a lot of moving parts. The key is to be systematic. Approach it one thing at a time and you will get there.

Time is an Illusion

The goal of regression-to-cause hypnosis is to uncover whatever life experiences have been contributing to the client's problem. But it takes courage for a person to face the things from the past that generate uncomfortable feelings.

As you resolve the thoughts, feelings, and decisions that are responsible for generating unwanted symptoms, the client's mind will come back into balance, restoring a sense of peace. But to do that, you need the cooperation of their subconscious mind.

Remember, the subconscious mind is holding onto the information needed to realize complete healing. You need to prove that it is safe for the client to go back into past events because you cannot override the subconscious mind's need to protect.

One of the easiest ways to set things up for regression to happen easily is to guide the client back into positive memories from childhood. This is incredibly useful because most of the problems we work with are rooted in childhood. Accessing *positive* memories from childhood can make it safe for the client to allow vivid recall of a past event. You can then use that event to teach a client how to work with you. This approach also gets you into the ballpark of the causal event without any of the drama.

The subconscious mind is duty-bound to protect. One of the ways it does this is by protecting the client from painful memories. The reason it does this is because those events were traumatic. Any traumatic memory will have a significant emotional charge around it. This is what holds the memory in place. But the problem isn't the feelings. The problem is that any unresolved event with a negative emotional charge around it is considered a current event.

As far as the subconscious mind is concerned, that event isn't over. It hasn't been stored as a past event. It's being held over so that the subconscious mind can keep working on it.

When an event from the past is unresolved in some way, the subconscious mind continues to keep trying to come up with a solution. But it can't. This is because it only has the resources that were available *at that time* – which are often the resources of a child.

The problem is that the subconscious mind doesn't keep time the same way as the conscious mind. The conscious mind needs to make sense of things. So, it organizes events along a linear timeline. It then creates stories about those past experiences because this provides a much-needed sense of control.

"I overeat because …" "I'm afraid of spiders because …" That's the conscious mind coming up with a story that makes sense of things. But the subconscious mind doesn't work that way. The subconscious mind is timeless. It has no problem with you being a newborn infant, a five-year old, and a fifty-years old, at the same time. This is what makes it possible to do Parts Work.

Parts Work is the ground floor for regression hypnotherapy because, most of the time, you're going to be going back into childhood. When you get there, you're going to be working with Inner Child Parts. The younger the age of the Child, the more impressionable they are, and the more vulnerable they are to any perceived threat. That, by definition, is trauma.

Trauma has been defined as the perception of a threat while in a state of helplessness[21]. It's about feeling vulnerable. And every Child is helpless.

Everyone has experienced some kind of childhood trauma. For example, birth is inherently traumatic. And a newborn is about as helpless and vulnerable as it gets. But this doesn't mean that an experience of trauma must develop into a lifelong problem. The problem is seeded when the experience doesn't end well.

---

[21] Dr. Robert Scaer

If the experience doesn't get dealt with and resolved at the time, it gets held over as a current event. This means that the threat is still present. That's going to continue to generate fear.

Most of the time what you'll find is that the event was misinterpreted by the Child. The threat was really no big deal. The real problem was that the Child lacked the information or maturity to make sense of what was happening. As a result, it felt overwhelming – at that time. This is what the subconscious mind is trying to protect the client from. It's the threat of being overwhelmed again. Naturally, there's going to be some resistance to going there.

If what happened during that event was too much for the client at age five, it's still too much, even though the client is fifty-five. The subconscious mind will try to block the memory to protect the client from it. That is subconscious resistance.

The subconscious mind doesn't know that they're not a child anymore because the Child that they once were is still stuck in that event. The way the subconscious protects the client is by preventing the memory from being brought to conscious awareness. This is because it's still a threat.

There can be conscious resistance, too. The conscious mind wants to be in control. But it doesn't have all the info. There are too many unknowns. The conscious mind doesn't want to face any uncomfortable feelings because it can't control them.

What this means for you is that you can end up with a real wrestle on your hands if you don't prepare the client for where you want to take them.

The solution is simple. Take them back to happier times. There's just no resistance to going back to happier times. Using a *positive* regression in the first session allows the client to have a *taste* of the process without any pain. Within the context of a safe, comfortable event, you can guide the client through the process quite easily. This makes the process familiar – which satisfies the conscious mind. And it makes it safe – which satisfies the subconscious mind.

This is how you can get both the conscious and subconscious mind of the client working with you before you start diving into painful events. Prepare the client for where you're going to take them. Then, when it comes time to guide them into an emotionally charged event, it won't feel weird or threatening to the client. It will be familiar and, therefore, safe.

Regression isn't always going to be the next logical step for a client. This is why I recommend using your first session to assess before you regress. It allows you to look under the hood and get a better idea of what you're dealing with. This will tell you what the next step in the client's program needs to be.

Some clients are going to need additional ego-strengthening before you ask them to face events in the past. Other clients will need to be educated more about the process to feel safe enough to allow feelings and emotions to come to awareness. Think of this initial positive regression as a "trial run" for you and the client without any of the pressure.

If the client needs to do some more work to be truly ready for regression, that's okay. That's what the client needs. And if you're just starting out, this gives you what you need, too, because it takes all the guesswork out of the equation by allowing you to uncover the information you need to feel confident guiding the process. Nice, right?

Parts Theory

Parts Work is central to regression-to-cause therapeutic hypnosis and involves a process of facilitating a dialogue between different Parts of the client. The three primary Parts we work with in regression hypnosis are the Child Part, the Adult/Grownup Part, and Parent or Offender Parts. All three are internal Parts of the client.

The Child is a feeling Part of the client and is the client's younger self. The Grownup Part is the adult consciousness of the client. This is the Part of the client that can use thinking, reasoning, and analysis to make sense of things. As a result, this is an important Part of the healing process. Parent Parts and Offender Parts or "perpetrators" represent other people who have contributed to the client's issue and have been internalized by the client. They are internal representations based on specific experiences in the past.

When you transform a Part, it changes how the client thinks, and feels, and behaves in their daily life. To create these changes, you need the cooperation of the Parts that are contributing to the problem. But what if the Part isn't willing to participate? What if the Child Part refuses to speak to the Grownup Part? What do you do? For example, let's say the Child Part isn't willing to communicate with the Grownup Part. When Parts aren't willing to cooperate, there's always a reason. It's because there's a block, an internal conflict.

When you bump into resistance, you might be tempted to switch to a different technique. But I wouldn't recommend it. This just gives the client permission to continue avoiding the real problem. Avoidance is always a major part of the overall problem. Realize that, when you bump into resistance, you're on the money! Don't try to push through or switch techniques. Stop right there and deal with the block.

Recognize that the block is a *symptom* of the client's overall problem! Grab the bull by the horns and focus on "that feeling" because, when there's a block, there's always a reason. Find out what that reason is. Regression-to-cause hypnosis is all about getting to the "why"? *Why* does the Child not trust the Adult Part? *Why* is the Child unwilling to speak to the Grownup? The answer to that question will give you the next logical step in the client's healing process.

Most of the time it comes down to the Child's need for safety. After all, you're dealing with the subconscious mind, and safety is the subconscious mind's primary concern. The block usually has to do with fear. But the subconscious mind is very specific. You won't know *why* there's fear blocking you until you ask the Part.

Stems Completion

When addressing a Child Part, avoid asking "why" directly. The Child doesn't use adult reasoning and logic. The Child is a *feeling* Part of the client. To the Child, "why" questions can feel like being interrogated. Interrogation is threatening and will cause *any* Part of the client to shut down. All Parts need to be treated with love and respect. Instead, tease out the answers by using a Sentence Stems Completion exercise.

Stems Completion is a process of offering the client a sentence to complete by putting an ending on it. This approach honors how the Child feels while framing things in a way that allows that Part of the client to reveal the reason for their resistance. For example, you could say something like, "Repeat after me and put an ending on this. I don't want to speak to Grownup *because* ...." Then, let the Child put an ending on it. If the Child says, "I feel scared" or "it's not safe", now you know what the underlying problem is. That's fear. But the objective is to find out *why* they feel scared. You need to avoid directly asking "why" because this could cause the Child to shut down. So, what do you do?

Use the same technique to grind down a little deeper. For example, you could have the Child say, "I feel scared *because* ...." or, "It's not safe to speak to Grownup *because* ..." "Because" gives you the "why". In this way, you can use Sentence Stems to quickly grind down to the underlying reason for the block.

Once you know what the underlying fear is, you can find a way to resolve it. Resolving the block will allow you to continue with the healing process.

Sometimes the Child Part won't talk to the Grownup Part because it is angry with Grownup. This is an internal conflict pointing to self-rejection and self-blame. Remember, the Child is a Part of the client. That anger is being directed towards themselves. They're at odds with themselves. They're blocking themselves. And they're very likely punishing themselves because of it. Internalized anger can generate self-punishing behaviors.

Your job is to find out what happened to cause that anger. If it looks like there's an anger issue, try using Stems Completion and have the Child say, "I *won't* speak to Grownup because ..." This can be very empowering for a Child Part. And when you give it permission to tell the truth of how it *feels*, it will trust you and gladly reveal the underlying reason for that anger being there.

Maybe they've been beating themselves up. Maybe they're being too hard on themselves. Maybe they're being critical, and the Child is taking the hit. For example, children are seldom listened to. Not being heard can be a source of frustration and anger that gets turned inward. (Who isn't listening? That's the question!)

Fear and anger are internal blocks that need to be released. To do that, you need to uncover all the contributing aspects. The more specific details you can uncover, the more effective you'll be at resolving the whole issue. For example, if it's not safe to speak to the Grownup Part, find a way to provide safety.

One of the ways you can do this is to suggest to the Child that "Grownup can't hear us. It's just between the two of us." Or tell Grownup to take a place in the background while you have a talk with the Child Part. Then invite the Child to tell you the whole story. Encourage the Child to express how she feels by telling you her side of the story without the Adult Part of the mind barging in and criticizing. That's often the underlying problem.

For the Adult Part of the client the problem is that the feeling isn't rational, it doesn't make sense, and the conscious mind has a need to control. This creates an internal conflict. The key is to validate the *feeling*. The Child is the feeling Part and "that feeling" has a right to be there. Let the Child know that she's *allowed* to feel that way.

Remember, the conscious mind is never completely out of the picture. You need that Part of the client to be present when the time comes to do the transformational work. When you place the Adult Part off to the sidelines, the client is still aware of everything that's going on. What this means is that the client is learning from you. They're learning how *you* interact with their younger self.

Modelling to the client how to treat a child with love and respect teaches the client to treat *themselves* with kindness. Witnessing how you treat their Inner Child can help pave the way for greater cooperation on their end.

Remember, when there's a block, there's always a reason. Find out *why* there's a block because *something happened* to cause that Part of the client to feel scared, or sad, or angry. Realize it's being brought to conscious awareness because it's relevant to the client's presenting issue. It may even be the underlying cause. That's why the best course of action is to deal with it.

Once you identify what the specific grievance is, you need to do something with it. Resolve it so the client can feel safe again because, when the client feels safe, the mind will open to allow learning. That's when healing will happen. The method you choose will depend on your training and what specific details you uncover. But you have a basic choice of how to proceed – either regress or release.

Regress or Release?

You can choose to stay in the event and release the feelings – the fear, or the anger, or the sadness, or whatever feeling the Child is holding onto - and give the Child some relief. Or you can choose to Bridge back off the feeling and regress back to a time when the Child is still feeling safe, or loved, or when it's okay for her to just be who she is and express how she feels. You can then find out what happened to cause the client to *lose* those good feelings.

How do you decide which approach to use? Purging the uncomfortable feeling will release the internal pressure. Once the internal pressure is gone, the Child will feel safe, again. Sometimes, releasing the feeling is quicker, while regressing back further can allow the Child to have an experience of what she most needs. This can give you a more resourceful client for doing Inner Child Work. Remember, the goal is to invite the Grownup Part back in to have a talk with the Child. The Adult can then reprogram the Child. But to do that the Child must be willing to listen.

If there's too much resistance – too much fear or anger – you might find it easier to regress back to an earlier event where you can gather up some resources for the Child. You can then bring a more resourceful Child back to the scene to continue the Inner Child Work.

Most of the time, all you need to do is just release the feeling to restore clarity and peace. When that happens, the mind will become open and receptive to learning. That's when you can re-educate and reprogram the Child to allow the changes that you're after.

How do you release an uncomfortable feeling like fear, anger, or sadness? I use tapping and pillow work. But you may have other techniques that work, as well. For example, some people use breath work or shaking to release a feeling. I found the most effective approach is to match the technique to the intensity of the feeling. When there's a lot of internal pressure, a lot of intensity, using a more dramatic approach will get you a deeper release.

How do you measure the intensity of a feeling? Quantify the feeling by taking a Subjective Unity of Discomfort (SUD). To take a SUD, all you need to do is ask the Part, "On a scale of one to ten, where ten is the *worst* that feeling has ever been, how *strong* is that scared feeling?" Or how strong is that anger? Or whatever the feeling happens to be. Then match the technique to the intensity.

The rule of thumb is - the bigger the feeling, the bigger the movement. It's more congruent. For example, if the emotional intensity is relatively low, like a four or a five out of ten, you could use talking and tapping to release the feeling.

If the intensity is higher - like ten or twelve - you'll get quicker results by using a bigger movement. That's when I would get out the pillow and have the client move the feeling out by pumping it into the pillow. The idea is to give the Part permission to feel better by releasing all the pain and the pressure that's been trapped inside. Then give the feeling a way out by giving it a way to express.

Once the energy of emotion has been released, the client will feel a tremendous sense of relief. They'll feel more peaceful and, as a result, they'll have more mental clarity. This is because the Child Part isn't holding onto all the pain and the pressure, anymore. That was the block. This is when you can invite the Grownup Part back into the conversation.

All Healing is Self-Healing

Before you can invite the Adult Part to speak to the Child, you need to make sure that you have a Grownup who is willing to be there for the Child and be loving and accepting of the Child.

For any change to be real and lasting, the change work needs to be done by the client. After all, it's their mind. You can't do it for them. You can guide the process. You can offer suggestions. You can model and coach. But the words that will have the greatest impact on the mind of the client will always come from the client. Remember, the Grownup or Adult Part is the conscious, thinking, rational, logical Part of the client. When you're speaking to the conscious mind, you need to make whatever you're about to ask them to do reasonable.

Make sure that the client understands that their subconscious mind is showing them what the real problem is, and that it has everything to do with "that feeling". Verify that the client understands that this is the key to their healing, and that the Child is not the problem. The Child is never the problem. The feeling is never the problem. It's a Part of them that needs to heal. Then ask the client if they would be willing to be there and support the Child.

With their agreement, you can then offer the suggestion, "Inside of you are the words that the Child needs to hear to *let go* of that (anger, or frustration, or fear, or whatever the feeling happens to be)." It's up to the client to *find the words* and tell the Child what she most needs to hear.

One of the biggest temptations is to try to *make* the client change. You can't. If you try, it will generate resistance. That will just add to the pressure. So, relax. Let the client do the work because these are the words *the client* most needs to hear.

Traumatic History

Some clients will come to see you knowing that they have a traumatic history. When you start talking about problems being rooted in past experiences, they'll tell you that they don't want to go there. That's understandable. But regression doesn't have to be a big, hairy traumatic reliving of all the gory details.

We're not interested in all the details. We're only interested in finding the feelings trapped in the event so that the client can let them go. Releasing all the feelings will drain off all the pressure, allowing the client to finally heal.

If you get a client who was raped, or witnessed a murder, or have some big-hairy traumatic memory from childhood, let them know that they don't have to relive all the gory details of the event. The only thing we're interested in is *the feelings*. That's how the subconscious mind communicates. The client just needs to be willing to allow the feelings attached to the consciously remembered event to come to the surface. Bringing them to conscious awareness allows them to be processed and released.

Begin with uncovering all the reasons the client doesn't want to go there. Address their resistance to facing the past. Remember, it's not what they consciously remember that's causing the problem. It's the aspects of the problem that are *hidden* from consciousness that can wreak havoc.

Start by identifying all the fears they have about what might happen if they ever look at those things. Then validate those feelings. Give them permission to feel that way. They're allowed to have their feelings. Those feelings are good. They're there for a reason. Something happened to cause them to feel scared, sad, or angry. They just weren't prepared for it. They were too young. There was no one there to protect them or help them make sense of things.

The problem is that their subconscious doesn't know that they're not a child anymore. It doesn't know that they're a Grownup, able to handle that knowledge and use it in a way that allows them to heal. Reassure the client that they don't have to spend the rest of their life feeling scared or vulnerable or alone - like they did as a child.

When you're dealing with a traumatic event, the goal is for the client's subconscious mind to realize that the event is over. It needs to realize that the client survived, they're still alive, that they're in the chair in your office, and they're all grown up. This allows that painful experience to be moved into long-term memory as a past event - where it belongs.

When you have established rapport with the client's subconscious mind, it will show you where it feels you need to go to get the healing. Be prepared, though, because just talking about a traumatic experience can bring on an abreaction.

Talking about the event will generate pictures in the client's mind. Attached to those pictures are emotions. That's what holds the memory in place. The stronger the emotion, the deeper the client is going into the subconscious mind.

The deeper they go, the deeper the hypnosis. Realize there's already some degree of regression taking place. As the client moves deeper into the memory, they could bump into something unexpected. That "something" could be the key to their healing.

Remember, you're just dealing with a story. The story is just how that experience got stored as a memory. This is based on the perceptions, thoughts and feelings of the client *at the age* at which the event occurred. Memory is not a recording of a factual event. It's a recording of perceptions, thoughts, feelings and responses. The younger the Child is, the more errors in perception there will likely be.

Whatever the Child couldn't make sense of, or cope with, or was too overwhelming for the Child didn't get stored as a past event. This means that, subconsciously, that event is still happening. If it was too much, the first time, it's probably too much now

Situations of severe trauma can sometimes be resolved simply by going immediately *after* the event. Get the client out of the hairy-scary situation and go immediately after what happened. Then, process the event using past tense language. This allows the client to get some distance from the source of threat which provides a sense of safety. That's what was missing the first time. You can then clear whatever happened in hindsight.

The client is still in a regressed state. You have just moved them to a point immediately *after* the big hairy, scary situation. Talk to the Child immediately after all the drama has played out and find out, "What just happened?"

Even if they don't have all the details, they're still feeling the feelings. That's all you need to know to drain off a lot of emotional intensity. Releasing the feelings and emotions after the event will allow the client to come to clarity about the details of what happened. You can then help the Child to realize that she's not alone, she's safe, she made it through that experience, and *it's over*.

Changing the Child changes Grownup. Once the client is stabilized, ask permission to go back to *before* anything bad happens in that event so that you can help the Child get through it without being negatively impacted by it. With the client's permission, guide them to go *before* anything bad happens. Then, support Grownup in preparing the Child for "what's going to happen."

Remember, if something truly happened, we can't change that. What we can change is how it feels. Draining off the emotional intensity after the fact, then front-loading the event with support will dramatically reduce the impact it had the first time, making it much easier to process the event.

Every client is different. It's different strokes for different folks. Not every technique is going to work for every client. Sometimes you can get the result you're after by using a surface technique. Sometimes imagery, metaphor, or dissociative techniques will get the job done. But there will be times when surface techniques won't be enough. That's when you need to go deeper to get to the root of the problem. You just need to keep the door open to allow for deeper work if necessary.

My approach is to introduce the client to the healing process in a gentle way. If there's any resistance to following your instructions, take a step back, and work on building compliance. Make it safe for the client to trust you to guide them. There's never any need to strong-arm a client into following your instructions. That's bullying. All you need is a Contract. And the Contract for regression says, "We go where we need to go to get the healing."

You can always begin a healing program using an imagery-based approach. It's gentle and non-threatening and you can use it to increase trust. Show the client that it's safe to follow instructions. You can use an imagined event to teach the client how to work with you. For example, introduce the uncovering techniques of regression hypnotherapy, or the concepts of Parts, or teach the client how to bring up feelings and release them.

Dreams and imagination both use the language of the subconscious mind and images come out of memory. As a result, a simple imagery technique can sometimes give you a back door into an actual event from the past. For example, when a client connects with any strong emotion, you have a Bridge to the past. This gives you the opportunity to convert an imagery exercise into real regression. You just need the client's permission to go there.

Chemical Lids

Doctors are struggling to help their patients find relief from *their emotions*. When the prescribed chemical lids fail to keep the feelings down, the only thing the doctor can do is to try throwing another drug at it. As a result, some people are taking two or three different antidepressant medications at the same time. This is not uncommon.

Women are twice as likely as men to take antidepressant medication (16.5 percent compared with 8.6 percent).[22] According to the National Center for Health Statistics (HCHS), the rate of antidepressants used among teens and adults (people ages 12 and older) increased by almost 400% between 1988-1994 and 2005-2008. The federal government's health statisticians indicate that one in every ten Americans takes an antidepressant.

Antidepressants such as Paxil, Celexa, Effexor, Zoloft, etc. may work but they are not selective. They work by putting a lid on *all* feelings – good and bad. The client doesn't feel *bad* anymore. But they don't feel good, either. They lose the ability to feel their good feelings. *That's* depressing.

People will come to you because they're sick and tired of feeling like a zombie all the time. They want to get off the drugs so that they can feel good again. Antidepressants are not usually a problem when it comes to bringing up a feeling for regression work. The feelings are still there. They're just muted. I have had clients on multiple antidepressants, and they were able to find and feel enough emotion to do the work required.

---

[22] American Psychological Association

If you get a client who wants to take the lid off, make sure you have a doctor's referral. They shouldn't just stop taking their medication. The patient needs to come off these chemicals gradually under their doctor's supervision.

Some clients just don't want to face their feelings. But feelings and emotions are there for a reason. What these clients need to know is that feelings are normal and natural. All mammals experience them. They are nature's biological feedback system. They're meant to guide us to be healthy and happy in life.

"Good" feelings tell us that we're satisfying our needs for safety, achievement, and connection. "Bad" feelings tell us we need to *do* something - change something or take immediate action - so that we can feel "good" again.

If you get a client who is on antidepressants, educate them about how *all* feelings are meant to be helpful. It's when we put a lid on our feelings that they become a problem. Reassure them that feelings naturally arise and pass away. Even the most uncomfortable feeling won't last very long when allowed to be felt fully. Then it finishes and it's over.

The feeling is like a Child tugging on the apron strings saying, "Mom, Mom, Mom, Mom." It's trying to get your attention because there's a problem. Ignoring, suppressing, and trying to shove the feeling down, only adds to the problem. The feeling isn't the problem. An emotion is a bio-chemical event that is felt in the body. It's a messenger signal coming from the brain, telling the body what to do. The signal tells the body how to respond so you can take care of yourself. For example, hunger is a feeling that says you need to feed yourself.

Fear is a feeling that says you need for safety. Anger is a feeling that points to a need for healthy boundaries. Sadness is a feeling that points to a loss of connection.

The way to resolve an uncomfortable feeling is to simply feel it. Feel it fully and it will finish. Then it's over. It's like a recurring nightmare. The "bad feeling" keeps chasing you. You keep trying to get away from it – but you can't. The way to *stop* the nightmare is to turn around and face it. Face the feeling. That's how you end the nightmare.

Intense feelings, especially those that are rooted in childhood, can seem overwhelming because they were overwhelming *for the Child*. Over time, these feelings can build up a lot of pressure inside. But feelings are finite. They don't last very long. Many people don't know this but even the most intense emotion won't last more than 90 seconds. That's 90 seconds – MAX – *if you just let yourself feel it.*

There's nothing wrong with any emotion. This is what a person who is taking antidepressants needs to understand. It's normal and natural to feel our emotions. Feelings only become problematic when we *resist* them, or avoid them, or try to get rid of them. That never works.

When you don't let the feeling express, it gets stuck in the body. That's when it becomes insistent. Like that kid going, "Mom, Mom, Mom, Mom." And like a child, the feeling is *never* the problem.

Once you end the resistance to feeling the feeling, you'll have a client who is ready to face the truth of their feelings. Then, you can help them to put an end to the nightmares for good.

Releasing creates space: Loving and approving of yourself, creating a space of safety, trusting and deserving and accepting, will create organization in your mind, create more loving relationships in your life, attract a new job, and a new and better place to live, and even enable your body weight to normalize.

~ Louise Hay

CHAPTER 8:
Ready for Regression Phase

Once you have completed the Conditioning Phase you should have successfully created your ideal client for *hypnosis*. The next step will then be to create your ideal client for *regression therapy*. During the Ready for Regression Phase, the focus shifts from hypnosis to assessing and preparing the client for regression-to-cause hypnotherapy. This is important because you cannot do it for the client.

Just because a client is *willing* to participate in their own healing process does not mean that they're going to be *able* to follow your instructions to go where you need them to go. You need to teach them how to work with you to get the results. This is a client-centered, rather than a technique-centered, approach that allows you to adapt to the needs of each individual client.

Being able to treat these two protocols as stand-alone sessions takes the pressure off you because you don't have to do everything at once. If you have a client who needs more time during the intake process, and you find that you are running short on time, you can wrap things up following the Conditioning Phase and you'll be all set up to pick up where you left off in the next session. This can help you to feel more in control of your sessions. If the client is in distress, they are probably not ready to dive into the hypnotherapy, anyway. Their greater need may be to talk and feel heard. That's okay. The power is not in the hypnosis. It's in the client.

Responding to the most immediate needs of the client will make it safer for the client to follow your instructions. Not only will this give you a more cooperative client to work with, but it will also make your job easier when it comes time to begin the process of regressing the client.

Strategizing

While you can easily facilitate the Conditioning phase as a stand-alone session, it works best when facilitated back-to-back with the Ready for Regression Phase. In most cases, you should find it fairly easy to guide your clients through both phases. But if you're running short on time, you can end right there with a session wrap up. The client's next session would then be a continuation, beginning with the Ready for Regression Phase.

The next session would begin with a preliminary check-in. Once you have completed the check-in, offer the client a blanket, ask, "Ready?" And with the client's permission, you can now proceed with the hand-drop induction.

1. Conduct preliminary check-in.
2. Offer the client a blanket.
3. Facilitate the hand drop induction.
4. Deepen immediately.
5. Quickly conduct test for state (eye catalepsy test)
6. Continue with Ready for Regression protocol.

If, on the other hand, you have plenty of time following the conditioning session, continue into the Ready for Regression protocol. Following any rapid induction, you must always deepen immediately. If you don't, the client will emerge themselves. I like the head-roll deepener because it feels very reassuring to the client, and it doubles as a test for compliance.

In the first session, however, when you deploy the hand-drop induction, you are merely testing the trigger. Because the client is still in a state of hypnosis, the hand-drop acts as a slightly dramatic deepening technique. Immediately follow this with add another deepener.

Stacking several deepeners on top of another makes for a really yummy experience for the client. And you want the client's first experience with you to be a positive one. Using lots of deepeners also helps the client to access deeper states of awareness which allow the client to vividly recall memories.

What follows the re-induction sequence is an imagery deepening technique. This is because we are going to be accessing imagination and memory. Imagination and memory are close cousins. They draw from the same databanks. And image and emotion are how the subconscious mind naturally communicates. In the first session, we want to make it safe for the client to access feelings and memories from the past because memories are stored at a subconscious level of mind.

Snow Falling Deepener

The Snow Falling Imagery deepener is a nice deepening technique that acts as a warmup for the Hypermnesia Exercise.

Almost everyone has pleasant memories of watching snow gently drifting down. It's quiet and peaceful. Safe and secure. This sets the tone for recalling pleasant memories from childhood!

Snow Falling Imagery[23]

And just like the way snow falls …. and every gentle flake of snow … comes down so slowly and so peacefully … you can allow your thoughts to just drift, drift … to a deeper level of rest … wrapping the trees and the ground in a soft blanket of quiet comfort ……. so peaceful and so safe …

And the longer you watch the flakes coming down, down, down … the more relaxed you become… sinking down to a more positive way of thinking, feeling and behaving, at that automatic, unconscious level …

And no matter how deeply you go in hypnosis, you'll always be able to go deeper than the time before. So next time it will be ten times more powerful because hypnosis is simply a shift from thinking to feeling. And if you can *feel it* – you can heal it.

And you know this brings you *all the benefits* that *you* desire … the benefits of change … And how change is a *good* thing for you now …. Change in a *positive* way … to allow yourself to feel better about yourself … And allow yourself to move forward with your life … feeling healthier, happier, and more successful in every way.

Pay close attention to your pacing and tonality. Remember to match the imagery by speaking slowly while using a deepening tone. "As you imagine watching the snow s-l-o-w-l-y drifting down … down … down … you naturally drift down deeper into hypnosis. It feels so good."

---

[23] Inspired by Maureen Imperial and Tom Nicoli

Remember

What makes any event memorable has to do with the feelings that got *associated* with that experience. This gives you a Bridge to the past. The feeling is a signal coming out of the event that caused it. The purpose of regressing to past events is to change the *meaning* the client has given to a painful past experience which, in some way, continues to cause them pain.

To re-member means "to re-assemble all the pieces." When we remember something, we mentally create an image. It is a creative process. We create a picture in our mind. This picture (thought) is an internal representation of that experience *based on the meaning we have given it.*

Research shows that every time a person remembers a past event, the memory is altered by their present interpretation of that event. When a memory is brought to mind it gets reinterpreted using the person's current level of knowledge and understanding. This is a natural process that allows us to learn from our past experiences.

Learning automatically changes the memory. This is a natural process that we utilize in regression hypnotherapy. Through the process of guiding a person's Adult consciousness back into painful events from the past, we encourage the client to review and reinterpret those experiences from a more mature point of view. This changes how a person *remembers* those events. The reason we can do this is because a memory is not a fixed event. It's changeable. You cannot change the *facts* of an event - if something truly happened, you can't change that. Nor should you try. Avoiding the truth about what happened is 90% of the client's problem. What you *can* change is how the client thinks about that experience. This changes everything.

Remember, every time something happens to remind the client of that painful experience, they get triggered. either consciously or unconsciously. When a person gets triggered, all the negative feelings associated with that experience come rushing up into conscious awareness. This can be quite distressing because the person often has no idea where it is coming from. As a result, they feel out of control.

What's happening is that they are re-membering. The problem is that they are reliving the memory without the benefit of consciousness. Because there is no conscious re-evaluation or re-interpreting of that experience, the negative associations trapped inside the memory get reinforced. This causes the underlying, unresolved pattern to grow stronger.

Our memories are constantly changing. This is why Subsequent Sensitizing Events (SSE) can flow back into the Initial Sensitizing Event (ISE) and make it stronger. It's because the more times we get triggered, the more emotional intensity gets added to the original event. This is why problems tend to get worse over time. But it's not what happened, that is the problem. The problem is that the client is still holding on to a negative *interpretation* of the event.

That's their story. But it's a story based on the knowledge and understanding they had at the age they had that experience. Most clients are stuck in a Victim Story because they're stuck in the understanding of the child they once were. They feel powerless to create the change they want because their inner child still feels powerless.

Through the healing process we will endeavor to transform painful past experiences into sources of empowerment for the client. This is accomplished by bringing the client's Adult consciousness back into the causal event to review and reinterpret what happened. Changing how the client interprets a past event will change how it *feels*. In this way, the client can transform their Victim Story into a Victory Story.

Memory Is Not Fact

Some people think that memory is factual. As a result, they think that regressing into a past event is going to reveal what really happened. That is seldom the case. Memory is dodgy, at the best of times. This is because the conscious mind is limited.

In any given moment, the conscious mind is being bombarded by information coming in from the environment. But it can only process about forty bits of information per second. The subconscious mind, on the other hand, can process 20,000,000 bits of information per second. That's 500,000 times more powerful than the conscious mind.

The subconscious mind is the emotional part of the mind. It's responsible for holding onto all our feelings and memories. Its primary concern is safety. If a situation is perceived as a threat, that information is going to be stored in memory to ensure that we'll know how to respond to similar situations in future.

It isn't like the information isn't getting in. It's just that very little of it is being processed *consciously*, which means the conscious mind doesn't have the whole story. The rest of the story is being processed and stored at a subconscious level of mind. This is what makes regression therapy so powerful.

Hypnosis gives us access to the subconscious level of mind. Regression allows us to access memories stored at that level of mind so that we can find out whatever happened to cause the problem in the first place. This ability to process information *un*-consciously certainly helped us to survive as a species. But it comes at a cost. Conscious recall of any event is only ever going to be partial. And if an event happened to generate uncomfortable feelings, and those feelings didn't get resolved, it can lead to unwanted responses and uncomfortable symptoms later in life.

Many of these problems have roots in childhood. This is primarily because children are downloading tons of information without the benefit of critical thinking. Remember, the Critical Faculty of the mind isn't fully formed until age five or six. This means that the child is wide open to suggestions.

Children are easily overwhelmed by their feelings and emotions, and they lack the maturity to be able to make sense of many of the things that are going on around them. As a result, whatever is happening to or around them is often mis-interpreted. These earliest impressions contribute to a person's core beliefs - which decide what we are going to get in life.

Regression hypnosis is a process of taking the conscious mind back into these events. This gives us access to more information about what happened to cause the problem in the first case, while allowing the client to review and then re-evaluate those experiences from a more mature point of view. Once they know the whole story, they can choose how that experience is going to influence them in their present life.

The reason they can create this change is because memory is not about fact. The subconscious mind makes no distinction between real and imagined. When a client goes back to a past event, they're not re-visiting is a factual event. It's just the story as their subconscious mind has it. The story is about the thoughts, feelings, and reactions that were shaped by that experience. These are based on how the situation made the person feel. That's what we're changing through the healing process of regression-to-cause hypnosis.

We're not changing what happened. We're changing how it feels. Now, if something really did happen, we can't change that. But the truth is that *that event is over.* It's in the past. It's just that the subconscious mind doesn't know this, yet, because there are painful feelings and emotions still trapped in that memory. The problem is that the subconscious mind only has the resources and understandings of the client at whatever age that event occurred. This leaves the client stuck in the fears and misunderstandings of the child that they once were.

So long as their subconscious mind doesn't recognize that the event is over, it's going to continue to generate symptoms. And because the subconscious mind must protect, it will continue to protect the client, even when those thoughts and feelings have no basis in fact. For example, a nightmare can be stored as an event.

Memory has nothing to do with truth or fact. Misperceptions routinely get stored as truths. The stories we overhear, the books we read, and movies that make an impression on us can all be incorporated into memory *as if* they were real experiences. What makes an experience "real" is how it feels.

That's the keyword here – *experience*. A subconscious event is a real *experience* because the feelings are real. The subconscious mind is responsible for holding onto our memories. And it's the feeling that makes any experience memorable. The problem is that the conscious mind's ability to process information is limited. It can easily be overwhelmed by too much information, especially strong emotions.

This is doubly true in childhood because children are vulnerable and easily overwhelmed. They are still developing the ability to regulate their feelings. And they are not always able to make sense of what's happening to and around them. Situations in life can easily get blown out of proportion. When that happens, it can, and does, lead to problems later in life.

When you're dealing with such an event in regression, you're not dealing with an actual event. You're dealing with a story. That story may or may not have any basis in fact. But the feeling is always true. Don't look for facts because memory isn't based on fact. It's based on perceptions, thoughts, and feelings. These things have everything to do with the age the memory was first formed.

The younger the Child is, the more suggestible they are, and the more likely they are to misinterpret things. Prior to the formation of the Critical Faculty, ideas are easily accepted uncritically. Without the Critical Faculty, there's nothing in place to discriminate between fact or fiction, real or imagined. But when misinformation and criticisms get accepted as truth or fact, that's when the party gets started.

Positive Memories

The Ready for Regression Phase begins with a simple Hypermnesia Exercise. This is a simple process of inviting the client to remember *pleasant* events in childhood. This is easy because most of these memories are readily available to the conscious mind.

Hypermnesia means "enhanced recall". Technically, it is not really a regression. Real regression involves revivification, not merely recall of past events. Revivification means "reliving" which requires the state of Somnambulism. Hypermnesia, on the other hand, is utilizing the heightened awareness of hypnosis to enhance the client's ability to *remember* things from the past. But because the state of hypnosis makes it easier to remember things, we can use it to enhance the client's recall of positive memories from childhood.

When a person is in Somnambulism, the images of past events become more vivid and clear. The client is not just thinking about those events. They're having a much more vivid and real experience of those situations. Not only is more information being made available to the client, but because they are feeling calm and relaxed, they are experiencing the optimum state for learning. You can use this state to teach the client how to step into an event and experience it fully.

In a regression session, we are usually looking to access an uncomfortable feeling to Bridge back on. The problem is that there's always going to be resistance to allowing uncomfortable feelings to come to consciousness. You can bypass this resistance by bringing up positive feelings and emotions, instead. As the client reviews those positive experiences in childhood, they begin to form positive associations to the process, making it safer for them to "go there."

Research shows that evoking pleasant memories from childhood can function as a safe lead-in to actual age regression. That's what we're going to do in the Ready for Regression Phase. We're going to *convert* the Hypermnesia Exercise into a real age regression.

A positive event provides a safe environment in which to teach the client how to respond to you when they are in a past event allowing you to prepare the client for the uncovering process. Allowing positive feelings and impressions to come to conscious awareness will also make other feelings and emotions more accessible, and available, for transformation.

Hypermnesia Exercise

The Hypermnesia Exercise can save you time by providing a much easier path to navigate and a shorter distance to the causal event. This approach can save you time as most issues we work with have their roots in childhood. When your client recalls a happy event in childhood you're already in the ballpark of the causal event.

When you land in an event in childhood, ask the Child, "Does the problem exist yet?" From there, with the client's permission, you could easily move backwards or forwards to locate the causal event. It's an option.

The Snow Falling Deepener acts as a warmup for the Hypermnesia Exercise. Once you have the client tuning into the peaceful feelings associated with that quiet, comfortable scene, ask the client to recall another pleasant memory from childhood. Most people have experienced being in or around water as a child making it a good place to start.

Water Memory

Ask the client to recall a pleasant memory of being in or around water. It might be a puddle or a pond or something else. Give them a moment to find that memory. Then verify when they're there.

When the client indicates that they have found that memory, help them to associate fully into the scene. Get them into the experience of being there and enjoying that experience, once more. Make sure that they are connecting with how it feels. Amplify the good feelings. Then, suggest they recall another positive experience.

Bicycle Memory

Another common childhood experience is being on or around a bicycle. Give the client a moment to find that memory. Then encourage them to enjoy that experience. The objective is to connect with the good feelings associated with happy experiences in childhood and feel them fully. Give the client time to associate fully into that experience before moving onto another positive memory.

Swing Memory

Invite the client to recall a time when they were on or around a swing. It might have been at a park, or at a friend's house, but a pleasant, happy memory of being on or around a swing. Repeat the process of guiding the client to associate fully into that scene, connecting with the feelings associated with that experience, and enjoying this return to happier times in childhood.

Each time the client associates into a positive, happy event it compounds the enjoyment of being a Child. As they feel those feelings, they *become* the Child. This means that they're already beginning to regress. They may be accessing conscious memories, but the feelings are coming from the subconscious mind. Regression is already happening to some degree.

Relaxation Memory

If you want to provide additional relaxation, invite the client to recall a time when they were feeling very relaxed and comfortable. It might be a memory of being snuggled up in bed or being in a special place like a garden or in nature. It might be when they were on vacation. I like to add, "Or even now" because some clients have reported that they could not recall ever feeling relaxed. Imagine that! When the client finds that memory, let them enjoy it fully.

Hypermnesia Script

Now, I'd like you now to allow yourself to experience some wonderfully peace-full, *positive*, happy memories from childhood. **Would that be all right?**

Good. And as soon as you become aware of those positive, pleasant memories, just let me know by saying "yes". **Okay?** *(optional: use ideomotor signals)*

As you continue to relax and listen, your mind can easily recall a happy time when you were just a child, when you were **in or around water**. A wonderfully positive time. It might have been a rainy day. It could have been bath-time, or a sprinkler, or a puddle, or a pond. It might have been at a pool, or the beach, but as that pleasant memory comes to mind, you let me know. (Good, deeper relaxed)

And now, a positive memory of a time when you were **on or around a bicycle**. It could have been your bicycle. It could be a friend's bicycle. Anybody's bicycle, really. As that happy time comes up, you let me know. (Good, deeper relaxed)

And now, a time when you were **on or around a swing**. It could have been *your* swing set. It might have been at the park or at a friend's. A pleasant memory where you are on or around a swing. And as that pleasant memory comes to mind you let me know. (Good, deeper relaxed)

And now, a time when **you are feeling really relaxed**. Feeling *so* calm and *so* relaxed. Comfortable. Peaceful and serene. Might be snuggled up in all comfy and cozy in bed. Or in a special place you l-o-v-e, like a garden or in nature. It might have been a time on vacation. But a wonderfully pleasant experience of feeling s-o-o relaxed and s-o-o at ease, that the only things you care about is how deeply relaxed you feel. And as that feeling comes on you let me know. (Good, deeper relaxed.)

> Now **just allow yourself to enjoy the simple pleasure of relaxing in this way.** Allowing relaxation to flow through you now, from the top of your head to the bottoms of your feet. And flowing wonderfully through tissue in your body. And every cell. And throughout the nervous system. And just noticing what that's like. **Feels good, doesn't it.**
>
> *This is optional but, if you like, you can anchor the state with a simple finger pinch technique. As homework, this can be a useful resource for some clients. They can use it as a daily stress-buster and this can help to increase their confidence in the process.*

Moment of Insight

Happy memories can evoke tears. If the client begins to cry, ask them, "What feeling are you feeling?" Never assume. Ask. They could be experiencing tears of happiness. Or they could be tears of sadness.

Usually, the client will tell you that they're feeling happy, or relaxed, or good. They will be tears of joy. But sometimes they'll tell you that they're feeling sad. And it is because they're experiencing a moment of insight. They're realizing that they have forgotten what it's like to feel truly happy, the way a child experiences happiness.

This is a moment of insight. Ask the client, "What's happening that you're feeling sad?" Often, the client will tell you that they are realizing just how disconnected they have been from themselves. This can be a profoundly healing experience for a client.

Give them a few moments to let that realization sink in while encouraging them to fully experience those "better feelings." Realize that this is a moment of healing. Remind the client, "You're allowed to feel all your feelings – *even the good ones.*" Encourage the client to let *all* their good feelings come back, fully, realizing that those feelings were there inside of them, all along. Then, encourage them to allow *all* their good feelings to come back to them now. Really fill them up with all the goodness. Then guide them to recognize that they have just *recovered* their ability to feel good. That's huge.

Finger Pinch Anchor[24]

I want you to know that you can recreate these wonderful feelings of calm relaxation any time you want. **Would you like that?**

Okay. **Place your thumb and index finger together** like this (*position fingers*). Now, rub your fingers together feeling calm and relaxed, calm and relaxed, calm and relaxed. And notice how that feeling grows stronger, as you rub your fingers together, feeling calm and relaxed, calm and relaxed, calm and relaxed. **What's that like?**

Realize that each time you do this, as you rub your fingers together, your ability to enjoy these wonderful feelings of being s-o-o comfortable and at ease, so calm and relaxed grows more powerful within you. **Won't that be nice?**

From now on, *any time* you want to feel more relaxed, and *more* calm and at ease, all you have to do is just rub your fingers together. And your ability to *f-e-e-l* comfortable, calm, relaxed, and at ease will return. So practice it frequently throughout the day. And notice how much better you feel. (PAUSE)

Age Regression

Any strong emotion can be used as a Bridge to the past. Once the client is feeling really good, you have a strong Bridge. Why not use it?

---

[24] Inspired by Cal Banyan, Banyan Hypnosis Center

Instruct the client to focus on "that feeling" and follow it back to an earlier time that they felt that way. Because you're guiding the client to go back to events that feel *good*, there's no resistance to going there. As a result, they'll regress very easily.

Just tell the client to focus on *that* feeling and go back to an earlier time that they felt that way. Do that and you effortlessly convert a memory exercise into an actual regression. Cool, right?

If you're not there already, direct the client to go back to *before* the age of five. As many of the problems we deal with have their roots in the vulnerability of childhood, the younger the Child, the better. This will get you into the ballpark of the ISE.

The ISE is almost always before the formation of the Critical Faculty of the mind which is formed by age five or six. The younger the Child, the more dependent they are on others to help them make sense of the world, and the more suggestible they will be. If you have time, you can lily-pad back through younger and younger ages.

I like to take the client all the way back to the womb. This can be a really lovely experience for the client.

The Womb

Any positive experience from the past can be used to remind the client that things weren't always this way because there was a time when they were free of the problem. There was a time when they felt good about themselves, a time when they felt safe and secure.

If you go back into the womb, there was a time when they were simply okay. That's when they felt whole and complete and at one with the Universe.

Regression Patter[25]

Realize that (happy/relaxed/good) feeling is connected to every time you ever felt that way. In a moment, I'm going to count from 5 down to 1. As I do, let your mind take us to an earlier time that you felt that way. And let it be sometime before the age of five.

Your mind can easily present to you a scene, situation or event in childhood where you feel relaxed, safe and secure. It might be five years old. It might be three years old. It might be one year old. *Or even younger.* And let it be a time before you ever knew what it was like to feel scared or angry or insecure in any way.

Now this is important. You don't try to think back or remember. Just let your thinking mind stay off to the side as you follow the feeling back. Just let the feeling guide you. And on the count of one, find yourself in a scene, situation or event feeling safe and secure.

5, going back in time.

4, to a scene, situation or event of significant to that feeling. A peaceful time. A time of feeling calm and relaxed. Safe and secure.

3, arms and legs may be growing smaller now, as your mind journeys further and further back.

2, moving right into that scene, situation or event of significance to the feeling. And on the next count, there you are, feeling safe and secure. You see what you see, you hear what you hear, and you feel what you feel....

And 1. **Be there**.

(Proceed to Uncovering Procedure)

The womb can be a blissful state, but not always. Regardless, it is a great place to test to see if the client's problem has gotten started yet. If the problem doesn't exist there, you'll have a wonderful opportunity to plant a few seeds.

Because the mind of the infant is wide open, you can provide understandings that were not there the first time. These understandings will be readily accepted. For example, you could use this experience as *evidence* that there is nothing wrong with the Child. This isn't a concept that the Child has even considered, and the Adult is not likely to argue with it.

But the Adult will be holding onto beliefs that conflict with the idea that there is nothing wrong with them. You can begin to undo those false beliefs by reinforcing the truth about the Child. The thing is, the Child and the Adult are the same persona. If there's nothing wrong with the Child, then there is nothing inherently wrong with the client.

Any changes that occur in the consciousness of the Child, are going to ripple up to the Adult Part of the client. You can encourage this process by suggesting, "Let all these new awarenesses and better feelings become a part of you now. You're *allowed* to let all your good feelings come back to you now." This is powerful stuff because these suggestions are going in before the problem ever existed!

When you get upstream of the problem, you can introduce positive thoughts and ideas that weren't there the first time. These thoughts and feelings will naturally flow forward along the client's timeline, changing subsequent events.

---

[25] Inspired by Cal Banyan and Stephen Parkhill

Remember, you're *before* the causal event. This means that as these thoughts and emotional energies ripple forward in time, they will flow *into* the casual event and change how it feels. These newer, better perceptions and beliefs can help to dislodge, and even dissolve part or all of the client's presenting problem. At the very least, the problem will get weaker, making it easier to resolve. Nice, right?

Regress to the Womb Patter

In a moment, I'm going to count from three down to one. As I do, your mind takes you back, further still, to a time when you're still feeling safe and secure and comfortable inside Mom. A time when you're still inside Mom. And notice how you feel what you feel, you see what you see, you hear what you here, and you know what you know inside Mom.

3, 2, 1 (snap!) Here you are!

Say, "Here I am/ And I feel (put an ending on it)."

CHAPTER 9:
Uncovering Procedure

The purpose of the uncovering procedure is to identify all the factors that are contributing to the client's problem so that you can resolve what is causing it. Once you know what is generating the problem, you can clear it. Clear everything and there will be nothing left to cause a problem. This is how you get a lasting result. But to do that, you need the client's cooperation. Regression therapy is an active process that requires the client's participation.

Regression hypnotherapy is an interactive process. Things will go much easier for you if you teach the client how to participate in their own healing. This begins during your educational pretalk. During the educational pretalk, let the client know that they will be very aware during the session.

Let them know that what comes to awareness during the session might not make sense, right away. That's okay. You're not interested in what the conscious mind thinks, anyway. You're only interested in what the subconscious mind knows. Remind the client that the only thing that can get in the way is trying to figure things out because that's accessing the wrong part of the mind.

The conscious mind doesn't have the answers. If it did, it would have sorted the problem out, right? The subconscious mind has the answers. It's just not what the client *thinks*.

How to Respond

The three keys to the Contract for regression hypnotherapy are:

1. Follow instructions.
2. Answer quickly.
3. Go with the first impression.

The client has already demonstrated a willingness to follow instructions. By following your instructions, they have relaxed into a state of Somnambulism. But relaxation is a passive process. The client needs to know how to respond to you during the uncovering procedure. A pleasant, positive, happy scene from childhood is the perfect place and time and place to teach your clients how to respond to questions - *not* when they have landed in a scene that was overwhelming for them as a child.

When you're guiding a client through the uncovering procedure, teach your client to respond to your questions *without thought*. Don't give them any time to think. If you do, their conscious mind is going to step in and get in your way.

Teach your clients to answer quickly and to go with their first impression. That's the key. There's no need to try to figure anything out. The client needs to learn to trust their first sense, their first impression because that's their subconscious mind speaking. And the subconscious mind has the answers.

This can be challenging for some clients, particularly the more analytical types, because subconscious logic seldom makes sense. The tendency is to want to question things. But the subconscious mind doesn't use reason or logic. The subconscious is the feeling part of the mind, it doesn't think. In fact, when something does not make sense, it could mean that you are right where you need to be. Reassure the client that there are no wrong answers and that *later* it will make sense.

Step into the Scene

2, moving right into that scene, situation or event of significance to the feeling. And on the next count, there you are . . .

You see what you see, you hear what you hear, and you *feel what you feel* . . . .

And ONE. **Be there!** Say, "Here I am . . ." (wait)

"And I feel . . . put an ending on it."

Be here!

The uncovering procedure begins on the count of one, with the command, "*Be there.*" Teach the client to use Sentence Stems by giving the instructions, "Say – 'Here I am . . .' (wait for the client to repeat the suggestion.) And I feel . . . put an ending on it."

The statement, "And I feel . . ." allows you to verify that the client is still feeling the feeling connected to the Bridge. It's a test. When you guide the client to go back to an event before the age of five, you are following a positive feeling such as "relaxed", or "happy." If the client is still feeling relaxed or happy, you will know that they're following instructions.

You can then proceed to guide the client through the following six basic uncovering questions of regression hypnosis.

The Six Basic Uncovering Questions[26]

1. Daytime or nighttime?
2. Inside or outside?
3. Alone or with someone?
4. How young are you?
5. What's happening?
6. How does that make you feel?

Notice that these are multiple-choice questions? This ensures that you're not leading the client. If you were to ask, "Is it daytime?" you're offering a suggestion. When you offer a choice, the client must sense which choice feels most true. That's what you want. Their first sense.

Your uncovering process will be more fruitful if you ask questions that offer a choice because – "Alone or with someone?" doesn't require thinking. It just requires an impression of which feels true.

The first three questions work like the Sounds Utilization Process used in the Conditioning Phase. You start with the broadest sense of things - daytime or nighttime?

Then, you gradually narrow down to the more specific details. Inside or outside?

Then, alone or with someone?

---

[26] Source: Gerald Kein, Omni-Hypnosis

As the client responds to each of these questions, the scene will start to flesh out and grow more vivid and real. This will allow more information to come to awareness, which in turn will allow you to guide and teach the client to respond with the key information needed to resolve the underlying problem.

1. Daytime or nighttime?

The first question is "Daytime or nighttime?" This gives you the broadest sense of where the client's mind has taken them. A more effective way to ask this question is to say, "Does it *feel* like its daytime or nighttime?"

This is a more subjective question. That's what you want. You want the client's first sense of where they're at. But here's the thing. As soon as the client answers the first question - you're in! Now *you know* that the client is stepping into the scene. You can now move to the next question which will help to flesh out the scene a little more.

What if the client isn't sure whether it's daytime or nighttime? When you're working with a positive memory, it's unlikely that you'll have a problem with the first question. But if you do, remind the client that there's no right or wrong answer. All that's required is that they give you their first sense.

They could be questioning themselves. Or it could just be that the client is not tuned into their feelings yet. That's okay. The purpose of the first session is to teach the client how to respond to your questions. All that is required is for them to give you their first impression. That's it.

If they're still stymied, tell them to pick one. It may just be that they're not trusting their impressions. Then, move to the next question. Often this will move the client through the block and the answers will start to come to them more easily to them.

2. Inside or outside?

The second question is, "Are you inside or outside?" Better yet, "Does it *feel* like you're inside or outside?"

This is narrowing the focus a little more. You're asking the client to locate their position in terms of space. If their sense is that they are "inside" you can then focus on getting more detail about where inside they might be. For example, "Where inside might you be?"

This process of eliciting more details helps the client to associate *into* the image. The more details they can give you early on, the more vividly they'll experience the event.

3. Alone or with someone?

The third question is, "Alone or with someone?" Or "Does it *feel* like you're alone or with someone?"

Sometimes the client will know right away. They'll say, "I'm with Mom." or, "I'm with my friend." And this will invite a little more detail to come to awareness. Just know that there are going to be feelings associated with that person.

This is where you need to identify whether that person is a source of good feelings or not so good feelings. Then make a note on your Session Worksheet.

> *Remember, the first three questions help to incrementally tune into the image of the event. Don't rush the process. Give the client time to find the answer before moving on to the next question. This will help them to associate fully into the image.*

4. How young are you?

The next question is, "First sense . . . How young might you be?" Notice I didn't ask, "How *old* are you?"

The reason for this is because, during the count back, the suggestion is, "growing younger." "How young are you?" is more congruent. This suggestion can help the client to associate more fully into being their younger self. That's what we want. We want them to *become* their younger self.

If the client says, "Little," this tells you is that you they have associated into a very young Child. The Child may not know his or her age.

If your sense is that you're speaking to a toddler, tap on the back of their hand and say, "Show me – how many fingers?" Small children often know how old they are by how many fingers.

If you suspect the client has regressed to infancy, say, "First sense. Does it *feel* like you are days, weeks, or months old?" This approach continues the multiple question approach while chunking things down.

Remember, there are no wrong answers. All you need is their first sense. As soon as you get an answer you can incrementally question the client until you pinpoint the age of the Child.

5. What's happening?

Question number five is, "What's happening?" But before you ask this question, make sure that the client has answered the first four questions.

Remember, you are teaching the client to set aside thinking and trust their first impressions. As their skill in responding to your questions improves, so will the amount of detail you have access to. They'll drop the hesitancy and just give you their first impression. That will allow the scene to come fully to awareness.

Once the client has associated into the event fully, they'll have a pretty good idea of where they're at and what's happening. That's when you can ask, "What's happening? Give me a report." This question gives the client permission to tell you the story as it's all playing out now.

6. What feelings?

The sixth uncovering question is, "What feelings are you feeling?"

This is *the most important question* because the problem always has something to do with a feeling trapped inside. That's what the client has been trying to avoid – *that feeling*.

The most important question you can ask is, "How does that make you feel?" Just don't overuse this question. That can get annoying because it can feel like an interrogation.

Keep your attention on the client and observe their responses. That way, when something happens to trigger a feeling, you'll see it. That's the best time to ask, "What's happening?" and "How does that make you feel?"

What's happening in an event will generate feelings. A positive event will generate good feelings. A painful event will generate uncomfortable feeling. You need the client to tell you what, specifically, is happening in that scene, situation, or event of significance to cause them to feel *that feeling*. Specifically, what emotion? That's where you'll find the healing.

Core Emotions

Good feelings and bad feelings are part of the human experience. Good feelings are associated with positive emotions which usually fall under the categories love and enjoyment. For example, happiness, joy, contentment, amusement, pleasure, satisfaction, bliss.

Love is accompanied by a general state of expansiveness, calmness and contentment and expresses feelings of tenderness, acceptance, trust, safety and security, adoration, satisfaction, gratitude.

Researchers are still debating which emotions can be considered primary or even if there even is such a thing as core emotions. But the primary negative emotions we encounter in our work as hypnotherapists are fear and anger, followed by sadness and shame/guilt. Complex or secondary emotions build on the primary emotions and involve more thought and interpretation.

Fear and rage are about survival. They come from the reptilian and mammalian brains. With fear, blood flow goes to the large muscles (e.g. legs) making it easier to take flight. A flood of stress hormones put the body on red alert in readiness for action. The face will blanch as blood is shunted away from the extremities. At the same time, the body freezes momentarily, fixated on the perceived threat, perhaps to evaluate what response to make. For example, run, hide, or fight.

Fear can be experienced from queasiness, wariness, on-edge, nervousness, apprehension, concern, scared, frightened, all the way up to terror. For example, phobia, panic attack.

With sadness there is a drop in energy and enthusiasm for pleasurable activities. When it deepens, it becomes depression, which then slows the body's metabolism. The purpose of this 'slowing things down' is to provide the opportunity to mourn the loss, come to grips with the consequences of this loss or disappointment in one's life and, as energy begins to return, make new plans. Sadness can be experienced as loneliness/aloneness, dejection, despair, disappointment, sorrow, self-pity, grief, and depression.

With anger, blood flows to the hands, making it easier to grasp a weapon. Heart rate increases and stress hormones like adrenaline send a powerful surge of energy through the system to support action. Anger can be experienced as irritability, annoyance, frustration, resentment, bitterness, outrage, fury, and at the extreme, hatred and violence. Anger is also a strong component in depression.

Rage "is the ultimate defense all animals draw upon." When we perceive that our lives are in mortal danger, when we are "up against the wall" with no choice but to attack, rage will move us to action.

Feelings like shame, guilt, and embarrassment likely come out of the pain of being isolated, i.e. *separation distress*. Shame can be experienced as regret, remorse, embarrassment and guilt.

Worthy of note is the feeling of "shock." Shock is the negative expression of surprise. With both shock and surprise, there is an accompanying lift of the eyebrows. This permits more light to hit the retina to allow more information about the unexpected event to be taken in.[27] According to E.A. Barnett, MD[28] primary negative feelings can be divided into three categories – hurt, fear, and anger. Hurt can be defined as the awareness of sensations of discomfort and pain associated with separation from the source of comfort and security, i.e. separation distress.

Hurt is felt in the body. Hurt *hurts*. Often it is accompanied by feelings of rejection, loneliness, or isolation (aloneness), as well as grief, sorrow, self-pity, dejection, despair, and in extreme cases, clinical depression.

Child psychology asserts that a child under the age of six months will not show any signs of separation anxiety because strong attachments have not yet been formed. However, in one study[29], the results suggested that human infants do recognize physical separation from their mothers and start to cry in pulses. When reunited with Mother, the child stops crying.

This postnatal cry has been likened to the "separation distress call" common to other mammals. These findings support the opinion that following birth, close contact with the mother is the most appropriate position for the child. The child is vulnerable and dependent on the primary caregiver. Crying is the child's only defense. When in distress the only thing an infant can do is cry more loudly.

When the child is older (between the ages of one and three years of age), he is more likely to show signs of separation distress when left by a primary caregiver. The feelings, however, are clearly evident at birth.

---

[27] Daniel Goleman, Emotional Intelligence, 1995
[28] E.A. Barnett, Theory of Analytical Hypnotherapy, 1989
[29] Karolinska Institute, Department of Women and Child Health, Karolinska Hospital, Stockholm, Sweden

Stages of Separation Distress

The stages of separation distress in childhood are defined as:

1. Protest: loud cries, frustration
2. Despair: very quiet, doesn't participate in activities
3. Detachment: withdrawal, doesn't interact with peers, plays by himself

Romantic relationships can trigger unresolved childhood separation distress leading to clingy/needy behavior, frustration/angry outbursts, quiet withdrawal.

Protest Stage: In adulthood, protest takes the form of crying over anything, frustration, and angry outbursts.

Despair Stage: The stage of despair can express as prolonged numbness, bad moods, depression, self-pity, a 'poor me' attitude, putting on a tough exterior, a needy search for love in adulthood.

Detachment Stage: The detachment stage typically involves withdrawal. Persistent hurt is often experienced as sadness. Sadness is meant to help us adjust to significant loss, such as the death of a loved one or a major disappointment (i.e. loss of a dream).

Sadness brings a drop in energy which can lead to unwanted habits and addictions. For example, eating for energy. As it deepens and approaches depression, there is a loss of enthusiasm for life's activities, particularly pleasurable diversions, and the body's metabolic functions slow.

This loss of energy may have served as a protective function for our ancestors by keeping them close to home at a time when they were more vulnerable. And withdrawal allows a person time to mourn a loss, come to terms with a frustrated hope, gain understanding and, as energy returns, formulate new plans.

Primary Emotions

The primary emotions we work with in regression sessions are Hurt, Sad, Fear and Anger. Hurt is the initial pain of separation from the source of comfort and security. Sad is the feeling of loss. Fear is the feeling that follows Hurt when the hurtful circumstances are perceived as life-threatening. Anger is the feeling that arises to defend ourselves against threat.

The normal physical response to anger or fear is a tightening of the body. Everything in the body mobilizes to protect us by either fleeing or fighting. This puts the body in a state of contraction.

Fear

Healthy fear is experienced as an immediate, intense, *short-term* burst of anxiety in response to a perceived threat. When allowed to be fully felt and expressed, fear arises quickly and then passes away as soon as the threat is gone.

Humans have only two natural fears: the fear of falling, and the fear of loud noises. All other fears are learned. In one study of five hundred people, over seven thousand fears were identified, making 6,998 of these fears unnatural and useless.

Common labels for the feeling of fear include:

- Apprehension
- Nervousness
- Concern
- Consternation
- Misgiving
- Wariness
- Qualms
- Edginess
- Dread
- Fright
- Terror
- Phobia
- Panic

"Fear is a feeling that says, "Something bad might happen." ~ **Cal Banyan**

Fear is the feeling that follows a Hurt when the cause of discomfort is perceived as life threatening. The purpose of fear is survival. We are hard-wired to respond to threat by either taking flight, to escape the source of danger, or by freezing to avoid detection (i.e. playing 'possum). Anxiety, terror, and panic express varying degrees of *intensity* of fear.

Fear causes blood to go to the large skeletal muscles, such as in the legs, making it easier to flee. As blood is shunted away from the core of the body, it creates the feeling of the blood "running cold". When the body freezes the circuits in the brain's emotional centers send a flood of hormones through the body putting it on red alert, making a person edgy and ready for action.

Unresolved fear from childhood results in chronic anxiety. An infant is helpless and incapable of running away from the perceived threat. Its only defense is to cry loudly until help comes. An older child, on the other hand, is able to move away from the source of discomfort and toward the source of comfort and safety, i.e. mother or surrogate[30]. Until feelings of safety and security are restored, the child's fear will persist. The memory of a past experience of hurt will trigger fear in order to motivate the person to avoid being hurt again.

Obsessive Compulsive Disorder (OCD) is an example of an attempt to push away fear.

Self-sabotaging behaviors are often attempts to avoid situations that are perceived as risky or dangerous. For example, procrastination, perfectionism.

A phobia is often displaced fear. Unresolved fear from the past is being projected onto harmless objects or situations in the present such as snakes, bridges, elevators, outdoors.

Fear can be generalized, resulting in the perception of the world as dangerous, others as untrustworthy, oneself as powerless (i.e. victim).

Fear can also generate psychosomatic illness. Many medical doctors would agree that a large percentage of diseases seem to be rooted in anxiety and fear. Fear is a root cause for many of our negative and depressive thoughts[31].

---

[30] Anyone who responds to the infant's cry for help functions as a surrogate mother in that instance

[31] Chester Tolson, PhD, and Harold G. Koenig, MD, The Healing Power of Prayers, 2006

Anxiety, on the other hand, is an unrelenting feeling of apprehension that lingers long after the actual threat has passed. Anxiety accompanies physical sensations such as sweaty palms, shallow breathing, rapid heart rate, and overall nervous energy. Anxiety has been linked to conditions like cardiovascular disease, IBS, and diseases related to inhibited immune function. Generalized Anxiety Disorder (GAD) is a chronic anxiety state where anything can become a source of worry for the sufferer.

Obsessive and compulsive behaviors (OCD) can develop to provide protection from disturbing ideas or images that flood the client's mind (obsessive). By creating routines and repetitive rituals (compulsive) the client seeks to rid the mind of these images. The movie, 'As Good as It Gets' depicts this condition with obsessive hand washing, door locking and eating rituals. Because tapping is a repetitive ritual it appeals to clients suffering with obsessive compulsive behaviors.

Panic attacks consist of overwhelming feelings of terror or anxiety surfacing suddenly and without warning. Symptoms include intense chest pain, numbness, racing heart, and shortness of breath. Because panic attacks can occur anywhere, at any time, anticipation of the fear is added to the client's overall feelings of vulnerability.

Anger

Anger can be defined as nature's "killer instinct" for self-preservation. The purpose of healthy anger is to increase energy for survival, assert one's needs, or correct injustice. (Gandhi described how he would 'conserve' his anger at oppression and injustice, not waste it.) Anger allowed our ancestors to survive by either scaring away or annihilating the source of threat (i.e. attacking).

Anger sends blood flow to the hands to make it easier to grasp a weapon or strike at a foe. Heart rate increases, and a rush of hormones such as adrenaline provides energy and strength. This is our biological 'fight response.'

Anger is associated with a strong sense of injustice which results in bitterness or resentment. When anger turns to revenge or hatred, it is a truly toxic emotion that can become volatile and dangerous. When there's a lid on anger, depression and psychosomatic illness can result. For example, migraine headaches.

Anger often expresses as:

- Frustration
- Aggressiveness
- Hostility
- Resentment
- Blame
- Exasperation
- Indignation
- Animosity
- Annoyance
- Irritability
- Being critical
- Silently withdrawing
- Explosive outbursts
- Tears (pseudo-grief)
- Hatred
- Violence

In childhood, yelling, hitting, and other 'acting out' strategies are used as defense mechanisms. In adulthood, signs of unresolved anger include habitually being late, making mistakes, "forgetting", failing to keep agreements, interrupting, giving the 'silent treatment', acting 'confused', accident proneness.

Hate

Kelly was nine years old when she went to live with her father and 'evil stepmother.' The new stepmother's demands of perfection from Kelly were interpreted as rejection. The young girl felt hurt (separated from her father's love), unwanted (rejection) and afraid (fear).

Kelly had never had cause to question her father's love, but now Dad was siding with his new wife, the 'evil queen.' Kelly felt vulnerable, helpless, and sad. With no one to support her, Kelly was left with a host of confusing feelings, including anger. With nowhere to put her feelings, Kelly's only option was to 'sit on them.'

Over time, her grievances toward both her father and stepmother compounded, developing into intense anxiety. This manifested as compulsive handwashing and, eventually, affected every aspect of her life.

Hate begins with a grievance which is a grudge strong enough to call for retaliation. It has its roots in something said or done by *someone* who was perceived as unjust or hurtful. It could be a real injustice, or it might be an imagined wrongdoing. Either way, the person takes the offense personally. As a result, the anger begins to simmer and boil within. Intense hate has its roots in rejection.

When an offense is taken personally, the offender is held responsible for how the person feels. The blame then keeps them stuck in the story. Every reminder of the past only serves to fan the flames of resentment.

What's the story?

The key to the uncovering process is to find out what caused the feeling in the first place. That's the story. The story is about the who, what, when, where and how that caused the person to feel a certain way.

The Six Basic Uncovering Questions give you the answers to these questions. Guiding the client through a positive event makes it easy to uncover:

- Who they are with ...
- What is happening in that situation ...
- What is being said/done ...
- What is *not* being said/done ...
- When this is happening .... (time of day, what age)
- Where they are when this happens (place)
- Where this is being experienced ... (in the body)
- How all these things make the Child feel ...
- And why.

This gives you all the information you need to facilitate the healing process. Remember to take notes in your sessions to ensure you don't miss anything. For example, who they are with may need to be forgiven.

There could be anchors which act as triggers which need to be removed. Anchors are aspects in the ISE connected to unwanted feelings including things seen (e.g., colors, expressions), things heard (e.g., tone of voice, machinery, argument), things smelled (e.g., alcohol, cigarettes) and things felt physically, in the body. (e.g., emotions such as fear, sadness, anger, etc.)

The Next Step

So far, you have guided your client through a simple memory exercise into a real regression. You've taught your client how to respond to you during the uncovering procedure. Once your client knows how to respond to your instructions, and to answer with their first impression, you'll have a client who is ready for regression. Bravo! Time permitting, the next step would be to guide the client back further. Guide the client all the way into the womb, conduct the basic uncovering procedure, and find out the following:

1. How does the Child feel toward Mom?
2. How does Mom feel toward the Child?

Mom is the most important person in the life of the Child. The question is – Does the Child feels loved by Mom? If the Child feels loved, you can reinforce those positive feelings and ripple them forward along the client's timeline.

If the Child feels unloved or unwanted, this is where the healing work needs to begin. Continue the uncovering process to identify what is causing the Child to form this belief. The goal would then be to disentangle the Child's feelings from Mom's feelings and restore the Child's sense of safety. Then, bring in Grownup to provide love and support and re-educate the Child.

We're not here to judge or sympathize but only face the Truth as the client's subconscious mind has it, then guide the Child to a place of acceptance. That's just how it was. Mom had a problem. No matter what happened, the Child is never the problem.

> **Uncovering Procedure: Womb Experience**
>
> - Daytime or nighttime?
> - Inside or outside?
> - Alone or with someone? (Who?)
> - How young does the Child feel?
> - Put attention on Mom. Notice feelings toward Mom.
> - Notice Mom's feelings toward Child. (Does Child feel loved?)

In some cases, there may be a need to release trapped emotional energy. For example, unresolved birth trauma. Birth is inherently traumatic but Caesarian birth is terrifying for the Child. If Mom required an emergency Caesarian, all the emotions associated with that emergency are not just being felt by Mom. They're also flooding into the baby. Separate Mom's feelings from the Child's feeling. Then, focus on releasing whatever rightfully belongs to the Child.

There may be other Players who are directly or indirectly contributing to the problem. Who are they? Doctor? Nurses? What Part are they playing? How is the Child perceiving what's happening and what decisions are being made because of those perceptions? Where's Dad? How does the Child feel about Dad?

If Mom didn't want the Child, realize that's devastating for a child. The goal would then be to find forgiveness toward Mom. This is relatively easy when the womb/birth experience is an ISE because nothing has been added to it via SSEs. But to get to the forgiveness, you first need to release the trapped emotions. This will restore peace and security to the Child, enabling you to uncover the "why?" Think about it . . . Mom went through giving birth to the baby. Why?

Might there be something going on that the client hasn't considered? What might that be? For example, what's going on in Mom's life that she feels she has no other options? Or what happened in Mom's life that she would reject her own child?

Child Feels Loved	Child Feels Unloved/Unwanted
Allow the Child a few moments to enjoy the state! "Isn't that nice? Let all those good feelings come back to you now. You're allowed to feel good, etc." *Continue with Autosuggestion Technique*	"That's why we're here. We're here to change things so that you can feel better." *Release emotional charge. Then, disentangle Mom's feelings from the Child's feelings. Continue with Autosuggestion Technique.*

Uncover the "Why?"

A useful method for uncovering this information and establishing the understanding required to allow forgiveness is the Windows of the Soul technique[32]. Forgiveness requires adult consciousness so let Grownup do the work.

Instruct Grownup to look into Mom's eyes and see her as a little baby. Establish that "that baby" is loveable and only wants to be loved and accepted. Then, establish that something must have happened to change that! Uncovering the reasons for Mom's hurtful behavior will open the door to authentic forgiveness.

---

[32] Gerald Kein, Omni-Hypnosis Training Center

Windows of the Soul

(Client), you've heard the eyes are the windows to the soul, right? That means that when you look deeply into a person's eyes, you can go further and further back in their time. It's by looking deep into their eyes that you can see them long before you ever existed in their lives. Understand?

Look inside Mom's eyes. Look deeper and deeper until you can see that little baby that she once was. (pause) Realizing . . . all that baby wants is to be loved. Isn't that true? (Of course, that's what every baby wants and needs!)

As you look at that baby . . . is there anything *wrong* with her? (Of course not! She's just a tiny little baby!)

And growing as a little girl, just wanting to be loved, and feeling so scared, and so powerless. (pause) That (fear/anger/sadness) that was installed in *you* was installed inside her in the same way - when she was just a child and had no choice either. (pause)

And then growing into adulthood, carrying all that emotional baggage, all the fear and anger and hurt inside. And even though deep down, she *wanted* to act in loving ways, she just couldn't figure out how to overcome all the pain. She had no choice but to act according to her inner programming. Can you see that now?

How much pain do you suppose she must have needed to bury inside because of the things she experienced in *her* life?

Optional: facilitate dialogue process and let Mom tell her story.

What if Things Go Sideways?

In the Ready for Regression Phase, we invite the client to remember some positive experiences from childhood. Accessing a positive event gives you the ideal conditions for teaching a client how to respond during the uncovering procedure we use for regression hypnosis. And accessing an event in childhood gets you into the general neighborhood of when most problems get started.

Bringing up comfortable, happy, pleasant feelings gives you a positive feeling that you can then use for Affect Bridge to regress back into actual events in childhood. In other words, real regression. Because the subconscious stores memory as image and emotion, using a positive memory to evoke feelings from the past can give you a backdoor to the causal event. The feeling – good or bad – can then be used as a Bridge to the past.

Usually, your session will go like clockwork. The client will follow your instructions and go back to happy, feel-good events from childhood. When they emerge from the session, the client will feel surprised and pretty amazed. They'll have gained some insight into their issue and positive shifts will have occurred internally. Having reclaimed some of their good feelings, they should be feeling pretty proud of themselves.

But not always. Sometimes things will go sideways.

You need to be prepared for this because the subconscious mind can zig when you tell it to zag. Remember, the client's subconscious mind knows why you are doing this. When you instruct a client to go back before the problem ever existed, what have you just done? You have just reminded the client about the problem.

Bringing the problem to mind will typically elicit one of the following responses: either the client will follow your instructions and go back to a happy event; they'll go back to a happy event and then abreact; or they'll dive into a painful event, instead.

Client Goes to a Happy Event

If the client follows instructions to go back to a happy event where they're feeling good, just encourage the client to enjoy those good feelings. For example, maybe Mom's cuddling them as a baby. Maybe she's brushing her hair when they're a little girl. Maybe they're with the family feeling safe and secure. If the Child is feeling good, encourage the client to just be there and enjoy allowing those good feeling to come back to them.

Remember, when a client is immersed in a feeling, their subconscious mind is wide open. This is the perfect time to offer a few targeted suggestions. It may not seem like much, but suggestions given at this time can have a dramatic impact on the client's overall state of well-being.

Client Goes to a Happy Event

- Brief uncovering procedure
- Validate good feelings
- Guide the client back into the womb

Children are taught that it's wrong to feel certain feelings. They're taught that some feelings are bad. Then, when the Child feels that "bad" feeling, they interpret it to mean that *they* are bad. This disconnects them from their intrinsic goodness and worth. What the client often doesn't realize is that their *good* feelings are still there.

You need to point this out to them because, often, they don't realize that their ability to feel good is still within them. Encourage the client to give themselves permission to feel all their good feelings.

Remind the client that it is *okay* to feel their feelings. Encourage them to take ownership of their right to feel their feelings. Tell them, "This is *your* feeling. You're allowed to feel *all* your feelings."

Be prepared for a few tears. These realizations can turn on the Water Works. When that happens, healing is happening. *Do not give the client a tissue.* That will shut down the feeling. If they're weeping, encourage your client to let herself feel the feeling while you gently dab her cheek with a tissue.

While you do this pour in the suggestions. Use a very maternal tone. For example, "That's right. You just let yourself feel it all. You're going to feel soooo goooood."

Client Abreacts

Sometimes, when a client goes to a happy event, they'll bump into an uncomfortable feeling and abreact. When a client goes into an abreaction, it's because something happened to trigger that feeling.

Remember, feelings don't come out of nowhere. When a client is abreacting it is because *something just happened.* But you may not know what that is. You need to ask them, "What just happened?"

Sometimes, revisiting a *happy* event has made them realize how disconnected they've been from themselves and their ability to feel good. Sometimes, realizing that they've lost a part of themselves will cause a wave of grief to wash over them. When this happens, encourage the client to feel the feeling fully.

Don't try to suggest the feeling away. Affirm that "that feeling" is allowed to be there. Recognize the client needs to grieve that loss before they can move on with their life. Then they can reclaim their ability to feel good again.

This sense of loss often surfaces when you are working with a client who suffers from depression. This is what happens when you learn to shut down your "bad" feelings. Putting a lid on your bad feelings puts a lid on all your good feelings, too.

This feeling of grief is about losing the Parts of them that feel good. You need to validate that. The client is recognizing the truth of how it has been for them. They need to honor this as a real tragedy. Then you can remind them, "We're here to change things so that you can feel better." The way to do that is to simply feel the feeling. Encourage the client to take back the Parts of them that have been missing.

Client Abreacts

- Provide relief by releasing some of the feeling.
- Validate any change for the better.
- Regress the client back to before the Child knew what it was like to feel those uncomfortable feelings.

Invite their good feelings to come back to them now. Remind them that *all* their feelings are good. Feeling the feeling releases the feeling. Encourage the client to just feel it fully. Remind your client that it's okay to feel all their feelings – even the sad, mad, bad, hurt, guilty, scared, and angry ones. Remember, these are Parts of the client. There's nothing wrong with the client. Those feelings are allowed to be there.

Encourage the client to release the feeling and let it all out. Once it is out, they'll feel better. Then let them soak up all the goodness. This only takes a few moments. It's very healing. Releasing the feeling creates a bit of a void at the subconscious level of mind. The space created by releasing feelings will tend to fill up automatically. What will flow into that space is a feeling of relief.

Relief feels good. This is where you want to encourage the client to send love and acceptance and forgiveness to their younger self so that Part of them can heal. Child Parts are feeling Part. What that Part of them needs, more than anything, is the client's acceptance. As this happens, the client is performing an act of self-acceptance. Nice, right?

Once the client is feeling better, regress them back to before the Child knew what it was like to ever feel those uncomfortable feelings.

Client Goes to a Painful Event

What if you instruct the client to go back to a happy event in childhood and they don't? What if their subconscious mind dumps them into a traumatic event in childhood? It happens. When it happens, you had better be prepared for it because you're going live, baby!

Remember, the Ready for Regression Phase is designed to *prepare* the client to face the past *before* diving into painful emotions. But if the subconscious mind is already going there, they're ready. When the subconscious mind takes you to a painful event from the past, realize that it trusts you enough to show you where the bodies are buried. It's willing to tell you the pain story and finally heal the wounds. That's good news.

The subconscious mind has just shown you the "owie." Realize that painful past event has everything to do with the reason the client is seeing you. There's a pocket of emotional pain trapped in that event and the client's subconscious mind is showing you that it trusts you to give it some relief.

Rub your hands together with glee because this is what you trained for. Then toss the protocol, roll up your shirt sleeves, and dive into the healing work because your client is ready to begin the transformational journey of regression-to-cause hypnotherapy.

Your best results will come from adapting to the needs of the client, not from following a script or a protocol. If the subconscious takes you back to a painful event, validate the feeling. Stay with the feeling. Make it safe for the client to be there. Remember, safety is Job One. Take charge and reassure the client that you know what to do.

The subconscious mind may be ready but that doesn't always mean the conscious mind is. It may have come as a surprise to the client to suddenly be dumped into a scene from childhood that doesn't feel very good. Give the conscious mind what it needs.

The conscious mind needs to have a sense of control. But it cannot control an emotion. It doesn't have the power. *You do.* So, reassure the client that you've got this. Everything is under control. All they need to do is follow your instructions and they'll get what they need. Then, immediately give the command to focus on "that feeling".

"That feeling" is subconscious communication. Keep the conscious mind focused on the feeling because that's what's calling for healing. Tell the client, "Your subconscious mind has just shown us what's calling for healing. Let yourself stay focused on that feeling." Then move straight into the uncovering procedure and find out what is generating that feeling. There may be some conscious resistance to allowing this to come to awareness. That's to be expected.

Remind the client, "Your subconscious mind knows why you're here. It brought us here for a reason - so that you can heal." Make it okay for the client to face whatever happened to cause them that pain. Then, move straight into the uncovering those first impressions.

The key is to work quickly. Don't give the client time to think or analyze. You need them to answer quickly with their first impressions. Then, as you move through the uncovering questions, coach to the positive. This encourages the client to continue following your instructions. For example, "First impression, does it feel like it's daytime or nighttime?" (Wait for an answer.)

Then say, "Good job! First sense, does it feel like you're inside or outside?" (Wait for answer.)

Then say, "Good job!" Move quickly onto the next question.

If you're short on session time, you can put a bookmark[33] on the event. This will allow you to come back to the event and process it to completion in the next session.

Alternatively, you can regress the client to an earlier scene where the Child is still feeling good. Before instructing the client to go back further, however, reassure the subconscious mind that you'll come back to this event and "take care of it." Make note of that situation/event for future reference. Keep your word!

---

[33] See chapter 12

> **Client Goes to a Painful Past Event**
> - Keep the focus on the feeling.
> - Put a bookmark on the event (so you can come back to it later)
> - Regress to an earlier scene where the Child is still feeling good.

Insight is Not Enough

Some regression hypnosis practitioners think that bringing conscious awareness to repressed memories is all that is needed to resolve a client's problem. They think that reviewing "what happened" will generate insight into the cause and that is all that is needed to clear things up. That's just not true.

Human beings have the ability to "forget" painful memories. The way that we do that is by either suppressing or repressing conscious recall of some or all of a painful event. This is a protective function of the subconscious mind. The idea is – out of sight, out of mind. But it's never completely out of mind because the subconscious mind never forgets. This is why the client still has a problem.

This ability to push aside memory is a coping strategy that is essential for a young child. It helps to reduce anxiety and allows a child to move on from experiences that were either painful, overwhelming, or traumatic. But it's a mistake to assume that simply bringing the memory to conscious awareness is the whole solution.

While it's true that bringing to light what happened can help to generate some understanding or insight for a client, insight isn't enough to achieve complete healing. People can spend years in therapy – decades, even. They can tell you all the reasons why they have the problem. They have plenty of insight and understanding. But they still have the problem. Simply reviewing an event isn't enough to resolve the problem. In some cases, it can even make things worse.

Here's why.

First, just going over a painful event can reinforce the underlying pattern. If you don't resolve what's causing the problem, repeatedly reviewing a painful event can have a compounding effect.

Second, reviewing an event can encourage false memories. This is particularly true when leading questions are employed. But memories are seldom based on fact. If the client assumes that what was revealed in the session must be true, that that is what really happened, *that's* a problem.

Let me give you an example. I once met a woman who was seeing a therapist. She told me that, through regression, she had discovered that she had been sexually abused. Based on this "insight" she made the decision to get the lawyers involved.

This is *not* the goal of therapy. The goal is always one of healing. We have no way of knowing whether her recall was in any way accurate. All we can know is that the feelings were real. The problem, for this woman, is that the issue hadn't been resolved. She was still carrying a boatload of blame, anger, and condemnation. And she wanted somebody to pay for her pain.

This is why insight isn't enough. It's because the problem calling for resolution isn't what happened. The problem is how the client interpreted the situation when it happened. And that has everything to do with the age at which it occurred.

Based on how the event was interpreted, at that time, decisions were made. Decisions are thoughts, thoughts become beliefs, and our beliefs decide what we're going to get in life. That's the problem. What needs to change is *the belief*.

Changing the underlying beliefs would have changed how this woman felt *inside*. When she finally came to peace with her past, she probably wouldn't have felt the need to keep reliving the pain by duking it out in a courtroom. She would have been able to move on with her life free of the past. That's the goal of healing.

Uncovering what happened is only part of the healing solution. Regressing into and reviewing past events will bring to light how a certain situation was perceived at that time. It can show you what decisions were made based on those perceptions. The client may even gain some insight into the cause of the problem. But merely bringing painful memories to conscious awareness isn't necessarily going to get rid of the problem.

To get rid of the problem for good you need to transform how it feels. And to do that you need to go beyond insight and transform all the erroneous thoughts and feelings that were shaped by those events.

Healing is in the Feeling

One of the most dangerous mistakes a hypnosis practitioner can make is to try to get rid of uncomfortable feelings like fear, or anger, or sadness. Yes, they're uncomfortable. But here's the problem. When you try to suggest away a feeling, it reinforces the client's avoidance strategy. That is a big part of the problem.

Repression or suppression is a way of trying to avoid negative feelings. It doesn't get rid of the feeling, though. The feeling doesn't go away. It just goes underground. From there, the pressure builds up inside. This can wreak havoc in a person's life by generating symptoms.

Unresolved emotions make the mind a living hell by generating negative self-talk. Any attempt to get rid of an emotion leaves the person wide open to getting triggered because situations in life can act as reminders of the event that caused them to feel that way in the first place. Many of the problems that people come to you for help with have their roots in traumatic experiences in childhood. This is because children are easily overwhelmed by stuff that *adult* consciousness would consider "no big deal." But when a child is in a state of overwhelm, that's trauma.

Current research into trauma therapy shows that the only truly effective way to resolve traumatic memory is to review and re-evaluate those past experiences with adult consciousness[34]. This is precisely the approach we use with regression-to-cause hypnotherapy.

Regression hypnotherapy is an exposure therapy because facing the feelings is what allows the client to release them – for good. Then, they don't have to carry them around inside, anymore. This is how you can get a complete resolution to the problem. The solution to any emotional issue lies in healing the feeling, not merely suggesting it away.

Feelings are never the problem. When you make the feeling a problem, you're making the subconscious mind the problem. This is the most direct path to losing rapport with the subconscious mind. The subconscious mind is the feeling part of the mind. Feelings are how

---

[34] Source: Unlocking the Emotional Brain: *Eliminating Symptoms at their Root Using Memory Reconsolidation* by Ecker, Ticic, Hulley

the subconscious communicates with the conscious mind. If you try to suggest away an emotion, you are just going to make things worse because the subconscious mind will stop trusting you.

Let me give you an example from a class I attended. The teacher was giving a demonstration of regression hypnosis. He regressed the client back to an event in childhood where the client was obviously feeling some uncomfortable feelings. That's good. Her subconscious mind was communicating loud and clear.

But then the therapist said, "That little girl feels so scared. She feels scared for herself. And she's scared for Mom, too, isn't she?" Without hesitation, the client responded, "Angry."

The therapist made three critical mistakes here.

First, he assumed he knew what the client was feeling. He didn't ask, "What feelings are you feeling?" He just assumed, based on *his* interpretation of what was happening, that the client must be feeling fear. But this wasn't the client's perception. She was feeling anger.

Never assume – ask. Your job is not to be a mind-reader. Your job is to uncover what happened and identify the perceptions, and thoughts, and feelings that are trapped in the event. Only then will you know what the real problem is.

The second mistake the therapist made was *suggesting* a feeling to the client. He said, "You feel scared."

Here's the problem. When a client is in a regressed state, they're hyper-suggestible. The therapist was instructing the client to feel scared. That's not helpful.

We all make mistakes. When the client said, "No, that's not what I'm feeling. I'm feeling angry …," all the therapist needed to do to correct course was to say, "That's right, there's the feeling." By validating the client's feeling, he would have been back on track. But he didn't do that. He didn't acknowledge the feeling. He didn't validate how the client was feeling. He didn't give that feeling permission to speak. That's when he made his third mistake.

His third mistake was instructing the client to melt the feeling away. He told her to push it out and get rid of it. He then suggested, "It's gone."

You can't just suggest away an emotion. If you try, it's only going to make things worse. When you try to suggest that a feeling is gone, or that the client "can't feel it," that suggestion is going to conflict with their innermost truth. That feeling is the truth as their subconscious mind has it.

Is it any surprise that the client said, "It's still there … I still feel angry"? That was her Truth. That's when the session went truly sideways. Instead of honoring the feeling, the therapist started arguing with the client. He said something like, "If you melted it away, it can't be there!"

He was arguing with the wrong part of the mind. Big mistake! You do not want to get on the wrong side of the subconscious mind. You cannot use reason and logic with the feeling part of the client. It won't work.

Remember, every feeling is a Part of the client. And every Part is valuable and worthy of respect. Your job is to honor the feeling. Child Parts are feeling Parts. Trying to get rid of a feeling is the equivalent of telling a Child to shut up and die. That's not very nice.

Realize you can't just get rid of a feeling – you can only transform it. The way to transform a feeling is to accept it and give it permission to speak. Give the feeling permission to express and it will tell you what the real problem is.

Feelings and emotions are how the subconscious communicates. Feelings don't come out of nowhere. Every problem is the result of a life experience. An emotion is a signal coming out of a specific past event. An uncomfortable feeling is a distress signal. The subconscious mind is trying to alert the conscious mind to an underlying problem that the conscious mind isn't fully aware of because the subconscious mind needs help!

If you were taught to "melt away" a feeling or suggest that it "dissolve away to nothing-nothing-nothing" or to instruct a client to "push it out" of their mind, or delete it, or put it into a box and then bury the box, this is simply the misuse of a technique. For example, think back to the Numbers Challenge/Losing the Numbers exercise. This is where you suggest that "all the numbers dissolve and fade away to nothing-nothing-nothing." This is a useful test for somnambulism because amnesia through suggestion indicates a state of somnambulism. What the Numbers Challenge is *not* is an effective way to deal with an emotion.

The goal is never to get rid of the symptoms. It is to locate the event that caused the symptoms so that you can uncover the real problem and find a way to heal it. Don't try to bulldoze the subconscious mind with reason and logic. Don't try to tell the subconscious mind how it should feel. Don't try to rescue your clients from their feelings. The feeling is never the problem. Don't *make* it a problem. Feelings like fear, anger, and sadness are always there for a reason. Your job is to honor the feeling and affirm that it has a right to be there.

Trying to get rid of a feeling is a very bad idea because avoidance is a big part of the problem for a lot of people. Avoidance strategies that attempt to suppress, repress, reject, judge-against, and disown the feeling don't get rid of the feelings. They just drive the feelings deeper underground. And when feelings get trapped inside, it makes the mind a pressure cooker.

You know what that means. Sooner or later, it's going to blow.

You can't just amputate a Part of a person. If you try to bury that feeling alive, *you* become a threat. You'll end up alienated from the part of the mind that has the power to create the change you're after. Don't do it. Affirm that the subconscious mind is doing its very best to take care of the client and meet important needs. Treat it with kindness. Show a little respect because, to get the results you're after, you need the subconscious to trust and work *with* you.

CHAPTER 10:
Inner Child Work

Inner Child Work is a process of self-change that involves bringing the client's (Adult) consciousness back into a painful event from childhood to provide support for the Child. This is because virtually everything we do is driven by some kind of feeling. And Child Parts are feeling Parts.

While the purpose of the uncovering process is to reveal the unmet of the Child in a specific event, the Inner Child Work allows the Adult Part of the client to find ways to meet those needs. The client is really the best person to help their Inner Child because no one knows the Child better than they do. Their job is to take on the role of a loving parent and respond to the Child in a way that provides support because that's what was missing the first time.

When you begin the process of regressing into painful past events, the primary goal is always to help the Child realize that the event is over, that she survived it. Your job is to guide the (Grownup) client to help the Inner Child make sense of the situation and to find a way to provide whatever the Child needs. Primarily, this is safety. Once safety has been restored, you can begin facilitating the Inner Child Work. But before you can proceed with the Inner Child Work, you need to take a pulse on the client's attitude toward the younger Part of them because, to be successful, you need a Grownup who can be loving and accepting of their Inner Child.

Not every client is going to feel love and acceptance toward their Inner Child. If you try to take a client back into a traumatic event in childhood carrying a load of hostility, it's going to add to the fear the Child is feeling. Not only will this increase the emotional charge trapped in the event, but it also means that now you've got two problems to deal with - a traumatized Child and a Critical Parent. This problem can easily be avoided by using your first session to assess and then teach the client how to respond to their Inner Child.

Realize there isn't just one Inner Child. There are many, many Inner Child Parts - one for every childhood event. Everything we do to act on our feelings is learned from our experiences growing up. The problem is that some of our Parts are in still in distress. This is because they got stuck in the traumatic event that caused them to form in the first place.

Remember, linear time is a construct of the conscious mind. This is useful for analyzing how the problem got started, and how it developed over time. But as far as the subconscious mind is concerned, all unresolved events are happening still and are occurring simultaneously - *now*. This is what makes regression hypnosis possible. It's also what gives us access to younger Parts.

In the Ready for Regression Phase, once you have converted the memory exercise into a positive regression to an actual event in childhood, the next step is to facilitate the uncovering procedure.

This process teaches the client how to interact with *you* in a way that allows you to uncover the information you need to guide the healing process. The uncovering procedure also helps the client to associate deeper into the Child Part. As a result, the client *becomes* the Child in that event, giving you access to thoughts and the feelings of the Child.

Because the client is seeing through the eyes of the Child, they are thinking the thoughts and feeling the feelings of the Child. This will allow you to uncover the underlying cause of the problem which has everything to do with the unmet needs of the Child.

Childhood Needs

Pioneering cell biologist, Bruce Lipton[35], suggests that our programming comes out of our environment and that most of it is installed before the age of six.

Healthy programming comes from growing up in a safe environment with primary caregivers who are tuned into and adequately meet the needs of the child. In such an environment, the child will grow up feeling secure and learn to trust.

Unhealthy programming, like when a person feels disconnected from themselves or others, comes from growing up in a childhood environment that failed to adequately meet the child's emotional needs. Dr. Spock was the first pediatrician to try to understand children's needs and family dynamics.

At the time Spock's bestselling book, *Baby and Childcare*, was published in 1946, conventional wisdom held that picking up babies when they cried would "spoil" them. Spock, on the other hand, encouraged

---

[35] Bruce Lipton, The Biology of Belief, 2005

parents to trust their own instincts, over external authority, and to be more affectionate with their children. He also counseled parents to treat their children as individuals.

But what happens when the child grows up with a parent who is insensitive to the child's needs? What if the primary caregiver is emotionally distant? Or neglectful? Or is rejecting the child? Or hostile? Think about an infant whose mother has been overcome with grief over the death of her two-year old child. Or a mother who, caught in the grips of post-partum depression, cannot connect emotionally with her child.

Think about a hungry infant crying for nourishment and comfort because of a rigidly imposed bottle-feeding schedule. Or a step-parent who perceives the child as competition for love. The younger the child the more confusing such unloving behaviors are to her. When the child perceives that the caregiver is not fully present to her needs, she will give up trying to seek closeness. She will simply disengage and withdraw.

A child whose strategy is avoidance will tend to feel isolated, first, from the parents, and later from partners. Having learned to stop seeking closeness, she will reduce her expectations of others and tend to be overly focused on herself while under-focusing on others. She may be dismissive. She may feel like an outcast. She may have difficulty reaching out for help from friends, partners, doctors, therapists, etc. because she doesn't know any way to ask for help that works.

Even when parents are loving toward their child, even when they are present to her needs, if they fail to be *consistent* in responding to the child, the child will become anxious. Because the child cannot predict when her needs will be met, she won't be able to relax. She will become overly focused on others to the exclusion of self. She'll show a preoccupation with relationships coupled with the feeling that it's not going to work.

When one or both parents interact with the child in a disorienting, chaotic or frightening manner, the child's energy system gets disrupted. The child's parent might be feeling a lot of fear inside. Or they may do scary things. Either way, the child experiences fear. This generates internal conflict for the child because she wants to move close to the person *and* wants to get away from them.

Picture a young child trying to contend with the chaos associated with an alcoholic parent whose moods swing from love and affection to stormy rages. Or a prenatal infant floating in amniotic fluid that's been contaminated by the mother's fears and anxiety.

A child whose energy system has been disrupted may become very chaotic (i.e., acting out). He may be hyperactive, run around in circles, or hit other kids. He may repeatedly get into trouble at school which will then amplify the difficulty he's already having as he tries to relate to others socially. The end result? Lots of confusion in relationships.

Mother Teresa said that the greatest disease of mankind is the absence of love. When we are treated in unloving ways, we feel hurt. When we behave in unloving ways, we feel guilty. When what we love is threatened, we feel fear or anger. And when we lose something that we love we feel grief.

'Bad' feelings are always related to love. The solution, therefore, is always the same. Work with the pain. Track it back to the Child and help her find love again. Invariably this will take you back to childhood because love is essential to survival.

Bonding with the people who are responsible for taking care of us improves our chances of survival. Bonding is also known as "attachment" and is always about the relationship with the primary caregiver. This person is the Child's source of protection and nourishment. Usually it's Mom, but not always.

Four Important Patterns

Studies in Attachment revealed four primary patterns which are installed before twelve months of age and have to do with emotional bonding. In one experiment with twelve-month-olds, the parent was asked to bring the child to a strange environment with toys. For example, daycare, play school. They would then leave the child with a stranger. When the parent returned for the child, they discovered that there were four distinct response patterns.

1. **Secure Attachment**

When the parent returned, the child would go straight to the parent and then go back to playing. This response indicates that the parent is sensitive to the needs of the child and responds in an adequate and timely manner. This results in the child feeling secure. Secure Attachment patterning results in healthy social, emotional and cognitive development.

2. **Avoidant Attachment**

When the parent returned, the child did not seem to care. It didn't appear to matter to the child whether the parent was there or not. This response indicates a parent who is not sensitive to the needs of the child. The parent doesn't know how to interpret the child's signals. For example, when the child cries the parent doesn't respond appropriately.

When the child cries because he's wet or tired, the parent tries to feed the child. Eventually, the child gives up. Avoidant Attachment patterning results in socially controlling behavior; avoids interacting with others; emotional distancing.

3. Anxious or Resistant Attachment

When the parent returned, the child would cling to the parent and was not easily soothed. The child would not go back to playing quickly. This response indicates a parent whose responses are often inconsistent. The child cannot predict what the parent is going to do. This generates uncertainty and/or ambivalence toward the parent.

Another cause of this pattern is a parent whose emotional state intrudes on the child's state. For example, if Mom is angry or anxious or grieving, the child takes on those feelings. The feeling is then associated with whatever is happening at that time. For example, feeding the baby while angry or anxious will anchor those feelings to food. This can lead to eating disorders.

The results of Anxious/Resistant Attachment often show up in the child's teen years. The unresolved nervous anxiety takes shape as insecurity, self-doubt, and an inability to regulate emotions.

4. Disorganized Attachment

When the parent returned, the child's behavior was confused. In some cases, the child would drop to the floor, bite his hands, or turn in circles. The child might completely ignore the parent, or approach and then avoid. The child might seek attachment but then not accept soothing easily. Disorganized Attachment is an indicator of some kind of trauma. It might be caused by abuse. For example, yelling at the child. It could be due to alcoholism in the family which produces out-of-control behavior. This generates terror in the child and creates a biological conflict[36] which can be expressed as physiological issues.

The problem is that the child needs to attach. Attachment is essential to survival because the child cannot take care of him or herself. Parents are a source of protection and soothing. When the parent becomes the source of threat, the child has nowhere to go to get his/her needs met. The only place they can go isn't safe. This internal conflict can be expressed as confused behavior. For example, move toward/run away. It results in social, emotional, and cognitive impairment.

Why is this important for you? These patterns will show up in your work with clients. They are often repeated in the client's primary relationship. They are learned responses that formed before the first year of age. These patterns developed in response to a specific relationship. This is who needs to be forgiven for what they did or didn't do.

It is not about the Child. It is how the Child adapted to the primary caregiver. The Child's response may be different to another caregiver. The problem is rooted in a specific relationship to a person who was responsible for meeting the needs of the Child. What is needed for healthy social, emotional, and cognitive development is the secure attachment pattern.

If your client regresses before twelve months of age, pay close attention to the Child's relationship to the primary caregiver. What are Mom's feelings toward the Child? How does Mom respond to the Child? How is the Child learning to adapt to Mom's behaviors/feelings? What is

---

[36] Dr. Gerd Hamer, The German New Medicine

Mom doing/not doing? What associations are being made? (Look for anchors.) What you uncover in the regression will indicate what was missing for the Child.

A lifelong pattern of the client's relationship with Mom could be reflected in the client's relationship with their spouse. Partners are often chosen as parental surrogates in an unconscious attempt to resolve the conflicts of childhood. This never works because the spouse cannot meet the needs of the Child. The problem is rooted in the client's past. Resolve it there and the client will finally be able to get his/her needs met. However, in some cases, this could negate the need for their current relationship, especially if it is conflicted.

Support the Child

What follows the uncovering procedure is a process of teaching your (Grownup) client how to interact with their Inner Child. In the first session, we use a positive event in childhood because this provides the ideal conditions for preparing a client to act as a loving support to their younger self. A positive event provides safety while allowing you to assess the client's attitude toward their younger self. You can then teach the client how to interact with their Inner Child in a way that promotes positive change.

Remember, children have a limited capacity for interpreting situations. The younger the Child, the less capable s/he is of making sense of the world of people and things around her. Things can happen that feel overwhelming to a Child. When that happens, the problem is often that there was no one there to support the Child or soothe the Child.

Bringing the Adult into the scene *with* the Child introduces a fundamental change to the original event; the Child is no longer alone. Now there are three of you there. There's the Child, the Grownup Part of the client, and *you*. You take on the role of guide and coach to the (Adult) consciousness of the client, while the client does the work of supporting and healing their wounded Child.

To accomplish this, you need to bring *awareness* to these two Parts of the self. This is the first step in setting up for Inner Child Work. The Inner Child Work begins with establishing a state of dual consciousness by *separating* the Adult from the Child.

Establish Dual Consciousness

The subconscious mind has no problem with you being five and fifty at the same time. They're just Parts of you in different timeframes. This is what makes it possible to go back and relive an event from the past. You do it by "becoming" the Part.

Realize that this state of dual consciousness has been there all along. While you're doing the uncovering work with the Child Part, the conscious mind or Adult Part of the client is still there. It's just off on the sidelines, taking the role of an observer. But to conduct the Inner Child Work you need to bring that consciousness into the event *with* the Child.

The way to do this is to offer a suggestion that is completely acceptable to the subconscious mind, "Let it be *as if* there were two of you there now. The Grownup Part of you and the five-year-old Part of you. And just be there with the Child you once were." That's it. From this point forward, both the Adult and the Child will both be present to the event. Whenever the Adult consciousness steps forward, the Child will take a place in the background. When the Child steps forward, the Adult will take on the observer role. The next step is to test to make sure that Grownup is going to be loving and accepting of the Child.

Assess Readiness

Assessing before you ask the client to do anything can really save your bacon! With just a few preliminary questions you can identify where the work needs to begin with each client. For example, if the client isn't ready to be a loving support to the Child, the next step would be to teach the client how to do the work that's required. This is an important part of preparing your client to be successful working with you in a painful past event.

Ensure that the client can *be there* for their Inner Child. Remember, you can't do it for them. The client needs to be willing to be a source of love and support for their Inner Child. That's what was missing the first time. Don't allow the client to interact with their Inner Child until you have assessed whether they're willing to treat the Child with love and respect.

1. Is the Child loveable?

Instruct Grownup to look at their younger self and notice how they feel toward the Child. Then ask, "Is the Child loveable?" If the client says that the Child is loveable, this tells you that they are *able* to give love to the Child. If the (Adult) client is rejecting their Inner Child, in any way, realize there is an underlying problem of *self-rejection*. In this case, go back further to a time when the Child was still loveable.

> Now, let it be as if there are two of you there, the Grownup you and the little one (inside Mom). And just be there with that little one, Grownup. And notice how all that little one wants or needs is to feel safe and secure and feel good about herself. Isn't that true?
>
> Notice your feelings toward her. What do you notice?

> If you had a little one like that in your life right now (daughter, niece, grandchild), you could love and accept her, couldn't you? (*If the client answers 'no', regress back to where Child is still loveable.*)
>
> *Yes* – Of course you can because the Child is completely loveable. And all she needs is to be loved and accepted. Take a moment to just thank her for being in your life because she matters. She matters to *you*. She matters because you share the same feelings. How does that make you feel?

> **Is that a "good" little girl?** Yes - Tell her, "You're good."
>
> **Does she hear you?**

No – Child does not hear	**Yes – Child hears Grownup**
What needs to happen so that she can really hear you?	Does she believe you?

No – Child does not believe	**Yes – Child Believes Grownup**
No one knows her better than you. Find the words that she needs to hear so that she can believe you. How does it feel to say that?	Say, I found you. / I'm so glad I found you. / You matter to me. / My mind brought me back to you. / So I can heal. How does it feel to say that?

2. Is there anything wrong with the Child?

Next, ask the client, "Is there anything wrong with the Child?" If the client says that there's nothing wrong with the Child, this indicates that they can *accept* the Child. This tells you that the client is ready to be a loving support to the Child. But sometimes there is something wrong with the Child. Sometimes there's a birth-defect or a genetic condition that the client is aware of.

If there is, you just need to do a little reframing. For example, if the client says, "Yes, she's got a cleft-palate" or some genetic abnormality, you can reframe this perception of being defective by asking, "Is the Child *able* to love and be loved?"

If the client says, "yes," then say, "Then there's nothing wrong with the Child. She has everything she needs to *be able* to give and receive love. Isn't that true?"

Example 2: Child is born prematurely. The Child needs to know that she is okay, that she isn't going to spend the rest of her life in an incubator, that she gets to grow up and become stronger and wiser for having had this experience.

Example 3: Child has a physical defect. Separate this from the Child's inherent worth and goodness. How might this have value later in life? Would it make her more forgiving or compassionate towards those less fortunate?

3. Would you be willing to be there for the Child?

It's important to establish that there's nothing wrong with the Child and that the Child is intrinsically loveable. This makes the Child deserving of the client's love.

Remember, this is a process of restoring self-love. Once this has been established, the next question is, "Would you like to always be there for the Child?" In other words, are they *willing* to support the Child?

Because there is no separation between these two Parts of the client - it's one person - you're asking the client to agree to be there for *themselves* by meeting their *own* needs.

"Would you be willing to always keep the Child safe?" Notice how this question transfers the role of protector from the subconscious mind to the conscious mind? What you're doing is setting up some ground rules for the relationship you're going to establish between these two Parts of the client – the Adult and the Child. What you want to know is this: is the client willing to take responsibility for the needs of their innermost self?

This is so critical to the Inner Child Work because, when you start regressing back into painful past events, you're going to be dealing with a traumatized Child. You need a Grownup who is willing to step up to protect the Child, and take care of that Child, and meet the needs of the Child. If you have a Grownup who is rejecting or judging or, in any way, unaccepting of the Child, the client is simply not ready to begin the Inner Child Work.

Remember, if the client doesn't accept their Inner Child, you can't take that energy back into a situation in childhood. That will only contaminate the original event, adding to the problem.

Most clients you work with will be resourceful enough to take on the role of a loving Parent to their Inner Child, especially if they have children of their own. But if they're not, you need to help them gain access to internal sources of empowerment. For example, maybe the client doesn't know how to care for a child and provide what a child needs because they never had children of their own.

This lack of understanding can be resolved simply by educating the client about what a Child needs. What the client needs to accept is that *every* child needs to feel safe and to know that they are loved.

Sometimes the client is carrying guilt from childhood. As a result, the Adult is blaming the Child. This anger towards self is an internal conflict that is going to generate anxiety. When the client is blaming the Child, you need to convince them that the Child *deserves* to be loved and cared for.

What Every Child Needs

The Child is never at fault for the things that happened to her. The client needs to know this. For example, the client might say that the baby cries too much. She's upsetting Mom and that's why Mom has a problem. Realize this is the reasoning of a Child. (This has everything to do with the problem that the client is seeing you about.)

Young children often take the blame for the things that are happening around them, even when it has nothing to do with them. That can be the root of the whole problem because decisions made in childhood color a person's opinion of themselves. But a bad opinion can block them from being as healthy and happy and successful as they want to be. You can change that.

The truth is that every baby is dependent on others to take care of it. Mom is responsible for the Child. If the Child is crying too much it's simply because her needs are not being adequately met. That's not the Child's fault. The Child needs to understand that (a) she is not the problem and, (b) Mom's got the problem. This restores innocence to the Child.

Autosuggestion Technique

Grownup, I'd like you to say something out loud and just notice how it feels. Tell her, "*I found you.*" (wait for client to repeat)

How does that make you feel? Feel true? (wait for response)

Now tell her this, "My mind brought me back to you ... so I can heal." (wait for client to repeat)

Tell her, "Your feelings are my feelings …. You matter to me." (wait for client to repeat)

(Her) feelings are *your* feelings …. How does that make you feel?

Realize . . . your mind brought you back to this event *so you can heal*. And now that you've *found* her, you can always *be there* for her. Would you *like* that? because … that would mean she never has to feel alone. And she can always know that she's loved and accepted by you. How would you like to give that to her?

Would you like to always *be there* for her and always keep her safe? (wait for response.)

Would you be willing to give (her) your *love and acceptance?* So that she can *know* that she is safe and feel secure and loved? (wait for response.)

Would you be willing to *give* her that? So that she can grow up feeling good about herself? (wait for response.)

Would you be willing to give her *all that?* (wait for response)

That's good because, that way, you can always know that *you're* loved and accepted. And always feel safe because you and the Child share the same feelings. Here's how we'll do it…. (*Proceed to transmit love*)

No one in the world knows her better than you do. Isn't that true?

No one understands her better than you do. That means no one is better able to be there for her than you are. How would you like to always be there for her?

That's good because *that way* you can be there to help and guide her to grow up feeling good about herself. And make *better* decisions for you growing up. Understand?

I want you to realize something else . . . That loveable little one is a human soul in the process of becoming. She has talents and abilities that are unique to her – maybe even more than you are aware of! She matters, doesn't she. Notice how, already, she's her own person. She can see, hear, feel, and know. Notice how she is choosing how to be and not-be, based on her experience. She's a unique individual. Her own person. She's not her father. She's not her mother. Nor anyone else. She's a whole being, unlike any other. So, you can thank her for being in your life.

And now that you've found her, you can always be there for her, so she never has to feel alone. She can always feel safe and secure and accepted. You can help her to grow in strength and wisdom. And learn good lessons in life that make her stronger and wiser for having been through them. And grow up to be the best person she was always meant to be. Would you like that?

That's good because that way *you* can always know that you're loved and accepted. And always feel safe. And grow up to become the person *you* were meant to be . . . because you share the same feelings. Understand?

Tell her, "I deeply and completely love and accept you."

How does it feel to say those words – feel true? *Proceed to Transmit Love*

Sometimes the client did something as a Child that resulted in a situation not ending well. The client could be beating themselves up over something that happened long before they were able to think for themselves. What they need to recognize is that it wasn't their fault because the Child is *never* to blame. The Child is never the problem because the Child is innocent. This is the message the client needs to carry back to the Child in those past events.

Help the Grownup recognize that mistakes happen and are an important part of growing up. Children make mistakes because that's how we learn. There's nothing wrong with a Child making a mistake because human beings learn through trial and error. Regardless of how things turned out the Child can learn from those experiences.

The Child needs to be given permission to grow up learning from life experiences, not being crushed by criticism. To achieve this, Grownup needs to recognize that mistakes are naturally going to be a part of growing up. This understanding makes the Child forgivable which, in turn, makes the client forgivable.

The Child is never the problem. The Child is innocent. If you've got a client who is blaming the Child, you need to find a way to make the Child loveable. The easiest way to do this is to regress the client back further.

Give the instruction to go back to a time when the Child is still loveable. Don't try to suggest to the client that the Child is loveable. They won't believe you. Remember, you're talking to the Adult consciousness of the client. That's the conscious mind. Instead, regress back further to *find* the love. Don't worry, it's there. Research shows that children who don't get enough love give up and die. The client must have received enough love to survive into adulthood.

Give the suggestion, "go back to a time when the only thing you knew was what it was like to be loveable." That's when the client felt worthy of love. If you can resolve this problem before you begin the regression work, you'll reduce some of the internal pressure. As a result, you'll have a better client to work with in those unresolved events in childhood.

Infancy is always a good place to start because an infant can't do anything worthy of blame. Take the client back to when they were just a tiny baby. Then, invite the client to hold that innocent, little baby in their arms and look deeply into her eyes. Then ask, "Is that baby loveable?" If Grownup affirms that the baby is loveable, you now have a client who is capable of giving love to that Part of them. You can then use this scene as an opportunity to access feelings of love and acceptance that can be transferred into other situations and events of significance.

What other resources can you find to support you in facilitating Inner Child Work? For example,

- "What does the Child *deserve*?"
- "Does that baby *deserve* to feel safe and secure?"
- "Does that baby deserve love?"
- "Does that baby deserve to have her needs met?"
- "Does that baby deserve to grow up knowing that she is loved and accepted?"

If the answer to these questions is "yes," the next step is to establish a contract by asking the client, "Would you be willing to *be there for her*? And keep her safe?"

"Would you be willing to *let her know* that she is loved and accepted?" "Does she *deserve* to grow up feeling good about herself, and know that there's nothing wrong with her?" "Would you be willing to give her what *every* Child deserves - to feel safe and know that she is loved?"

Questions to Establish a Contract[37]:

- Is there anything wrong with the Child?
- Is the Child loveable?
- Does the Child deserve to feel safe?
- Does the Child deserve love?
- Does the Child deserve to have her needs met?
- Does the Child deserve to grow up feeling loved and accepted?

If the answer to these questions is, "Yes", follow up with:

- Would you be willing to be there for her?
- Would you be willing to protect her and keep her safe?
- Would you be willing to let her know that she is loved and accepted?
- Would you be willing to give her what every Child needs and deserves – to feel safe and know that she is loved?

Every child deserves to grow up feeling safe and knowing that she is loved and accepted because the Child is innocent. This is the understanding the client needs to accept to realize that *they* are loveable. They need to realize that they are loveable so that they can accept themselves. They are loveable and nothing can ever change that. And

---

[37] Inspired by Cal Banyan, 5-PATH and 7th Path Self-Hypnosis.

because they are loveable, they deserve good things in life. These are the gifts of healing you will resource the client with. Then, during the Inner Child Work, you will be asking the client to give these gifts to *themselves* by offering them to Child Parts that have been stuck, trying to get her needs met.

The Steps:

1. Guide the client back into a positive event from childhood.
2. Associate the client into the Part of the Child.
3. Conduct a little uncovering to deepen the association
4. Separate Adult consciousness from Child consciousness.
5. Teach the client how to be a loving support to the Child.
6. Transmit love to the Child.

How to Communicate Love[38]

1. Physical touch. e.g., cuddling, comforting
2. Words of endearment. e.g., encouragement, appreciation
3. Quality Time. i.e., undivided attention
4. Gifts. e.g., rewards, treats, surprises
5. Service. i.e., doing nice things for the child, helping with chores

---

[38] Source: Five Love Languages of Children by Gary Chapman

Transmit Love[39]

Once you have established that the client is capable of being a loving support to the Inner Child, the next step is to guide the client to "find the love" and then transmit that feeling of love to the Child.

Realize this is what the Child most needs. While this process can be facilitated in any childhood event, the ideal place to introduce it is in the womb experience. This is because, most of the time, the womb provides a safe, warm, pleasurable experience.

1. **Find the Love.**

Suggest to the client that there is a love inside of each of us that can be accessed for the purposes of healing. Then, invite the Grownup Part of the client to go inside and find the love. Give the suggestion to go into their heart and, "Find the love, it's there." Then, verify that they're feeling the feeling.

Sometimes it's obvious by the look on their face, but not always. Verify that the client is feeling the feeling. Then, ask them how it feels. It should feel good. It may only be a flicker to begin with. That's okay. What we pay attention to we get more of.

By offering a few suggestions, you can fan the embers into a cozy fire. For example, "I want you to notice that there is a love inside of you. Go into your heart and find the love. It's there. Dig down deep into your heart and when you find the love, let me know." (wait) . . . "What does it feel like?"

---

[39] Inspired by Gerald Kein (Omni-Hypnosis Center), Cal Banyan (Banyan Hypnosis Center), and Randy Shaw (Advanced Hypnotherapy of Utah)

2. Validate the Feeling.

Validating a feeling gives it permission to be there and encourages more of the feeling to come to awareness. For example, if the client says they're feeling a warm, comfortable, feeling in their chest, you can say, "That's right ..." Or "There's the feeling ..." Find out where the client is feeling that love in their body. Then encourage them to feel it fully.

3. Amplify the Feeling.

Using the client's own descriptions will help to amplify the feeling. For example, "There's the feeling. It's a beautiful warm, comfortable feeling in your chest. It feels so good. Just let that feeling of love grow strong within you, now. The more you feel it, the better you're going to feel."

The amplification process will provide the information you need to create suggestions which will feel true for the client. Don't make this up. Get it from the client. Remember, emotions are felt in the body. The client might say they feel it in their heart. Or it might be a pleasant sensation that's flowing throughout the body. Just find out how they are experiencing that feeling. What else are they noticing?

The important thing is that the client is feeling the feeling. Everything else is just details. For example, you might ask them to notice if it has a color. What color might it be? (Most of the time it's either yellow or pink.) Ask the client if that feeling has a temperature. (Most of the time they'll say it feels warm.) Take it a step further by suggesting that it might have a quality of vibration. (Sometimes the feeling has a bubbly, giggly quality to it.

Often, the client will have a big smile on their face because it feels really good.) Sometimes there's even a sound that goes with that feeling. (I've had clients remember songs from childhood during this exercise. When that happens, you can invite the client to hum that song to the Child and notice how good that feels.) The idea is to bring that positive feeling up powerfully within them by giving the client time to experience it fully.

> "That's good. Just go inside and let yourself feel it fully, it feels so good. Feelings and emotions can sometimes express as a color. If that feeling of love had a color, what might it be?" (wait)
>
> "That's right. You might also notice that it has a quality of vibration to it. What does *that* feel like?" (wait)
>
> "Does it have a temperature? What temperature might it be?" (wait)
>
> "Sometimes, there's even a sound that goes with it. What sound, if any?" (wait)

4. Send Love to the Child.

Love feels good. Encourage the client to just let themselves have that experience and enjoy it fully. Then, once they're feeling the feeling full, ask them to give it to the Child.

Have the client transmit that specific quality of love *into* the Child by sending it from their heart to the heart of the Child. This gives the Child Part the experience of the one thing it needs the most. As this is happening, bring the client's attention to how good this process of giving and receiving love feels.

This can be a really yummy experience for the client because they're flooding their system with endorphins. Realize that this is very healing. Continue to *amplify* the feelings by pouring in suggestions to encourage more feelings of pleasure and enjoyment.

Use whatever words the client gives you. If you need more information, ask the client to tell you what else she is noticing. For example, "There's the feeling ... It's a feeling of love ... You can feel it in your heart ... It's that warm, comfortable bubbly pink feeling ... It feels so good ... And as you allow yourself to feel that feeling ... notice how it grows stronger within you...."

> That's right. And as you allow that love to grow stronger and stronger within you, realize that you can allow that love to go into the little one. Just let it flow from your heart into her little heart. Send your love into that loveable little Child. And notice how *good* that feels. (pause) Feel good?

5. Verify Child is Accepting Love.

Verify that the Child is accepting the love by asking, "Does it seem like the Child is *accepting* your love?" This is the kind of positive energy you want to get *into* the Child because this will allow the client to feel good again. If the Child is accepting love from the Grownup, tell them to keep sending it in until the Child is "completely filled with love." It doesn't take very long. Just let the client tell you when the process feels complete.

Remember, the Adult and the Child share the same feelings. Grownup knows what the Child is feeling. So, ask, "How does the Child like that?"

> That's good. Just keep sending it in until the Child is filled with your love. Does it feel like (she) is *accepting* your love? (wait for response.)
>
> That's good. How does (she) *like* that? (wait for response.)
>
> Keep sending it in until (she's) completely filled with your love. And let me know when it feels complete. (wait for response.)

The moment the client indicates that the process is complete, you have successfully prepared your client for the Inner Child Work. Bravo! When it comes time to dive into painful events from the past, you'll have a client who is ready to do the work of self-healing.

Self-Acceptance

Once you have confirmed that the Child is accepting that beautiful energy, encourage the client to keep sending it in. As they do that, have them tell the Child, "I deeply and completely love and accept you[40]." This is a suggestion you cannot use enough in hypnosis. Just don't use the "love" word until you have verified that it's actually true. The client needs to be *feeling* the love. When the suggestion is true, each time they say these words to the Child, the client will be giving themselves a suggestion that is completely acceptable.

Remember, the Child is just a Part of the client at a younger age. There's no real separation between them. What the Child needs is also what the Adult needs. When the Child gets her needs met, that change will ripple outward into the client's adult life. This changes everything.

---

[40] EFT Self-Acceptance Phrase

Guide the client to fill the Child up with their love and acceptance. As they feel the feelings, the energies of love and acceptance are also flowing into Adult consciousness as well. This will change how they feel about themselves. And because they are speaking to a Part of *themselves*, they are giving themselves a suggestion that is wholly true. This becomes an act of *self*-acceptance and *self*-love.

This is the Core of the healing work of regression hypnosis - reconnecting a person with themselves by healing how they feel. Healing isn't something we "do." It's something that happens when the client lets it happen. All you need to do is encourage the client to go inside, find the love, then give themselves permission to feel it. This reconnects them with the source of all healing. Nice, right?

It's good for you, too, because you will have created your ideal client for Inner Child Work. You will have taught the client to treat themselves as a loving parent would, the way they should have been treated when they were growing up. As a result, they can be kinder to themselves, and more patient and forgiving. And because you have given them the experience of having what they most needed as a Child - safety, love and acceptance - you have *resourced* the client in a way that will support them, not only through the healing process, but in their daily life. Just realize that you can do so much more than that!

> Just allow all those good feelings to become a part of you now. And realize that she *trusts* you. In a moment, I'm going to ask you to just have a little heart-to-heart talk with her and tell her some nice things about herself. Would you be willing to do that? (wait for response)

> That's good. But *this is important.* Only say it if it's true, okay, because if you were to ever say something that wasn't true, the little one would *feel* it. Understand?
>
> It's important that you always tell her the truth. Would you be willing to do that? (wait for response)
>
> Okay. Tell her this – "I love and accept you." (wait for client to repeat)
>
> Feel true? How true is it? Absolutely? 100%? So, you can love her unconditionally? (*If it's not 100% - go into the heart and find what's needed to be to love and accept the Child unconditionally. Alternately, go back further.*)

If the Child is feeling safe and good, the client is feeling safe and good. The stronger the client feels the positive emotions associated with this state, the deeper they'll go into hypnosis. This means the mind is wide open to suggestions. Suggestions offered at this time will have a powerful impact on the client. So, once the client has filled the Child up with love, the next step is to pour in some suggestions - but only suggest what is true.

Tell the Truth

A Course in Miracles says, "Only what is loving is true." This is especially true when it comes to Inner Child Work. The things a person says to themselves, in the privacy of their own mind, have the power to affect how they feel.

Everything the client says to the Child must feel real and true. If it doesn't, the Child will feel it. This will then reinforce the internal dissonance. You want the client to take responsibility for their self-talk.

Once you have verified that the Child is accepting the client's love, you can invite the client to say a few things to the Child. Tell them to say some things that are kind and loving – but *only if they're true*. This is important because you're establishing a bond of trust. You don't want clients to merely repeat everything you say to them. They need to carefully choose their words based on how they feel. It needs to be true. It needs to come from the heart. If it feels loving – it's true.

By teaching the client how to communicate with their Inner Child, by speaking the truth, you are setting up for the dialogue work of regression hypnosis. In the first session, this conversation can take place in the privacy of the client's own mind. But if the client says the words out loud, you can monitor what they're saying to themselves, and offer corrections as needed.

When the client is giving themselves suggestions, this is called Autosuggestion. Make sure that what they're saying is good and wholesome and empowering for the Child. What I like about this approach is that it gives you a way to test the truth of a suggestion.

Any time you want to test the truth of a suggestion, just instruct the client to go inside and, as they say the words out loud, notice *how it feels*. Then ask, "Does it feel true?" They'll know. The subconscious mind is the feeling mind. If it feels true, that means the suggestion is acceptable. The next thing to ask is then, "How true is it?" If the client says it 100% true, or that it's absolutely true, you *know* that suggestion is going to have an impact. This allows you to gauge the efficacy of a suggestion.

Remind the client that they share the same feelings with the Child, and if they were ever to say something to the Child that was unkind or untrue, the Child would *feel* it. To get the kind of change they want the

Child needs to feel safe in trusting them. The Child needs to believe what they say. Stress how important it is that they *only say it if it's true*. Remember, only what is loving is true.

Establish an agreement from the client to always tell the Child the truth. Then, have them say to the Child, "I'll never lie to you. I'll always tell you the truth." That's the agreement. It's one they're making with themselves. Then, offer them a few suggestions that they can say to the Child that are true of any child. For example, that they're good, that they matter, that they're loveable, that there's nothing wrong with them, etc.

This acts as a warmup and helps to set the tone for the process. You can then invite the client to "find the words the Child most needs to hear." The client knows better than anyone what that Child needs to hear. All you need to do is get the ball rolling and then let the client do the work.

The objective is for Grownup to tell the Child all the things the client *wishes* they had known back then. That way, the Child can grow up feeling good about herself, and develop strength, and confidence and whatever else is needed. This is a way of resourcing the client. Just come up with a few suggestions that are relevant for the client. Then let the client find their own words and say them out loud.

Have them notice how it feels to say those things to the Child. It should feel good. Remember, only what is loving is true. If it doesn't feel good, it's not true. And if it's not true, the Child doesn't need to hear it. If it feels good, the more they say it to themselves, the better they're going to feel. Repeating an acceptable suggestion has a compounding effect.

This is the key to getting rapid results. Compounding a suggestion means that it will get stronger. So, if it feels good, have the client say it again, and notice how much better they feel. Remember, the one suggestion a Child can never hear enough is, "I love and accept you." The more the client repeats this suggestion, the more self-acceptance they're building within themselves.

This is such a versatile suggestion, too, because you can offer any number of variations on it. For example, the client can simply say, "I accept you." Or "I accept you just as you are." Or you can deepen the level of acceptance by saying, "I *deeply* and completely love and accept you." Mix it up to make it feel new.

You can also use this suggestion to qualify another statement by adding it to the end. For example, "You're allowed to feel good about yourself *because* I deeply and completely accept you." Or "Even though (something might be true), I accept you anyway."

This is especially useful when the Child is feeling responsible for something. Maybe they did something wrong. Maybe they're just taking on the feelings of others. But you can validate the perceptions of the Child and still affirm their acceptability.

Ask the client to say to the Child, "I'm so glad I found you." Then notice how it feels as they say *those* words. If it feels good, it's true. What this tells you is that the client has just recovered a Part of themselves that's been missing. *That's healing.*

Have Grownup say those words again. "I'm so glad I found you." Then, have them add these words, "You matter to me." Tell the Child, "Your feelings are important to me." This reinforces the value of the *client's* feelings.

Remember, everything they say to the Child is what the client most needs to hear. Whatever the *Child* needs to hear are the words the *client* needs to hear. What they *most* need to hear is that they matter. That's music for the Soul.

A suggestion I use a lot is, "You are a worthy soul on an important journey. You're here for a purpose." Isn't that nice? You are a worthy soul on an important journey. We all are. We are here to give and receive love. To do that we need to know that it's safe to give and receive love and know that we deserve to be loved and forgiven - no matter what.

Only what is loving is true. Test to make sure that everything the client is saying to themselves is true. If it feels good, it's true. That's a suggestion that will have an impact on the client's life. So, play it again, Sam, and notice how much better it feels.

Test Acceptability

There are two Parts involved in the Inner Child process: the Grownup Part and the Child Part. For a suggestion to be accepted at a subconscious level of mind, both Parts must agree that it's true.

Once you have verified that a suggestion feels true to the Grownup Part, the next step is to test how it feels for the Child. If it feels true to the Child, that suggestion will have impact in the client's life.

To test to see if the Child is willing to accept the suggestion, direct the Adult Part to go into the background. Then, speak directly to the Child Part and say, "As I touch you on the shoulder, or snap my fingers, be FIVE." (Or whatever age the Child is.) That's it.

Ego Strengthening[41]

I want you to notice something else - that she is a complete person. Notice how she has her *own* body and her *own* mind. She has a *body* so that she can see and hear and feel and do in the world. She has a *mind* so she can think for herself and *learn* from her experiences. So she can grow and evolve in a way that supports *you* in becoming who you were always *meant* to be.

She matters, doesn't (she)? Tell her – "You matter. You have a purpose for being here."

Are you glad that you found (her)? Tell her!

So, you can thank the little one for being in your life. And even though she is still growing inside Mom, she's *not* her mother. She is her own person. Always has been. That's how she started out - as an individual cell … growing inside Mom. But she's *not* her mother. Nor is she her father. Or anyone else. Sure, she may share some genetic material with some people but she's her own person! She simply cannot be compared to another because … there is no one exactly like her. Never has been. Never will be. She is one of a kind.

There's nothing wrong with her. This is who she is right *now*. She can see, and hear, and touch, and feel. She can say and do! And she will continue to experience life through all her senses. And continue to grow and learn from life growing up. So, *you* can learn and grow and evolve. Understand?

You can change. You can be better. It's just that … we forget sometimes … After all, no one ever *prepared* us for this experience we call "life." Sometimes we forget … that we're loved. And those are the hardest times. Those are the toughest times - when we forget. We're here to change that. How would you like to always be there for her and *help her* to grow in a way that *empowers you* both?

That's great because, that way, it all gets to play out *much better* for her than it did for you because she'll know something *you* didn't know back then. That she gets to grow up. Here you are! Living proof that she's going to make it through! How might that have changed things for you growing up, if you'd known that then? It changes everything.

Does she have your permission to go through life knowing that ... and just learning from her experiences?

Does she have your permission to feel good about herself - no matter what? ... because life is going to happen, no matter what.

And is it okay with you if she surprises you with how well she will do?

You might just be amazed at how she can grow through situations that, for *you*, were challenging... simply because you didn't know then ... what you know now. And you'll be there for her to help and guide her. Would you like that?

That's good because she trusts you. And you're the only person whose opinion truly matters. Now, she's going to make a few mistakes, growing up, isn't she? Sure, she is! That's how human beings learn! We learn through trial and error. That's what helped us to survive as a species! When we make a mistake, we can *learn* from it - and that makes us smarter. So, we have the ability to change.

When somebody *else* made a mistake, maybe in a way that affected us, we can learn from that, too. Or we find can some value in it ... to enrich us. Or find a blessing ... or whatever... because it's in our nature to learn and forgive and move on. And we can always find *some* good in our experiences in life ... *if we look for it.* There's always *some* good to be found there ... to make us stronger and wiser for having been through it.

---

[41] Inspired by Virginia Satir

> And it's *this ability* - to forgive ourselves and forgive the past - that can help us to *thrive* in life. And live long and happy and productive and prosperous lives because ... we always have a choice. Because as soon as we discover something no longer works, or it causes us pain, or it holds us back in some way ... we can let it go. And when you release something, you set *yourself* free to move on with your life. You become *more* free to be the person you were always *meant* to be. Happy. Healthy. Confident. Vibrant and alive. Because the things of the past no longer have any power over you.
>
> Are you ready to be there for her?
>
> And help her to change ... so you can set yourself free?
>
> Take a moment to have a little heart-to-heart talk with her and tell her some nice things about herself. Tell her all the things you wish you had known back then . . . that she matters, that you love and accept her, that there's nothing wrong with her, that she's smart, capable, good. All the good things about her that you want her to always remember.
>
> Really fill her up with your love and acceptance so that she will always remember and grow up feeling good about herself. Strong and confident. Learning from her experiences in a way that empowers her. Take as long as you need. Tell her to always remember. And I'll sit quietly and you let me know when you're done, okay?
>
> How does she feel now?

"BE FIVE" or "BE GROWNUP" will switch the focus of attention, bringing the Part you want work with to the forefront. Simple, right?

Once the Child steps forward, say, "Grownup just told you something ..." Then repeat the suggestion the client just gave themselves. Ask the Child, "How does it feel to *hear* those words?" It should feel good. If it feels good, it's true. But you can take it one step further by asking the Child, "Do you *believe* it?" This is another test. The Child might *want* it to be true. "Want" is a feeling. But do they *believe* it? If the Child believes the Grownup, ask one more question, "Is it *all* true?"

Verify that the Child believes everything Grownup has said. If so, the subconscious mind has permission to go ahead and generalize those beliefs. This will generate real change.

If the Child doesn't believe it, find out what part of what Grownup just said that isn't believable. You can then call in the Grownup to do the work of convincing the Child that it really is true.

This is how you make the client responsible for the results. If there's *any* doubt or hesitancy in the Child, that's a block. It's an objection. The Child is saying, "Yah-but …" That's *not* a resounding yes.

You need 100% yes to get a change. To resolve the objection, you need to switch back to Grownup. Give the problem of resolving that doubt or objection to the Adult consciousness of the client. Tell them, "(Child) doesn't believe you. Inside of you are the words *she needs to hear* to know that what you are saying really *is* true." Then, instruct them to say whatever needs to be said to *convince* the Child that it's true.

1. **Verify the Change**

Make the client responsible for creating change. You can't do it for them. You can't *make* them change. All you can do is guide the process and get to the underlying truth. The truth is that there's nothing wrong with the Child. This means that there's nothing wrong with the client.

The truth is that the Child deserves to feel safe. This means that *the client* deserves to feel safe. When it's safe enough to *allow* change, change will happen naturally.

> **Find the Words**
>
> Okay, I want you to go inside and find the words that she most needs to hear to *know* that she is loved and accepted. Tell her what you *wish* you had known back then … that she's good … That she's loveable … That there's nothing wrong with her …
>
> Tell her that she gets to grow up … and that she's allowed to grow up feeling good about herself …just learning from her experiences growing up … And she's allowed to learn from her experiences in a way that empowers her … because you love and accept her … exactly as she is.
>
> Tell her she doesn't have to change to be loved by you. Tell her all the good things about her … And tell her to always remember because you'll always be here for her. Okay?
>
> That way, she can grow up feeling strong and confident … and feeling safe secure … because now she knows … there's nothing wrong with her … Understand?
>
> Okay. Go ahead and really fill her up with all the things you wish you had known back then … so that she will always remember. Take as long as you need. And when you're done you let me know. (wait for response.)
>
> How does she feel now? Does she *believe* you? Is it *all* true?
>
> *Switch and ask the Child directly – Is it true? Is it all true?*

Let the client convince herself that it's safe to change. Then, once the client has accepted all the suggestions, ask the client to tell you what's different. Ask, "What's changed?" In other words, let the client verify that there has been a change.

You can ask the Grownup Part, "How has the Child changed?" Or you can say to the Child Part, "You've changed, haven't you? What's different?" This can generate a moment of insight. (You would be well advised to take notes because the information the client gives you, at this point, will be GOLD. You can use it during your session wrap-up[42] to validate changes that are true.)

2. Integrate Change

Once the client realizes that the *Child* has changed, all you need to do is transfer those changes over to the Adult. The way to do this is by integrating these two Parts of the client.

One of the ways to integrate the Adult and the Child is to have the Grownup go into their heart and find a place where the Child can go. This is a nice way to reclaim a Part of them that has been missing. It's like bringing it home and giving it a place in their life.

Instruct the client to place their hand over their heart when they do this so that they can feel it. As the Child goes in there, ask the client, "How does the Little One like it in there?"

Often the client will say it's like a womb or a cocoon. It's warm and safe. You can then suggest that *from now on* the Child can always feel safe and secure and always know that they are loved. And because the Child feels safe, the client can always feel safe and secure because they're the same person. They are one person.

---

[42] To learn more about how to tweak your session wrap-up, get Ditch the Script: *Get Everything You Need from the Client and Set Up to Wrap Up with Results*

Something else you can suggest is that, now that they've got this Part of themselves back, they can always know that they have something special inside of them – *because they do.*

At the end of the session, I used to give each client a small Teddy Bear to act as a reminder of this reclaimed Child Part inside of them. I would then encourage them to put it somewhere special where they can see it every day. This would act as a reminder to always be loving and accepting of themselves. When they talked to themselves, they were to remember to only say nice things because "the little one is listening." This encourages positive self-talk in an ongoing way.

Another way to integrate the Adult and Child Parts is to invite the client to hug the Child. The way I do this is with a little Butterfly Hug. Have the client place each of their hands on the opposite shoulder, then give themselves a hug. Then, give the suggestion that as they hug, these two Parts will merge or melt together. It feels really good. Remind the client that they're *one person*: the Child is simply a younger Part of them. There's no real separation.

As they accept this Part of themselves fully, they merge or melt together. Have the client take a moment to notice how good that feels. Then, before you break off from the hug, tell the client to give themselves a little pat on the back because *they've* changed.

Invite them to realize that all the changes that are happening to the *Child* are happening inside of *the client*. And it's because they gave themselves permission to let love back into their life.

Validate Change

She's changed, hasn't she? What's different?

Realize as she changes, you change. The changes that have occurred in the little one are changes that are occurring inside of you, *right now* …. What's that like?

Allow all these positive changes, all this new learning, and all these good feelings, to become a part of you now.

Optional: Move forward to birthing process and have Grownup receive the little one.

You've done well. Feel proud. Because you've given yourself permission to change in a positive way, you have allowed yourself to feel better today. So you can feel healthier, happier, and more successful in every way. That's the gift you've given yourself today. Because the secret to happiness is not looking outside or looking for more. It's in your ability to simply love and accept yourself. Understand?

In a moment, we're going to move forward along your timelines, just learning and growing, and bringing these newer, better energies with you. And as that happens, all these changes become available to all Parts of you now. So, the benefits can be more pervasive.

Grow the Child up through SSEs or simply give the suggestion to "ripple the changes all the way up to the Grownup you. (pause) What's that like?"

At this point you can wrap up the session and emerge the client.

Optional: Autosuggestion Integration/Compounding Patter

Are you ready to be there for her? Then tell her, "There are some things I want you to always remember." (Now only say it if it's true, okay?)

Tell (her) - "You are loved. / There's nothing wrong with you. / You are precious to me. / I deeply and completely love and accept you."

"You matter. / You're here for a reason. / You matter because … (put an ending on it)"

"You're allowed to grow in kindness and understanding./ You're allowed to be happy – no matter what. / And always love yourself …"

"That is what you are – the Love. / And nothing can change the fact and the truth about you …/ You are made of the stuff of the Universe …/ No less than the trees and the stars. / You have a right to be here."

"You are precious to me./ A priceless jewel … / You deserve a special place in my heart …/ And to always know that you are loved."

"I forgive you. / I love you and accept you and I forgive you. / Even though you've done nothing wrong - I forgive you."

"I am your greatest ally. / I am here for you. / From now on I will always be here for you…. because I found you…/And I love you …/ And I accept you …"

"You are you …/ And you are me …/ And we are one together. / We are together now."

"That changes everything / That changes me for the better/ Because I found you … I can heal."

"LOVE heals … / And to heal is to make happy. / You deserve to be happy and healthy …/ And grow and evolve to be the best person you were meant to be/ And always know that you are loved."

"And like a jewel of great price, that was found lying there at my feet, I accept you now … into my heart./ We are one."

PAUSE.

Notice how it feels to say those things. Feel good?

Would you like to make it feel even better?

Then go inside now. Deep into your heart. Find those feelings of love and acceptance. And appreciation and gratitude. And let yourself feel them. It's okay. And just thank the little one for being a Part of you. And in whatever way feels right for you … send that love from your heart to her heart. Send her *your* love and *your* acceptance … and forgiveness and gratitude because … **you got an important Part of you back today**.

Keep sending it in until she's completely filled. Send it in until she's beaming. You might even notice there's a color that goes into the little one. What color?

Realize that's what was missing.

Really fill her up completely. Just let that radiant (color) flow from your heart into the little one. Really fill her up until she's beaming with your love and acceptance and forgiveness and gratitude. And if words come send them silently from your heart. And I'll sit quietly. Anything that needs to be said is just between the two of you. And you let me know when you feel complete. (wait)

Feel better? *(Client may like to hug the Child)*

She's changed, hasn't she?

What's different?

Love changes everything. Help the client realize what a wonderful gift they have just given themselves. The client can *feel* that something has shifted inside of them. It might be a little. It might be a lot. It doesn't matter.

The subconscious mind is not quantitative, it is qualitative. It's the quality of feeling that will motivate the subconscious mind to take these changes and generalize them in a way that creates real and lasting change. So, pat yourself on the back because something wonderful has just happened.

Not only did you create your ideal client for regression hypnosis, but you also just helped your client get a Part of themselves back today. That's no small thing. Realize they're not the same person anymore. And now they *know* that they *can* change for the better and that, by following your instructions, it's possible to heal.

Well done!

Many adults abused as children have no specific memory of the trauma itself and have a vague sense only of being traumatized. When memories themselves are "recovered," they often are remarkably distorted. This distortion or suppression of traumatic memories may be proportional to the severity of the freeze response, or dissociation at the time of trauma. ~ **Robert Scaer**

CHAPTER 11:
Introduce Forgiveness

Forgiveness Work is important to regression hypnotherapy because, in order to get a complete resolution to the problem, the client must be willing to face the people and situations that caused them pain. Releasing the thought and emotional energies attached to those experiences is what allows healing to happen. The goal is to guide the client to the point where they're willing to let go of their pain story. That's forgiveness.

Forgiveness is simply a letting-go. It's letting go of the pain story. The problem is that not everyone is going to be willing to do that. This is why you need to educate your clients about what it means to forgive. It's because there are the people in the client's life who need to be forgiven.

During the healing process you are going to ask the client to forgive themselves and the people who hurt them. But before you ask them to do that, you need to prepare them for the forgiveness work because forgiveness is not what most people think[43]. Sometimes, letting go of

---

[43] For a more in-depth exploration of therapeutic forgiveness, see The Devil's Therapy: *Hypnosis Practitioner's Essential Guide to Effective Regression Hypnotherapy*. Also,

the pain story can be perceived as a loss of identity. Forgiveness will then be interpreted as a threat which will naturally bring up resistance. Resistance is fear. The Ready for Regression Phase provides the perfect opportunity to bypass a lot of unnecessary fear by showing the client that it's safe to let go of the pain story. This is a process that begins during the intake.

The intake acts as a preliminary uncovering procedure that allows you to take a pulse on how the client feels toward the people who were prominent in their lives in childhood. You can also use your intake to get a sense of how the client feels about forgiveness and uncover any resistance they might have. This will allow you to customize your pretalk to address their concerns before you begin the hypnosis.

The roots of the client's pain story often turn out to be unresolved conflicts from childhood. And the people responsible for causing the Child pain often turns out to be Mom and Dad. This is because the Child is dependent on the parents to meet important needs. Unfortunately, this doesn't always happen. Children don't come with an owner's manual, parents are perfect, and even the most well-intention parent can't be present to the needs of the Child 100% of the time. When a parent or someone else is abusive toward the Child, it leaves behind unresolved trauma that can generate unwanted symptoms.

Clients are not always aware that there was a problem with a particular relationship in childhood but, when they are, often what they'll tell you is that they've dealt with it and that there's no need for them to forgive that person. They may make excuses for that person by saying, "They

---

Radical Healing: *Hypnosis Practitioner's Guide to Harnessing the Healing Power of the Educational Pretalk.*

were doing the best they could." Some clients will provide sound reasons why they don't need to forgive that person. They may even argue that they've already forgiven the person who hurt them. For example, they went to counseling and through the counseling process were able to forgive that person. They may truly believe that there's no longer any problem. But if you watch carefully, you'll see it.

The moment they start talking about that person, the feelings will start to bubble up to the surface. They'll get agitated. Their faces will change color. This is clear evidence that they still have a problem with that person.

When a client starts trying to convince *you* that there's no need to go over old ground, what they're telling you is that they don't want to go there. And the reason they don't want to go there is because it's not finished. This is uncomfortable territory for them and they're trying to convince themselves (and everyone else) that they've been there, done that, and they shouldn't have to go there.

This is the mask of forgiveness. They're not being dishonest. They may honestly believe that they have put the past behind them. But the feelings are still alive. That's the problem. The forgiveness they're talking about is head forgiveness. Head forgiveness is not real forgiveness. Forgiveness based solely on reason doesn't allow the grievance to be acknowledged and released. If anything, it just buries the hatchet deeper into the heart.

Some people believe that they "should" forgive. When forgiveness is seen as an act of saintliness, they'll convince themselves that they have forgiven when, in fact, they've just buried all the pain deep inside. They don't realize it, but feelings buried alive make the mind a living hell.

Buried Emotions Don't Die

When a client tells you they have forgiven, don't believe them. That's just their conscious mind speaking. Meanwhile, their subconscious is screaming out to be heard and, until somebody has the heart to listen, the mind and body will continue to suffer.

The heart feels what it feels. When the head tries to reason away an uncomfortable feeling, it just drives the problem deeper into the psyche. That's a problem because, when emotions get stuffed down deep inside, and a lid gets pushed on top of them, those feelings don't go away. They just find another way to express – usually through symptoms.

If the client truly believes that they have forgiven, there's no point in trying to convince them otherwise. Show them. When you guide them back into events from the past, the truth will win out. The client will be shocked to discover just how much emotion is still attached to those events and people.

During the Ready for Regression Phase, you can give your client a little taste of what it means to forgive[44]. How you do this will really depend on where the client's mind takes you during the session. For example, let's say that your client goes back to a positive experience where Mom is holding them as a baby.

This is a common positive regression to an event where the Child is feeling good with the most important person in her life, Mom. To introduce forgiveness in this situation, have the Child look at Mom and notice how she feels toward her.

---

[44] The Devil's Therapy provides a more in-depth look at Forgiveness Therapy.

If the Child feels safe and loved by Mom, there's nothing to forgive, right? Not necessarily! There's always stuff around Mom. It's just that in this specific moment in time, the Child is feeling good.

Emotionally, children are more like animals who, unlike humans, don't have mixed emotions such as love-hate relationships. A child's brain is limited in its ability to make connections. As a result, their feelings are more separate and compartmentalized. This means that a child can feel angry one moment and completely forget about it the next.

This phenomenon that is wonderfully portrayed in the movie, "*The Boys Are Back*" in which a sportswriter, played by Clive Owens, is left with a young son to care for after his wife dies suddenly. The movie illustrates how the child's grief surfaces through irrational behavior and moods which shift rapidly.

One moment the boy is chattering away happily and the next moment he is morose. While playing with friends, suddenly and without warning, the boy begins angrily shouting and breaking things. Some people would call this 'acting out.' This behavior is normal because feeling mad and feeling happy are two separate states. How the child feels depends entirely on the situation in the moment.

When a young animal/child engages with others it develops social and communication skills. These interactions are responsible for building confidence, self-control, and competence. Social bonding is the seed-planting for future relationships. Attachment styles are developed in childhood. And how a person feels in a relationship is often a reflection of how they interacted with their primary caregiver. Most of the time this is Mother. It's important to recognize that in childhood, Mother is the primary source of security, comfort and peace.

According to Temple Grandin[45], there are four basic feelings common to all mammals, including humans. Those feelings are fear, rage, prey chase desire, and curiosity/interest/anticipation.

Prey chase desire is, as it suggests, the feeling of desire to chase down prey to eat. This predatory aggression is a potential behavior in all animals, including humans. It is triggered by the perception of sudden or rapid movement. For example, in a tense situation sudden movement can trigger a person holding a weapon to use it. You can see this response in any Western gunslinger movie.

The feeling of **curiosity/interest/anticipation** or "seeking" is experienced as a pleasurable feeling of *intense interest*, *engaged curiosity*, and *eager anticipation*. Go to any shopping mall or nightclub and you'll see this drive in action.

What's interesting is that enjoyment isn't dependent on the object of interest. The search itself is pleasurable. For example, if the object of interest is food, it's the *anticipation* of eating, rather than the actual eating of food that brings pleasure.

Grandin states that the feeling of play also provides a sort of life rehearsal that serves to facilitate social bonding. Play is a feeling essential to developing brain function. Play teaches a child to rapidly process tons of incoming sensory data, set goals, and make predictions based on learning. Because early life experiences lay the foundation for future experiences, negative perceptions can become self-fulfilling prophecies.

---

[45] Temple Grandin, Animals in Translation, 2005

Repression

Keeping a lid on feelings, or repression,[46] begins as a means of escaping from feelings of pain, fear, frustration, helplessness and rage. The consequence, however, is a denial or disowning of Parts of one's being leading to feelings of self-alienation or loss of self.

Repressed feelings generate tension in the body. For example, a knot in the stomach, tightness in the throat, pressure in the chest, headaches. Tension inhibits blood flow to the tissues, generating pain. Unexpressed emotions drive unwanted behaviors including smoking, overeating, emotional meltdowns, addictions, OCD, etc.

It takes a lot of energy to keep a lid on emotions. Over time, this loss of energy is experienced as fatigue (often chronic), lack of motivation, depression, or inhibited immune function. When there isn't enough energy left over to run the body's natural healing functions, physical symptoms of disease appear

The more obvious causes of repressed emotions include childhood sexual, physical and emotional abuse, public humiliation, and severe rejection. Extreme strictness, rigidity, and lack of affection are perceived by the child as rejection and can cause inner rage. This rage can find expression through abuse against others (acting out).

When a parent suffers from depression or a prolonged illness, a child's needs can go unintentionally neglected. This can cause insecurity, fear, and sometimes deep anger in the child. Any circumstance where a child feels overwhelmed will, of necessity, result in repression.

---

[46] The unconscious exclusion of painful impulses, desires, or fears from the conscious mind

War, violence, and terrorism, divorce and marital separation, adoption, extreme poverty, moving frequently, alcoholism and drug addiction are perceived by a child to unpredictable, unstable, or insecure situations.

Repressed emotions are not always caused by trauma. Often, they will go back to seemingly innocuous situations. For example, because a young child cannot discern real from imagined, childhood nightmares and imaginary shadows in the closet can haunt a person in adulthood. For this reason, it is imperative that you simply assume an attitude of curiosity and openness. By staying naïve, you give the subconscious mind permission to render up its 'truth' through the process.

We really only have two emotions – love and the absence of love. Love feels good; it's a feeling of expansion and lightness. The absence of love feels bad; it's a dark feeling of contraction that hurts. When we perceive love to be absent, we feel lost and vulnerable. At the ISE there is always the *perception* of separation from comfort, safety or love. This perception finds expression by generating sensations of tension and discomfort in the body. For example, loss generates emotions of sadness and loneliness.

When the source of the hurt or danger is Mother herself, the normal emotional response is *confusion*. When Mother is neglectful or abusive toward the child, feelings of hurt cannot be expressed because doing so would only attract more hurt. Fear cannot be expressed because there is no safe place for the child to escape to. The safe place, Mother, has become dangerous. Anger cannot be expressed because to attack the source of hurt would destroy any chance for security. The only option available to the child is to block these emotions by repressing them. Buried emotions, however, do not go away. Their cry is expressed through symptoms (behavioral, physical, mental).

Healing these symptoms requires releasing the original feelings that got trapped inside. The Child within must be validated, embraced, and allowed to release the unresolved grief of childhood. Restoring comfort and safety can be facilitated by providing the adult self as a surrogate source of nurturing, love and acceptance in daily life.

Releasing

Hurt is the pain of separation. The loss of connection to feelings of comfort, safety and security can feel devastating to a young child. David Hawkins writes, "Grief is the notion of the irreplaceability of what's been lost or that which it symbolized. This is a generalization from the particular so that the loss of a loved one is equated with the loss of love itself." [47] Unresolved grief can find expression through feelings of sadness, loneliness, aloneness, and depression.

An infant's primal need is to feel good. Good, to the infant, is synonymous with pleasure and relaxation. Bad is associated with the pain of constriction or fear. To feel good, the child needs a great deal of attention. She needs to be fed, held, and attended to by people who show the child love and express encouragement and appreciation. This tells her that she is wanted, that her needs matter, and that *she* matters.

Because the infant does not have the ability to reason or understand what happens to her, when these basic needs are not met, she feels hurt and afraid. The shift from feeling good to feeling bad is confusing to an infant and will cause her to become unsure of herself. If her cries for help continue to be ignored, the Child will begin to interpret her helplessness as a weakness. This will then form a part of her self-

---

[47] David R. Hawkins, Power vs Force: The Hidden Determinations of Human Behavior, 2002

concept as inadequate and worthless. Repeated incidents will re-stimulate the initial wounding, reinforcing the perceptions, feelings, and thoughts that will determine her behavior.

All injuries to and overloads of the infant human being's primal integrity arise from the negation of its needs. Neglect, disregard and unreasonable demands – combined with the recurrent experience of receiving too little good, and too much bad, treatment – will overload and disturb the young person's system. Usually this is not done intentionally. It is simply passed on blindly from generation to generation.[48]

According to J. Konrad Stettbacher, initial wounding occurs on three levels and, therefore, must be released on all three levels:

1. Somatic level (physical sensations)
2. Emotional level (feelings)
3. Cognitive level (understandings)

Perceptions awaken sensations and feelings in us which are then given appropriate evaluations. An event that makes an impression on the nervous system of the body automatically produces sensations in the body (pain/pleasure). An emotional response then gives voice to how we are being affected by the situation (positive/negative). Thoughts form as we attempt to make sense of the event and other's behavior. Our (mis)understandings regarding the situation result in decisions (beliefs) about self, others, and what we deserve from life.

Physical sensations can arise anywhere in the body, but the gut, chest and throat are the most common target regions in the body. Discomfort in the body (hurt) is almost always associated with an uncomfortable, blocked emotion.

---

[48] J Konrad Stettbacher, Making Sense of Suffering, 1930

These feelings can be stored in layers - as one feeling gives way another can quickly surface in its place. As a result, a systematic approach to thoroughly releasing each feeling that presents will yield the best results.

The ancient yoga systems of India describe an energy system in the body comprised of spinning vortices called 'chakras.' Physically, six of the seven major chakras correspond to nerve plexus in the body. The throat chakra is considered the center of communication and creativity. Communication involves both listening and speaking, so this chakra is associated with our ability to express our true thoughts, feelings and emotions as well as our capacity to listen.

A sensation of tension or tightness in the throat, a 'lump' in the throat, or involuntary swallowing reflex are often physical signs of trapped feelings. For example, a cry being choked off, words being swallowed away, putting a lid on your feelings.

The heart chakra is related to love and forgiveness. Mind and body meet in the heart. If the heart chakra is blocked, we suffer to the core of our being. Our breathing becomes shallow, metabolic function slows, and physical energy diminishes.

Neuroscience has recently discovered that the heart actually has its own nervous system that has at least 40,000 neurons – as many as are found in various parts of the brain. The heart apparently is in constant communication with the brain and the rest of the body through nerve impulses, hormones, neurotransmitters, and pressure waves.

Growing scientific evidence suggests that the heart and brain may also communicate through electromagnetic field interactions, i.e. energetically. In fact, the heart may be the source of information regarding emotional and intuitive thoughts and feelings we are experiencing. The visceral area of the body is especially significant. That's where the body's Enteric Nervous System (ENS) is located.

The ENS is comprised of two networks of neurons embedded in the wall of the gastrointestinal tract (gut). It is governed by the central nervous system, sensing and responding to tension in the gut.

The ENS has been described as a "second brain" because it can operate autonomously and because it consists of between 200 - 600 million neurons. This is similar to the number of neurons in the spinal cord.

The feeling of hurt is often first experienced in the gut as constriction, clamping down, or cramping. And research shows that stress, anxiety, and irritable bowel syndrome (IBS) are related to this response. The same stress that causes a tension headache can also trigger a migraine. With tension headaches, the muscles in the upper neck and back tighten. As they become overly fatigued, they spasm, causing headaches. Migraines are caused by the dilation of blood vessels in the head as the body internalizes the stress in the blood vessels rather than the muscles.

When tension and pressure are present in the head and neck area, it could be a symptom of the body holding onto a physical injury. For example, upper cervical (neck) injuries are common during the birthing process. Often the birthing practitioner will pull or twist the head to assist the birth causing misalignment of the spine.

Forceful traction due to forceps and breech delivery are both identified as high-risk factors for trauma to the newborn's upper neck, spinal cord, and brainstem.

While children often struggle with understanding their feelings, grownups often struggle with *feeling* their feelings. Unlike grownups, young children don't have the ability to experience mixed feelings. They're either feeling good or they're feeling bad. If the Child is feeling good, all this tells you is that, *in this moment*, the Child is feeling okay (with Mom).

Pay attention when the Child reports a feeling of confusion. Confusion often suggests that the Child is trying to make sense of something new which could indicate that you have located an ISE. Releasing the confusion will reveal the authentic feelings of the child.

Vulnerability generates emotions of aloneness, fear and guilt. Anticipatory fear (anxiety) is always based on memory. Releasing the fear will allow you to find the underlying hurt. Releasing the hurt will restore the awareness of love and security allowing healing to happen naturally.

When There's Anger

There is an Aesop's fable about a slave who came upon a lion roaring in the woods. A thorn had gotten lodged in the lion's paw and festered, causing the noble beast insufferable pain. The slave carefully removed the thorn, bringing relief to a very grateful lion, and the wound was finally allowed to heal. Hurt is felt in the body. It's a thorn calling for release. Remove it and healing will follow.

Releasing is the process of safely moving out the burden of stored-up hurt, fear and anger from the past. As stress hormones, such as adrenaline and cortisol, are discharged from the tissues, healthy function is restored to the body. Releasing the internal pressure and stress provides the mental and emotional space necessary for insight and wisdom to be applied to past events. Unfortunately, a mistake you see a lot of new hypnosis practitioners make is trying to use a script to get rid of an uncomfortable feeling like fear or anger. You can't suggest away an emotion, you can only transform it.

Remember, you're working with the feeling Part of the mind. Feelings are how the subconscious mind communicates. If you try to suggest away a Part of the client, you will only reinforce the problem and add to the underlying conflict. That's not healing. The client is already alienated from their feelings and emotions. Don't add to the problem by trying to use a surface technique on a deeper issue.

There's nothing wrong with the client. There's nothing wrong with the feeling. Every feeling is a Part of the client. Trying to suggest away a feeling is like trying to amputate an arm or a leg. Don't do it. The feeling is merely a symptom. Symptoms are how their subconscious mind communicates.[49] And the subconscious mind has a very good reason for doing what it's been doing. You just don't know what it is, yet.

The purpose of the uncovering work is to find out what's generating the feeling, and what purpose that feeling serves. Then you can change it. But the feeling is never the problem. When you're dealing with an emotional issue, you need to find out what *caused* the feeling in the first place.

Every problem is the result of a life experience. That's where you need to do the healing work. But to gain access to those events you need to be on good terms with the Parts that are still stuck there. That means accepting them and giving them permission to express. Not judging and criticizing by trying to get rid of them.

---

[49] See The Devil's Therapy for Symptom Imperative.

What you'll find quite often is that the client's mind will take you back into events that seem like they're no big deal, at least to adult reasoning. But you're not dealing with the adult part of the mind. You're dealing with the mind of the Child. The subconscious mind is the irrational part of the mind. For some reason, that situation generated uncomfortable feelings. The reason it's still a problem is because the Child couldn't come to resolution.

The event may have just been misinterpreted by the Child. But the feeling is real. This is what keeps the client trapped in past events. It's because a very young Child lacks the maturity to be able to figure things out.

A Child is acutely aware of how dependent she is on others for its survival. When there's no one there to look after the Child, or help the Child make sense of things, the Child feels incredibly vulnerable. This makes the situation a very real threat for the Child. With no one to look after her, the Child knows one thing – she could die.

When there's a hurt involved, either physically or psychologically, it's often overwhelming for the Child. For example, when Mom and Dad are not paying attention to the Child, or taking care of the Child's needs, this leaves the Child feeling abandoned. Abandonment equals death.

If there's abuse, you'll find there are multiple feelings all contributing to the problem. There can be fear and anger and sadness. Often the Child will lose the ability to trust herself or others. This can develop into unconscious vigilance as an attempt to make sure those things never happen again. It can result in anxiety or armoring. The person can end up carrying a burden of weight just so they can feel safe in the world.

The problem is that the subconscious mind is timeless. It doesn't know that the event is over. If the Child got hurt, and there was no one there to make it better, the subconscious doesn't know that there isn't more hurt on the way. If the Child concludes, "I'm the problem," or "I have done something wrong," this generates guilt. When guilt gets turned inward, it generates fear and anxiety. When it gets projected outward, it generates anger.

There's nothing wrong with anger. Anger is simply the subconscious mind trying to protect. But for most people, anger is like the elephant in the living room. Nobody wants to admit that they feel anger because displays of anger are socially disapproved of. As a result, people tend to hold onto their anger. That's a problem.

It's not that anger is the problem. Anger is good. Anger is an emotion that empowers us when we need to set boundaries or defend ourselves or someone we love. But anger that doesn't get expressed can be vented in unhealthy ways. And unresolved anger from the past can cause harm to self and others.

Anger is an uncomfortable emotion. And emotions need to move. That's their job. They motivate us to take action. But when you stuff a feeling down, it has to go somewhere. If it can't get out, it gets turned inward. When anger gets turned inward, it takes the form of self-abuse. This generates anxiety and self-punishing behaviors.

When anger gets turned outward it gets projected onto others. It's like a toxic spray that gets spread around indiscriminately and unconsciously, and this generates guilt. Guilt is a gift that just keeps on giving by keeping the pain story alive.

Anger is the hurt trapped inside the pain story. And suffering is what happens when you're attached to that story. You hold onto the hurt. Anger steps in to protect. And it doesn't feel good.

When anger roars like a lion, it is because we have been *stuck* in hurt and fear. Anger is a defense in the face of a perceived threat. When we feel threatened, vulnerable, afraid, and backed into a corner, anger arises to protect us. The answer to anger is let it go.

When a person releases all the anger that's been trapped inside, forgiveness will follow. The goal of regression-to-cause is to get to the heart of the problem and release everything unlike love. *All* the fear. *All* the sadness. *All* the anger. That's when authentic forgiveness happens.

Release the anger and you'll find the underlying fear. Release the fear and you'll find the thorn. Remove the thorn and feelings of gratitude will flow through the body-mind system to allow healing. That's forgiveness. It happens automatically when an emotional block is released.

I used to follow a standard protocol which focused on convincing the client to forgive. But what I discovered is that forgiveness is not something we do. It's something that happens, automatically, given the right conditions. Releasing the trapped emotions of fear and anger creates precisely the right conditions for forgiveness to happen.

This makes the Forgiveness Work a very organic process. The client doesn't *have* to forgive because forgiveness is not something we *do*. It's something that *happens* as a by-product of letting go of all the hurt associated with the pain story.

When a person decides to let go of their pain story, they experience true freedom from the pain of the past. As a result, they no longer *need* to hold onto the anger.

Forgiveness is not a religion. Nor is it merely words. It's an experience of letting go. When a person let's go of the problem – healing happens. The key is to release everything.

The goal is 100% freedom from the feeling. Leaving a wee bit of emotion trapped inside is like leaving a little infection behind in a wound. How do you know if the problem is gone for good?

You need to test to see if there is any emotional charge left. If the client is still holding onto a grievance, the issue isn't fully resolved. As a result, it's going to continue to grow and fester. It's only a matter of time before the symptoms recur.[50] But to release the hurt and the anger trapped inside, you need to give it a place to go. This is the purpose of Pillow Therapy.

Pillow Therapy

Pillow Therapy is where you place a firm pillow in the client's lap and invite them to pump the feeling into the pillow. But this is important - Pillow Therapy is not about hitting or punching. That can be interpreted as violence or aggression which will generate fear. The purpose of Pillow Therapy is to *discharge* the energy that's been trapped in the body by giving the feeling a way out.

Even if things go sideways in the first session, you can use whatever comes up to teach your client how to work with you. That is the fundamental purpose of the Ready for Regression Session. It is to

---

[50] For more on symptom recurrence, recidivism, and symptoms conversion, see The Devil's Therapy: *Hypnosis Practitioner's Essential Guide to Effective Regression Hypnotherapy*

prepare the client to be ready to regress back into painful past events. They just need to be willing to feel the truth of their feelings. Then, they can let them go. That's what real forgiveness is.

You don't usually need to introduce Pillow Work in the first session because, typically, you're going back to positive events. But if a client dives into a bucket of anger, and you don't have any other tools you can fall back on, then the answer to anger is to give it a place to go.

Pull out your pillow and tell the client to pump that feeling into the pillow. Give it a place to go. Moving the body physically can help to quickly discharge the trapped energy. Even if you don't get a complete release, the client will still let go of some of the pressure. Any measure of relief will prove to the client that you can help. They'll know that they can trust you with their more vulnerable feelings.

Forgiveness

Forgiveness of others, self, and even God can effectively transmute past hurts into strength and wisdom. Using your Ready for Regression Phase gives the client the opportunity to experience forgiveness in a non-threatening way. This will allow them to discover some of the benefits which will bring down resistance.

Most of the time you'll be able to give the client an experience of what it's like to forgive. All you need to do is have the client say the words out loud. "I forgive you (Name)" and notice how it feels.

If the client tells you that it feels good, amplify that feeling by having the client repeat those words and notice how much better it feels each time they say it. Forgiveness feels good *because* it is a letting-go.

A positive experience of forgiveness teaches the client that it's safe to forgive. (At the very least, it proves that nothing bad will happen if they forgive a person.) Providing this experience can make it easier to obtain forgiveness when the client regresses into stickier situations. Remember, forgiveness feels good. This realization will make it easier for the client to be willing to forgive in more challenging situations from the past. That's what we want.

All forgiveness is self-forgiveness. Allowing even a little bit of forgiveness will make the client more forgivable. This will open the door to allow more forgiveness to happen. The place to begin the Forgiveness Work is with the Child simply because it's easier to forgive a Child.

1. Forgive the Child

The Child still needs to be forgiven because *all forgiveness is self-forgiveness*. First, establish that the Child is innocent and that there's nothing wrong with the Child. If there is nothing wrong with the Child, the Child is forgivable. If the Client doesn't agree with you on this point, the next step in their healing process is to make the Child forgivable.

To heal, the client needs to able to accept that there's nothing wrong with the Child. There is nothing a Child could ever do to deserve hate or condemnation or rejection.

Remember, these judgments are being directed toward a Part of the client. These judgments generate anxiety and rage. That's a problem. The client must accept that the Child is worthy of love and acceptance and deserves forgiveness because, if the Child deserves to be forgiven, the client deserves to be forgiven. After all, they're the same person.

The Child doesn't need to do anything to be worthy of love and acceptance. The Child is intrinsically loveable and there is nothing the Child could ever do to diminish their love-ability. If the Child did something wrong, it was merely a mistake. Certainly, it wasn't intentional. It's just that human beings learn through trial and error.

Here on Planet Earth, mistakes happen – especially in childhood. This ability to make mistakes has made it possible for the human species to survive. Thrive, even! This is the foundation we want to establish because love heals.

Learning is an important concept because it involves curiosity, and curiosity is a positive emotion. It's a resource state. Get your clients invested in learning from their past experiences and they'll gladly give up their self-condemnation. Mistakes happen. Mistakes serve the purpose of learning. Learning is good. This is the understanding that lays the foundation for forgiveness.

Start with the Child because the Child is always forgivable. The Child is innocent. There's nothing wrong with the Child. The Child is allowed to learn. Learning is empowering. And it feels good. It's a reward state. Reinforce the idea that the client is learning something by asking, "What did you learn?" Or "What are you discovering?"

Remind them that the Child is allowed to learn and grow through experience and that it's okay to make mistakes. If the Child makes a mistake – that's forgivable. By learning from experience, they will grow stronger and wiser. And so, will you. Your clients will always be your best teachers. As you guide your clients to heal, you will learn and grow and become stronger and wiser, too. This will make you a much more capable healer. Give yourself permission to make mistakes!

Mistakes Are Good Patter

There was a stage in our evolution where human beings learned to walk upright. Unfortunately, this created a problem for the female of the species. To be able to walk upright, our hips needed to be slimmer. This meant that we could no longer carry a child to the point where it could walk immediately following birth. A baby giraffe can stand on its own two feet as soon as it is born. A baby horse is scampering around within just a few hours following birth. But a human child must be born prematurely and, as a result, it must learn how to walk.

If you've ever watched a baby try to figure out how to walk, you know what I'm talking about. The baby starts by pulling itself up and holding onto something like the coffee table or a chair. The muscles in the hips, thighs, knees and ankles haven't learned how to coordinate into walking yet. When the baby takes that first step, it plunks down onto its butt. Is this a failure? Is this a mistake? Hardly, because the child has just learned something very valuable from that experience, hasn't she? The child has learned how *not* to walk. It may take a thousand more trials before she finally learns how to get it right. But that's something Thomas Edison figured out. Edison said that he hadn't failed a thousand times before inventing the light bulb. He said that he learned a thousand ways *not* to make a lightbulb. That's nature. That's evolution. That's life!

Eventually a Child learns how to coordinate all these micro-movements that go into walking. And through repetition it becomes automatic. That's when you don't have to think about it anymore. It just happens. But we all had to learn how to crawl before we could walk. And we had to walk before we could run. And it's because human beings learn through trial and error – which means mistakes are bound to happen. And **that's forgivable.** Mistakes are meant to be learned from. And learning is good. It's what helped us to survive as a species. Without this ability we'd all still be crawling around in the dirt. So, mistakes are good!

The key understanding for the healing work of regression hypnosis is that *all forgiveness is self-forgiveness.* The Child is a Part of the client. Forgiving the Child is an act of self-forgiveness. This is also true of the people who show up in events from the past. They're not people. They have been internalized as Parts of the client. That's why they have the power to influence how the client feels. This means that when a client forgives that person, they are forgiving themselves.

Once you have established that the Child is worthy of love and forgiveness, invite Grownup to say, "I forgive you," to the Child and notice how it feels. You're using the client's first session to plant a kernel of truth in their subconscious mind and that is that forgiveness feels good.

Forgiving the Child will give the client the experience of *being* forgiven. This will open the door to allow more forgiveness to happen. All the work you do from this point on will take on a deeper, more transformative quality.

2. Forgive Mom & Dad

There will be other people from the past who are contributing to the client's problem. But the top of the hit list is always going to be the primary caregiver. Usually that's Mom or Dad because Mom and Dad are the most important people in a Child's life. Even when the client is convinced that they had a perfect childhood, or that Mom and Dad are blameless, there is always an emotional charge around Mom and Dad.

These are the people who are at the top of the forgiveness list because these are the people who had the greatest influence on the Child growing up. They need to be forgiven for the things they did to cause the Child pain, or for failing to meet the needs of the Child, either through what they did, or what they didn't do. If the client goes back into an event in childhood where they're with Mom or Dad, check out the Child's feelings toward that parent because this can be very revealing.

Often what you'll find is that there will be an event where the Child feels "not wanted." Usually, it's because Mom and Dad are having problems. As a result, they're preoccupied. This makes them less-than attentive to the needs of the Child. But the Child doesn't know how to make sense of this.

If you do a little uncovering work, you'll often find that the Child is misinterpreting the situation. The Child will think, "I'm a problem," or "I'm not wanted," or "I'm not important." This is a decision that, left unchallenged, can continue to impact a person for their entire life.

Remember, the problem is not what happened during the event. The Child survived that experience, the client is still here, and they can learn from their past experiences in a way that empowers them. The problem is that the Child lacked the maturity to be able to figure things out and there was no one there to help them make sense of things. That's reasonable. If you can't make sense of your environment, you don't know how to respond appropriately to take care of yourself. That's going to generate fear.

Fear is the mother of all negative emotions. 90% of the time the root of the problem you're dealing with is *fear*. Events in childhood can generate a lifetime of despair simply because the Child wasn't able to make sense of things. You can transform these kinds of fears very quickly.

The first step is to provide safety. Bring in the Adult Part of the client to support the Child and help the Child to feel safe, again. Once the Child is feeling safe, they'll be able to relax, and the subconscious mind will open up to allow learning. That's when you can ask the Adult Part of the client to educate the Child about what's really going on.

Help the client to reinterpret the event so that the Child understands what's happening. Help the Child realize that she hasn't done anything wrong. Whatever's going on, the Child did nothing to cause it. Really, it was just a mistake so there's nothing to forgive. Then, ask the Child to forgive Mom or Dad.

Instruct the Child to look at (Mom) and say, "I forgive you (Mom)," and notice how it feels to say those word. That's it. Just say the words, "I forgive you (Mom)," and notice how it feels. Usually, forgiveness will happen automatically. The Child will say, "I love you (Mommy)," and the client will come to peace in some regard.

Often, the client will tell you that there's nothing to forgive. Recognize that that's the conscious mind stepping in. That's head forgiveness. Authentic forgiveness comes from the heart. What you want to know is how does it *feel* to forgive Mom?

It's a test. It should feel good. If there's a little hiccup or a hesitation, that indicates a block. There's no need to explore what the block might be. In the first session, your prime objective is essentially to introduce the concept of forgiveness. When there's a block, make a note. This is a relationship you'll want to pay closer attention to in future sessions.

Once the Child has forgiven Mom, ask *Mom* if there's anything she needs to forgive the Child for. This can be very revealing because sometimes the client will be carrying guilt. Maybe they were colicky as a baby. Maybe Mom had a difficult birth. These are common issues for a lot of clients because children have the tendency to take the blame. But you won't know if there's a problem unless you ask Mom to forgive the Child.

If *Mom* says there's nothing to forgive, that's the right answer. This confirms that the Child is innocent. Now you can let Mom be a source of positive suggestions for the Child. The Child will readily accept suggestions from Mom because they are coming from the most important person in the Child's life. Nice, right?

Realize that Mom's opinion matters to the Child. And the words the Child most needs to hear from Mom are, "I love you." Ask Mom, "Is the Child loveable? Is there anything wrong with the Child?"

If Mom has just told you there's nothing to forgive, you know what the answer will be. You can use this as an opportunity to lay the groundwork for deep healing by letting *Mom* do the Inner Child Work. Invite *Mom* to fill the Child with love and tell the Child, "I love you. I forgive you. There's nothing wrong with you."

Fill the Child with *Mom's* love by having Mom say, "You're precious to me." Realize that this is an act of self-love. The client is forgiving a Part of herself.

Time permitting, you can even invite the Child to forgive Grownup. This might sound a little weird, but the Adult Part of the client may be feeling guilty for having abandoned themselves, or for letting themselves down, or for having neglected some Part of their life for too long. Being forgiven by *the Child* will result in the client letting go of some of the guilt.

If you're pressed for time, a quicker way to introduce forgiveness is to simply have the Grownup Part of the client look at the Child and say, "I deeply and completely love and accept you. I forgive you. I set you free ... to be ... who you are." Then, ask the client how it feels to say those words. It should feel good. Really good.

Now, obviously, not every session is going to be this simple. Things can get complex when there are unresolved problems in childhood. Maybe the Child was put up for adoption. Or Mom was an addict. Or there was abuse in early childhood. But even when there are larger issues to be resolved, this little bit of forgiveness can make a big difference with respect to how the client feels about herself.

Don't worry if you don't get complete forgiveness at this point. This is just a warm-up. There will likely be other situations in the past involving Mom and Dad where forgiveness is called for. In the first session all you need to do is establish the willingness to forgive. This will open the door to allow more forgiveness to happen. That's where the healing lies.

"In the beginning of my work, I matter-of-factly presumed that emotions were in the head or the brain. Now I would say they are really in the body." ~ **Candace Pert**

CHAPTER 12:
Wrap Up Powerfully

By the end of the Ready for Regression session, your client will have experienced many things with you. Through the process of being guided into hypnosis, they will have been wowed with the incredible power of their own mind. They will have used their imagination to experience positive memories from the past which have been converted into a real regression to childhood. You will have taught them how to respond to you during the uncovering procedure, introduced them to their Inner Child, and taught them how to love, accept and forgive this younger Part of themselves so they can heal. They have likely gathered up some internal resources that will help them to feel better. In fact, they could be feeling better already!

The client has just experienced a journey into the territory of their own mind. Through an amazing process of self-discovery, they may have gained some insight into themselves. They may even have had a few insights into what's causing the problem. As a result, they're probably feeling much more hopeful than when they first began. To wrap up this session, your goal is to turn this experience into a powerful learning experience.

Your Session Worksheet gives you everything you need to wrap up your sessions powerfully by making the experience meaningful and relevant for the client. You do this by turning it into a revelation.

Revelation Wrap Up

A revelation is "a surprising and previously unknown fact, especially one that is made known in a dramatic way." First, remind the client of their Therapeutic Goal. Remember, that's what they're paying you for. It's *why* they are taking this journey with you. But the client's Therapeutic Goal is not merely a change they want to make. It's their vision of who they might become for having made this change. It's the dream that they want you to help them to grow into.

What does a positive future look like?

Help the client connect all the dots between what they experienced during the session and their therapeutic goal. Connecting the dots sets the client up to face a brighter future. Hypnotherapy is a learning process that changes how a person thinks and feels about themselves, others, and life in general.

First, remind the client of why they're taking this journey with you. That's their Therapeutic Goal. What did the client discover? What do they know now that they didn't know before? How might this provide evidence that it's *possible* to create the change they want? How is this experience *relevant* to the client's Therapeutic Goal?

Second, remind the client of their list of Conditions for Change by inviting the client to imagine what it's like to be *effortlessly* taking appropriate action. Guide them to imagine it vividly by bringing in all of their five senses - seeing, hearing, tasting, smelling, feeling. How did they make the right choice to create their desired change? Easily. Why? Because their subconscious mind has the power to make them into the kind of person they want to be. For example, a thinner person, a stronger person, a calmer person, etc. It's all in them *now*. Remind the client that they're *allowed* to change - change for the better.

You don't have to *make* the client change or do anything at all. You just need to create a space that allows for a new sense of possibility. Then, fill that space with suggestions to *allow* change. Think of it as filling their tank. Fill it with their permission to allow change to happen. Fill it with permission to take those few steps and take action to make those changes that will allow them to enjoy all the rewards of change.

Third, bring in all the benefits they can look forward to because they were willing to take the action necessary to create that change. Go through the Benefits of Change list and invite the client to experience what it's like to be enjoying the rewards of having achieved their goal. Instruct them to experience it *as if* it were already true.

This can be an interactive process, or you can just deliver a few suggestions. It's up to you. But the language of the subconscious mind is image and emotion. When the client imagines having the results, they experience a reward state. This reduces resistance to taking action to create those changes.

What feelings are associated with the picture they're holding in their mind?

What emotions correspond to the experience of having made that change? That's the motivating factor.

Now you know . . .

What did the client discover? What, if anything, has changed? How does this change things from now on? This forms the basis of the revelation – a surprising and previously unknown fact.

Use the client's own insights and realizations to formulate, "Now you know . . ." suggestions.

If you needed to wrap up your session following the Conditioning phase, your suggestions would focus on the power of the client's own mind. For example, "Now you know . . . hypnosis is a safe and effective way to create real change, from the inside out. As we continue to work together, releasing all remaining blocks, more and more you can discover what it's like to really be enjoying life free of the past."

Most of the time your client will follow your directions to go back to a positive event in childhood. They'll associate into a Child Part and experience some positive feelings. If the session brought them into some good feelings, yay! Mission accomplished. During your session wrap up you can turn this experience into a celebration by reminding the client that they found their good feelings. Now they know that those good feelings are still inside of them. Use this as evidence that they're *allowed* to feel their feelings.

Finally, get the client looking forward to their next session with you by suggesting that they are now in the process of healing. It is a process that involves learning and growing and changing from the inside out. If the client is feeling calmer and more relaxed, or has let something go during the session, use it as evidence that change is already occurring! (And there's more where that came from!)

From now on . . .

The re-induction process following the Conditioning phase often comes as a surprise. The client experiences a kind of whoosh into a deeper state of hypnosis. That's when they realize, "Wow! This is powerful stuff!"

That's the Wow Factor. Remember to review the instructions for the re-induction trigger before emerging the client. This will cause the client to mentally rehearse the induction, helping to reinforce the response to the trigger you've installed. For example, "You've done well. From now on, whenever we do hypnosis together, you'll find it easy to return to the state of hypnosis. This ability is going to be so helpful to you. Next time, it will be much more powerful. When that hand goes "plop!" into your lap, you'll go right back down to the same beautiful state. And each time you will go deeper than the time before. Okay?"

Guiding a client back into a positive event from childhood doesn't always go the way you'd expect. Sometimes the subconscious mind will go to an event that seems happy, at least to begin with. Then, as you move into the uncovering process, the client will start to experience feelings of sadness or grief and loss. That's okay. During your session wrap up you can remind the client that those feelings are allowed to be there, too. Make it okay for them to feel *all* their feelings.

There's no such thing as a "bad" feeling. Just feelings that don't feel good. But all feelings are meant to be helpful. They're part of our internal guidance system which is always pointing toward what we want. This understanding will encourage the client to allow more feelings to come to awareness which will give you access to a deeper level of healing.

Everything in a session is helpful. It's pointing to the direction of healing, and you can use it to guide the process. When it comes time to wrap up your session, do it powerfully. Show your clients how relevant what they have just experienced with you really is. Make it a revelation. Reinforce all the positive changes they can look forward to as you continue the work together. And you'll be all set for the next session.

Zig-Zag

If the subconscious mind zigged when you told it to zag and, instead of going to a happy event, it dumped the client into a traumatic event in childhood, that's okay. It happens. But when it happens, you need to toss the protocol aside and do what you were trained to do and get to work on identifying and resolving what's brought to consciousness.

The idea is to work with whatever the subconscious mind gives you. If it's showing you a pocket of pain, work with it. Just know that you don't have to resolve the whole problem in a single session. All you need to do is show the subconscious mind that it's possible to get some relief.

Do that and, not only will this give you a more cooperative client to work with in future sessions but, their subconscious mind will trust you enough to show you where the bodies are buried.

Big Bucket of Pain

If the client stepped into a painful memory and experienced some uncomfortable feelings, then use your wrap up to acknowledge that they just faced a big, hairy-scary feeling - and *they're still here.*

The client needs to realize that they made it through. Nobody died. As a result, they can feel proud because they faced their feelings! That's huge! Validate it by saying, "Good job!" or "Well done!"

Remember, that's what the client has been trying to avoid. Now they know that it's okay to feel their feelings. Give the suggestion, "You're allowed to feel all your feelings – *even the good ones.*" The client just learned that feelings don't come out of nowhere! Those uncomfortable feelings are connected to past events that have everything to do with the problem the client is seeing you about. This understanding can provide a sense of control and safety.

The client needs to understand that their subconscious mind is not the enemy. It only wants what's best for them. It wants the same things they want – to feel better, to be happy, to feel in charge of their life, and let the past be the past. The fact that their subconscious mind took them to any event tells you that their subconscious mind wants this problem resolved. That's good news! This proves that the subconscious mind wants the problem resolved. It's willing to show where the "owie" is!

If the client bounced back into an event where the Child was feeling scared, or sad, or conflicted in some way, the revelation needs to be that it's safe to allow uncomfortable feelings. Remember, the feeling is never a problem. The feeling is just the messenger.

If the client found an uncomfortable feeling, they did well. The revelation needs to be that their subconscious mind has just shown them something very important. Now they know that this is what's calling for healing.

Whatever happens, when it comes time to do your session wrap-up, it's all good. It's relevant to the client's issue because it is connected to the problem through the feeling. Even if what was revealed through the session didn't feel good, even if it came as a shock, you could still use it as evidence that their subconscious mind wants them to heal. Turn it into a revelation because the client now has experience that proves what you're telling them is true.

No matter what they discovered during the session, it's helpful. It's a step toward achieving their goal because now they know something that they didn't know before. This is knowledge that can empower them. That's worth celebrating and appreciating. In fact, something I like to do during the session wrap up is to invite the client to transmit a feeling of appreciation to their subconscious mind.

Remember, there's a split between the conscious and subconscious mind. There's a conflict. Anything you can do to encourage greater rapport between the conscious mind and the subconscious mind is going to help restore internal harmony.

Gratitude is a healing state. A feeling of gratitude can help to encourage rapport between the client's conscious and subconscious mind. It only takes a moment. Just invite the client to go inside and say "thank you" to their subconscious mind for being willing to show them these things so they can heal. That's it.

Healing is a process. Wrap up each session with a vision of the reality the client is *living into*. Get them seeing and feeling and experiencing what it's like to be creating those changes and what it's like to be living into their desired goal. Then, fill their tank with suggestions that allow them to go the distance.

The images that come to mind will become more believable as you resolve the blocks and resistance within. And the behaviors that contribute to making this new reality will become more do-able in daily life.

Social approval is a strong motivator. Invite the client to imagine sharing these changes with others. Give them the experience of what it's like to have others recognizing and approving of them for having made these changes. Help the client discover how this *reinforces* the pride of accomplishment that they *already* feel for having given themselves this wonderful gift. And how achieving their goal is the natural consequence of having made the right choices for *them*.

Remind the client that all that is needed is to decide on the direction and then commit to taking the next step. Then suggest that they have *already* taken the first step. The journey has already begun. As a result, they can feel confident that success is only a matter of time.

Finally, suggest that the subconscious mind now has all the information it needs to begin making these changes. And use a formal count up to emerge the client from hypnosis.

Buttoning Up

When there's so much internal pressure that the subconscious bounces back into a traumatic event, you won't always have enough time to process the whole event. That's okay. You can still help the client to get some relief. This will help to instill confidence in the process.

Even a slight shift for the better can be used to remind the client that the subconscious mind is qualitative, not quantitative. All it takes to change a person's entire trajectory in life is one small shift in the right direction. And then another. Before long, they will have walked themselves right out of the problem.

Sometimes the event turns out to be no big deal. In this case, you may be able to process the whole thing and take the client from "ow!" to "wow!" But if you're pressed for time, there's no problem. Rome wasn't built in a day, and neither was the client's problem. Just work with what the subconscious gives you. When it is time to wrap up your session, button the client up so that you can come back to the event and clear it in the next session.

Buttoning up allows you to come back to where you left off. Remind the client that they just discovered something valuable. Something important has been revealed to them through the process that is relevant to their Therapeutic Goal.

The idea is to set up reasonable expectations about the process. Make it reasonable for the client to go where you need them to go. You can do that by validating what they have just experienced.

1. Validate the Feeling.

Because the subconscious mind is the feeling mind, when you validate a feeling, you are recognizing and acknowledging the subconscious mind. You're valuing what it has to say. "That feeling" is an important Part of the client and it has been brought to awareness for a reason.

Don't make the mistake of trying to suggest it away or defaulting to reading a script. All that will do is cost you a rapport with the subconscious mind. It could even make things worse. The first step is always to validate the feeling. Give it permission to be there.

We learn from a very early age to put a lid on our feelings. When a feeling gets trapped inside it generates pain. But every feeling is a worthy Part of the client and deserves to be loved, accepted, and forgiven. Give it permission to be there.

Whatever comes up, validate it. Point out that it has value to your client and to the healing process. Remember, this is their subconscious mind speaking and it has the power to create the kind of change they want. Then show how what was revealed to them in this session has everything to do with what the client wants.

2. Reframe the Event.

Reframe the event to make it a revelation. What have they just discovered? What are they learning about themselves? Make it a breakthrough moment in the client's healing.

3. Make it Relevant.

The goal is to tie everything together and make it relevant to the client's healing goal. Reinforce any insights they might have had and turn them into revelations to empower the client. The weight problem. The skin problem. The relationship problem. Whatever it is, it's coming out of the "owie."

The owie is the real problem and that's coming out of an uncomfortable experience in the client's past. Whatever the client has just discovered has everything to do with the reason they're seeing you. That's their Therapeutic Goal.

What has been revealed is that the *problem* the client has been struggling with has everything to do with past events. That's big. Help the client make the connection because now they know that the problem is rooted in childhood. For example, "*Now you know* ... that fear (or sadness, or anger, or whatever came up in the session) ... *that feeling* got stuck inside of you *long* before you were old enough to make sense of things. But you're not a Child anymore. You're a grownup. And you have the power to change things for the better. That's what we're here to do."

Help the client realize that it's not their fault. No *wonder* they've been stuck! No wonder they couldn't fix things! The problem they've been struggling with started long ago, when they were just a Child! The fact that their mind took them back to that event can be used as evidence of the power of their own mind. This is how the mind works. It's perfectly normal. And now they know things about themselves that they didn't know before. They can use this knowledge to create a real and lasting change. By giving themselves permission to release the *real* problem, they can take back this part of their life that's been missing.

4. Remember the Rewards

When it comes to realizing real and lasting change, a painful event from the past is a gold mine of transformation. But there can be resistance. And the client may not see how it's relevant. You need to remind the client of why they're doing this work with you.

Make what you're doing relevant so that they won't give up on themselves - or you. Then, stoke the fires of motivation by reminding them of all the rewards that come from allowing themselves to face their feelings.

The Benefits of Change are all the rewards that come from releasing the underlying problem. What does life look like once they're finally free of that problem? That's the motivating factor.

5. **Bookmark the Event.**

Before emerging the client, instruct them to put a bookmark on the event so that you can come back to it later. This is a post-hypnotic suggestion to return to this event in a future session. This will give you a starting point for the next session.

In the next session, you can either return to the same event to continue the process, or you can bring the feeling back up and continue Bridging back to locate the causal event.

Buttoning Up

1. Validate the feeling. Give the feeling permission to be there.
2. Reframe the event. Make it a revelation. What is the client discovering? What can be learned from this experience?
3. Make what happened relevant by connecting this experience to the client's Therapeutic Goal and Benefits of Change.
4. Put a bookmark on the event so that you can continue the work in the next session.

Quick Polishing Techniques

Something I like to do is have the client gently tap on their thymus. Alternately, you can just have them place their hand(s) over their heart. Physical touch has a calming effect on the body which means that while they're tapping or touching the heart, they're relaxing. You can then offer a few suggestions to validate all the shifts and better feelings that have occurred.

You can even make this an interactive process by using autosuggestion. Just remind the client to only repeat a suggestion if it's true. Then, give them a few suggestions to validate change. For example, "I've changed/ I can feel it/ I feel better/ I accept this change/ I accept this healing / I accept it now / with gratitude ..."

When a client goes back to childhood and discovers some good feelings you can turn this into a revelation by suggesting that they have just given themselves a wonderful gift. They got a Part of themselves back today. They know this is true because they can feel it. What this means is that they haven't lost their ability to feel good. All their good feelings are still there inside of them.

The subconscious mind knows why the client is seeing you. Often the Child Part it shows you has, in some way, been rejected or disowned by the client. This experience can be a wonderful opportunity to bring a Part of the client home to them. This experience is going to help the client to heal.

The client may not realize that accepting all Parts of them – all feelings - gives them permission to feel good again by restoring them to wholeness. To heal is to make whole. Feeling Parts are Child Parts. To feel safe, that Part of the client needs love, and acceptance, and forgiveness. Giving this to the Child gives the client back something that is truly priceless and that is the ability to feel safe and know that they are loved. This is no small thing.

If the client is feeling better by the end of the session, it's because they have given themselves permission to feel better. They have reclaimed a Part of themselves. That allows them to feel better.

Now they know that *it's possible* to feel better. They're *allowed* to feel better. They're allowed to have *all* their good feelings come back to them so they can heal. These are suggestions that you can incorporate into your session wrap up.

Remember, every feeling that comes to conscious awareness is a Part of the client. So, every feeling needs to be acknowledged, and accepted as good and worthy, and valuable. And it needs to be given permission to express.

If their mind took them into a painful event, then you want to validate the truth of that experience. Just have the client say, "Even though (whatever happened) happened … it's over/ I'm okay/ So I can relax now." You can then set up for future healing to happen by inviting all Parts of the client to be a part of the process.

TAT Wrap[51]

TAT is an alternative medicine therapy developed Tapas Fleming. It's used to clear negative emotions and past traumas. I found this Patter makes a great polishing script for wrapping up a session. The idea is that, when you're working with a Part, all the other Parts are listening in.

Give the suggestion that all Parts are aware of what's happening and are benefiting from these changes that are occurring inside the client. Then, have the client say, "I accept these changes /Allowing all Parts of me involved in this to heal now/ Thank you / Thank you subconscious for healing whatever is left."

---

[51] Inspired by Tapas Acupressure Technique (TAT)

This acknowledges that healing has happened. And it invites the subconscious mind to continue the healing. You can then add a few statements to help integrate change. For example, "I accept this healing / I accept it now / This healing is now fully and completely integrated now …"

TAT Wrap

1. Validate all the Parts involved in the problem.
2. Validate that change is happening.
3. Validate that whatever happened is over.
4. Give thanks.
5. Give permission for more healing to happen.
6. Integrate all changes.

Then, finish off by giving the suggestion that some of these Parts are being transformed by this experience. Others are learning from it. As a result, the client is allowed to experience positive change with respect to their specific goal.

Validation of Change

Have client tap on thymus or gently place hands over heart while you guide them to repeat the following suggestion using autosuggestion.

I have changed / I can feel it / I feel better / My *body* feels different /
I know I have changed because now I feel (put an ending on it) /
I accept this change / I accept this healing / I accept it *now* /
With gratitude / Thank you

This gives you a yummy way to polish off your session – especially when the client dove into some uncomfortable feelings - and it can help to make it safe for other Parts of the client to step forward and be heard in future sessions.

Validations of (Painful) Truth

Even though it happened / It's *over* / I'm okay / I can relax now /

And I can feel better about myself for having made this change /

This helps me to feel good about (specific goal / behaviors) /

I'm allowed to feel good about (specific goal/behaviors)

Permission to Heal (Future)

Allowing all Parts of me involved in this to heal now /

Thank you (God/Subconscious) /

Thank you for healing all the Parts of me involved in this (pause) /

Allowing whatever is left about this to now heal /

Thank you (God/Subconscious) for healing whatever is left (pause)/

I accept this healing (pause) / I accept it now (pause) /

This healing is completely integrated now (pause) /

With my grateful thanks

Generalize & Integrate Change

To integrate means to pull all the pieces together. It means connecting the dots in a way that makes the information relevant to the client. The objective is to encourage the client's subconscious mind to continue the healing after the session by integrating all changes in a way that is most beneficial to the client - physically, mentally, emotionally and spiritually. This is something you can do at the end of every hypnotherapy session to deepen the healing. The subconscious mind naturally generalizes all learning. A powerful way to encourage this natural process is a technique called Timeline Generalization[52].

Timeline Generalization

Instruct the client to gather up all the newer, better thought and emotional energies and send them back to the moment right before conception. Then, drop all those beautiful healing energies down into their timeline, sending them forward in time, all the way up to themselves in the present moment. Instruct the client to notice, as those energies flow forward along their timeline, how just *having* these energies, right from the start, changes things for them.

What's happening? You are planting a seed *before* anything bad happens. As a result, the better feelings, understandings, and insights that the client has *now* can be there for them right from the start. This can really help with the regression work because that seed is going to grow as the client grows up. It's going to influence all the subsequent events along their timeline. As a result, the client will have installed greater awareness growing up.

This imagery is a set of instructions to their subconscious mind. It tells the subconscious mind to make this new information a part of the client's story line. As a result, when you move the client forward along their timeline, these new energies will be transforming events which occurred in the client's childhood and teens.

---

[52] Core Transformation, Connirae Andreas

As the energy flows forward in time, it flows into and through experiences growing up. This changes situations from the past that match the old pattern, weakening the overall problem. Changing the thoughts and feelings associated with any situation – past or present - will change how similar situations are going to be perceived - consciously and subconsciously. This changes everything because we're not changing the events. We're changing how the client perceives those situations.

The idea is that if they'd *had* that awareness from the start, events in life would have played out differently for them. They would have responded differently to similar situations growing up. This changes how they remember things.

Memory isn't static. To re-member something, you need to bring up all the pieces into conscious awareness. You literally reconstitute the event. Research tells us that every time you remember an experience it changes the memory of that event. This is why memory can be so dodgy. If there are aspects of an experience that didn't get recorded, those pieces aren't going to be there to be re-assembled.

We all learned to repress certain aspects of memory. Repression is a decision to disconnect from certain aspects of an experience. This is a healthy, self-protective skill we all learned early in life. The problem is that it contributes to problems later in life.

Bottom line, memory is, at best, incomplete. The process of regression hypnosis involves uncovering the missing pieces, releasing the emotional charges, and re-assembling all the pieces in a way that makes the client more resourceful.

As new information is brought to light through the uncovering process, the client will often discover unresolved emotions. The emotional charge is what keeps the memory current, rather than a past event.

The releasing work serves to discharge that energy. Discharging this energy results in greater clarity because trapped emotions generate internal stress. Stress inhibits cognition. Releasing trapped thought and emotional energy releases the blocks, allowing insights to start bubbling up to the surface of awareness. When that happens, the mind becomes wide open to allow learning to take place.

New information can then be introduced to encourage positive changes. Remember, we're not changing the event. If something happened, we can't change that. What we can do is change the perception of the event by helping the subconscious mind to realize that the event is over. If it's over, it's no longer a threat. That's the essential change.

Change work has to do with how the client sees themselves and the world around them *as a result* of those events. This then changes how they will respond to similar situations in future. The timeline generalization process is a visual suggestion to do just that. You're giving the subconscious mind instructions to take all these "learnings" – these changes in thought, feeling, and perception - and "change everything" associated with the old pattern.

You are also installing resources that the client didn't have earlier in life. This empowers the client at their core. It also sets them up to allow more change to happen. Nice, right?

Embody Change

When you instruct their subconscious mind to take all the changes back to the moment just before conception, realize this is transformation in the making. But it must come from the client. This isn't guided imagery. Let the client create the image. Guide them to use all their senses – seeing, hearing, smelling, tasting, touching and feeling. Then, let them describe their experience to you as it happens.

Constantly bring them back to noticing how they are feeling. For example, when they drop into their timeline, what's that like? As they ripple those changes forward in time, what are they noticing? Ripple those changes all the way up to the present moment - right into the client's present moment, into the body. That's where the client lives – in the body.

Bring all the changes home to them. Then, pause for a moment and ask the client to go inside and notice how they feel *now*. What's changed? How is it different, now?

Compound Change

The timeline process is a way to compound change. This helps to get a deeper level of integration. It deepens the healing by amplifying the perception of change. If that change is a better feeling, the client is going to feel much better than when they began the process. Give the client a moment for these changes to register.

Let it "land" that something interesting has just happened. Bringing this *felt* sense of change to conscious awareness helps the client to realize that *they* have changed.

When they "get" that - give them a moment to enjoy it, realizing that powerful change is occurring at both conscious and unconscious levels of mind. The subconscious mind is a quick study. It learns very quickly. And once it has learned a process, it can perform it automatically - at lightning-speed. But the first time you guide the client through the integration process, you need to be very detailed in your instructions.

Once the client has been through this process, their subconscious mind will know what to do. Then, it will only take a few moments at the end of each session to repeat the process and reinforce all the changes.

1. Validate Change

Usually, the client feels better by the end of the session. They'll feel more relaxed. They may have had a few insights. You can validate these things as evidence of change. The most powerful way to validate change is to use autosuggestion. Have your client say it out loud, "I feel better."

Saying it out loud is a statement of self-validation. It's empowering to the client. Then, ask the client to tell you how they *know* that there's been a change. Once they recognize there's been a change, you can have them say, "I've changed."

Ask how it feels to say these words. Does it feel true? If this suggestion feels true to the client, have them add this suggestion, "I know I have changed *because* ..." And put an ending on *that*. "Because" is a powerful word. It satisfies the conscious mind's need for reason. Making any suggestion reasonable increases its acceptability.

Let them tell *you* how they know there's been a change. Usually the client will say, "... because I can *feel* it!" That's validation. This is when you can encourage the client to take ownership of the better feeling by inviting them to feel it fully and saying out loud, "This is *my* feeling." Get the client to notice how *that* feels.

Usually, it feels incredibly powerful because it's true. They *know* this is their feeling because they can *feel* it. This encourages a deeper level of integration. And when the client gives themselves permission to feel their feelings it opens the door to allowing *more* feelings to come to consciousness. That's a *good* thing.

2. Elicit a Commitment

One small shift toward the better can be used as evidence that more change is possible. Once the client realizes that something has shifted, the next step is to get them to take ownership of that newer, better feeling. Nothing changes without a change in consciousness. After the client validates change, ask them to commit to keeping the change.

Any statement of choice validates the idea that the client *has* a choice. If they want it, they can *have* it. For example, "I feel better. I choose to keep this change," or "I feel more calm and relaxed. I choose to keep this better feeling."

All it takes is the decision to *keep* what they want and let go of what they *don't* want. That's forgiveness. Forgiveness is a letting-go. We choose to keep the better feeling and forgive the rest.

3. Integrate Change

Once the client makes the decision to *keep* the better state, you can guide the client to integrate all the changes – physically, mentally, emotionally and spiritually. You can do this by amplifying and generalizing all the changes that have occurred. Start by bringing the client's attention to the body and having them notice what's changed in the body. Then, instruct the client to gather up all the insights and all the better feelings and send them through the nervous system of the body.

Saturate all the cells and tissues of the body with these positive energies created through the process, transforming every part of the mind-body system. People are generally identified with their body. This teaches the client to *embody* change and make it a part of their identity.

If you're working with a physical issue, be sure to amplify those positive energies powerfully. Then, send them directly into the area that's calling for healing. (Remember to always touch the owie and give that extra attention it needs.)

You can make the healing more powerful by bringing in the healing power of the Universe. Or the healing power of nature. Whatever fits for the client. Use it to bathe and rinse and cleanse and heal every part of the mind and body.

4. Send it Forward

So far, what have you done? You have had the client gather up all the shifts and changes, and insights, and better feelings. You have had them send those things back to before the moment of conception. They have dropped these newer, better energies into their timeline. And they have sent them forward in time, with the instructions to transform all their experiences growing up, all the way up to present time.

You have had the client bring these energies home by bringing them into the body. You have then had the client validate how they feel. This validates the change as a present experience. The next step is to send those changes into the future.

Time permitting, you are now going to project these changes into the client's future timeline to create a "new vision" for themselves. They may have imagined a better future but now you are going to give them an experience of a better future that is based on changes that have already occurred in their past. This makes it much more believable.

To begin, invite the client to, once again, gather up all the better thoughts and feelings, and insights, and greater awareness, and all the good stuff. And this time, send it *forward* along their timeline. There's a couple of ways you can do this. You can do future pacing, which is where you have the client move forward along that timeline. They can then describe to you their experience of what it's like to be living into this newer, better future. But if you're short on time, you can simply suggest that they send it forward along the timeline.

The goal is to establish a positive expectation for the future by suggesting that this now becomes their vision of the future that they're now living into. Then test. Have the client check inside to see how it feels. It should feel good. If it feels good, bring that energy back to the body in the here-and-now. Bring awareness back into the body and what it's like to be resting comfortably in the chair.

You can even anchor that vision, if you like, by touching the client lightly on the forehead, or on the chest, as you give the suggestion that this vision goes into their heart, or into their mind. It becomes part of them, there to remind them of the future they are now living into.

> **Future Pacing**
>
> In a moment, we're going to wrap up. And as we continue to work together, releasing all remaining blocks, more and more you can discover what it's like to really be enjoying life free of the past. So, I'd like you to take a moment now to imagine what it's like to be moving forward, into your future, taking with you all these wonderful, positive changes *you* have created for yourself. And as you do, let yourself *experience it vividly*, as if it's already true. Sense it, see it, hear it, feel it. Use all your senses. And experience what it's like to be doing things free of the past. And able to enjoy all the benefits of change. (*benefits list*)

Tie it to the client's goal. And you're done.

The subconscious mind now has the information it needs to begin creating positive change because you've changed the story line – past, present, and future. As a result, you can feel confident that the healing has begun.

There will be other aspects of the issue that need to be brought to light and resolved. But the subconscious mind will work on this piece between sessions. It will continue to integrate and generalize all changes. And the seeds will grow, making it easier for the client to allow more change to occur in future sessions.

Optional: Mental Rehearsal

And now, imagine a situation in your daily life where this ability to feel calm and at ease will be helpful. Might be a situation at home … or a work … or some other place, but as that situation comes to mind, find yourself in that situation as you rub your fingers together.

As you do, you find yourself enjoying your ability to feel comfortable, calm, relaxed, and at ease in that situation. That's right, comfortable, calm, relaxed, and at ease.

What's that like? (Okay, stop rubbing your fingers together.)

And now imagine another situation in your daily life where you would like to feel more calm and at ease. As you find yourself in *that* situation, place your fingers together and enjoy that wonderful feeling coming on. That's right, comfortable, calm, relaxed, and at ease. Feels good, doesn't it?

And each time it feels better and better. So practice it frequently throughout the day. Okay?

Each time you do it grows ten times more powerful.

Okay. Stop rubbing your fingers together and go deeper relaxed. (Client), I want you to know we've made excellent progress. And you can feel confident that positive change is occurring, and you *will* succeed. (tie to goal)

Homework assignment: practice finger pinch technique frequently

Emerging Statements

In a moment I'm going to count from 1 to 5 to bring you back to your ordinary level of awareness.

As I count from one to five you become more and more alert to everything around you realizing you are in a process of re-creating yourself. Allowing yourself to finally become the person you were always meant to be, by releasing everything that has been getting in the way of you feeling good about you. (tie to goal)

On the count of five those eyes will open. You'll feel alert and energized, as if you've enjoyed a wonderful, restful night's sleep, feeling comfortable and alert, with all your energy back. Really feeling good. Get ready …

CHAPTER 13:
Debriefing

One of the main reasons for allowing a little time to debrief the client following a regression session is to reinforce all the positive changes that are occurring, at a subconscious level of mind. It also gives the client a few minutes to consciously process where their mind just took them. This gives you the opportunity to explore any thoughts or feelings the client might be experiencing immediately after emerging. You can then address any questions they might have about what just happened in the session and build positive mental expectancy toward the results of the healing process.

During a session there can be a lot going on behind the scenes that you're not aware of. The mind processes information a lot faster than a person can speak. Not everything that is being revealed to the client during a session is necessarily going to get shared with you. This is why we want to take the time to debrief the client after emerging them. It's because, when a client emerges from hypnosis, they're still processing everything that happened in the session. There may be things they haven't shared with you, yet. And there can be more stuff bubbling up to the surface.

That little post-hypnosis debriefing session gives the client an opportunity to share thoughts, feelings, and insights that they may not have mentioned during the session. This gives you the opportunity to continue the healing work by reframing or reinforcing certain things in a way that brings them into alignment with the client's Therapeutic Goal.

It's like putting the candle on the cake. The debriefing session happens immediately after you emerge the client. It only takes a couple of minutes. And the purpose of this short debriefing session is to remind the client that healing is a process.

Most people don't turn to hypnosis first. As a result, there can be multiple factors contributing to the client's issue. It can take time to resolve all the aspects. If the problem isn't completely resolved, the client still has the problem.

Sometimes you get lucky. Sometimes the client's issue is a simple fix, the client is ready to embrace change, and there's no resistance whatsoever. Sometimes there are only a couple of aspects contributing to the problem, they're brought to light right away and they're easy to resolve. Sometimes you hit the nail right on the head in the first session and the client emerges from hypnosis completely transformed. When that happens, mentally do a little Snoopy Dog dance. Then, pray that the client will integrate those changes fully. Pray that when they go back to their daily life, they'll be met with support and approval for having made those changes. Pray that they'll be able to hold onto the transformation – for good.

It can happen. But I wouldn't count on it. The single-session miracle is largely a myth. What's more common is that you'll emerge the client from hypnosis, they'll be feeling all warm and fuzzy, you'll give yourself a pat on the back as you send them off and back into everyday life. Then, something will happen *between* sessions to send them right back into the crapper.

Now, if you've set things up right, they'll come back and tell you about it. Whatever happens will then give you the next step in their process. But you need to prepare your clients for this eventuality because, if you don't, they're going to feel upset - and understandably so. After all, wasn't hypnosis supposed to help them to feel better? And it did, right? Only it was temporary. Now they've taken a dive into the emotional dumpster.

The debriefing process is a valuable part of the client's healing process because a regression session will often bring to light something the client wasn't consciously aware of. Sometimes they'll go back into an event they have conscious recall of. But then they'll discover that there are aspects of that experience that have been missing from memory. This can often provide the key to their healing.

Debriefing Doubt

Sometimes the client will bump into something that has been hidden from their conscious awareness. This has to do with the subconscious mind's protective function. But because the subconscious mind has been blocking this awareness, the client will find it hard to believe that those things really happened.

They may have some doubts about what their subconscious mind has shown them. The client may doubt that any of those things are real or true. This can cause them to doubt the process.

If the client expresses any doubts, you need to address them, right away. Don't let them take those doubts home with them. Take care of them during your post-session debriefing. For example, if the client were to say, "I don't think I was hypnotized," that little bit of doubt can undo all the good work you've just done with them.

You need to nip that in the bud because they're invested in the hypnosis being the answer. If the client doesn't believe that they were hypnotized, they won't believe that anything has changed. Their disbelief has the power to undo any positive change that might have occurred.

If the client emerges from a regression session and asks, "Did that really happen?", realize their subconscious mind has just thrown them a curve ball. It has shown them something they were not consciously aware of. They're thinking, "Did I make that up?"

Even when it's an event that they had conscious recall of, there's something about that event that was previously hidden from consciousness. Then, when it's brought to light, it's hard to believe. The client starts to question whether it's even true.

Sometimes the client will regress back into an event that they had no conscious memory of. This may be because the event happened very early in life. Or it could be that their own mind has been protecting them by blocking conscious recall of those aspects.

Either way, when the regression reveals something that's hard to believe, they're going to question whether they just made the whole thing up. That's the conscious mind doing what it does best – trying to make sense of things.

For regression hypnotherapy to have any real effect, the client needs to be willing to set aside reason and logic long enough to listen to what their subconscious mind has to say. That's not always easy because the subconscious mind has a different kind of reason and logic from the conscious mind. What the client needs to accept is that their own mind has just shown them where the real problem is coming from.

When a client asks, "Did that really happen?" or "How do I know that event was real?" my answer is always the same, "True or false – you were feeling the feeling."

Now, this is important. Never ask a question that you don't know the answer to. Only ask this question if you *know* the client was feeling the feelings. That way, when the client says, "Yes, I was feeling it," you can ask the next question, "Was the *feeling* real?" This opens the door to reminding the client that the only thing we're concerned about is the feeling because that's the language of the subconscious mind. The subconscious mind holds onto all our feelings and memories. What makes any event memorable is the emotion that got attached to it.

1. True or false, you were feeling the feeling.
2. Was the *feeling* real?
3. The only thing we're interested in is the feeling.

Truth versus Fact

Regression-to-cause hypnosis is not about revealing the facts of what happened in a past event. It's about healing the feeling. Your job is not to verify the facts of a past event. It's to uncover the underlying perceptions and thoughts that are generating the client's problem.

Perceptions generate thoughts. Thoughts form the basis of our beliefs which generate feelings and emotions. This is what drives all our behaviors and responses in daily life. It has everything to do with the feeling. While we can't change what happened, we can change a thought. Changing a thought will change how it feels.

The subconscious mind is the repository of all our learning. It holds onto all our feelings and memories from the earliest age. This serves the purpose of survival. The subconscious mind's prime concern is protecting us from harm. This is based on what we learned growing up. This means that our past experiences have value. They shaped our lens on life. They taught us how to be and how not to be.

Even the most painful experiences can become a source of empowerment when viewed through the right lens. The problem is that many of the issues that clients come to you for help with have their roots in childhood. And not everything that was learned at that time is necessarily based on truth or fact.

The younger a child is, the more chance there is that situations are going to be misinterpreted. This is because children have a limited knowledgebase from which to make sense of the world of people and things around them. And children lack the maturity to be able to process strong emotions. Children are wonderfully imaginative and creative. But they don't have the ability to think critically about things. They're like little sponges, soaking up information from their environment including things said, and things done. They're making decisions based on those impressions.

Our earliest decisions have to do with "who I am", "how I have to be to get my needs met", and what to expect from others, relationships, and life in general. These decisions form the basis of a person's Core

Beliefs. The problem is that mistakes get made because there's nothing in place to reality-check perceptions and decisions before the age of five or six. Information is being processed without the benefit of critical thinking.

Remember, the Critical Faculty of the Mind isn't fully formed until around age five or six. Before this, information and suggestions are being accepted unconsciously. This ability to direct-download information gives us a real advantage in terms of survival because thinking slows us down. Not having to think, and not having to evaluate everything, gives the child a sort of superpower.

This ability to learn unconsciously makes the child a super-learning machine. But not everything that gets in is necessarily based on fact or truth. It's just perceptions that make an impression on the child and, based on those impressions, decisions are made.

It's been said that more learning occurs before the age of two than will happen over the rest of a person's life. This means that the thoughts, feelings, and decisions of a two-year-old can be running a person's adult life! This is what we find through the work of regression hypnosis. Many of the issues we work with are rooted in decisions that the client made before they were able to think for themselves.

Much of the stuff we work with in regression is rooted in some kind of trauma. But trauma is not what most people think. Trauma is simply any situation that is *perceived* as life-threatening while in a state of helplessness. That covers a lot of territory in childhood.

The younger the child is, the more helpless they are. The more helpless they are, the more dependent they are on others to provide safety and to help them to make sense of things. Unfortunately, that doesn't always happen. And the child has a limited capacity for reason and logic. The logic centers of the brain aren't fully developed until around age twelve to fourteen. That leaves a lot of wiggle room for making mistakes! Even the most harmless situations can be misinterpreted and lead to traumatic memory.

The most helpless child is the infant. Every infant instinctively knows that it cannot survive without someone looking after it. The only defense an infant has is the ability to cry for help. When help doesn't come quickly enough, or consistently enough, the child will interpret this as a threat to survival. This will plant the seeds of fear. That's trauma.

A rigid feeding schedule, a parent who is distracted by work, or too many kids, or a demanding spouse, or who is grieving the loss of a loved-one can be interpreted as abandonment. Biologically, abandonment means certain death for a child. When there's no one there to respond to the needs of the child, or comfort the child, or care for the child - that's trauma.

When a client says, "Was that real?" your job is not to try to figure out whether the event really happened. Your job is to find out how that experience affected the child, and how the perceptions, and thoughts, and feelings shaped by that experience have continued to affect the client. How might these things be responsible for generating the symptoms of the problem the client is seeing you about?

The subconscious mind does not make a distinction between real and imagined. If you have ever walked in the garden at dusk and mistaken the garden hose for a snake, you know what I'm talking about. Even though the snake was imaginary, your heart still leaped up into your throat. All the physiological responses associated with facing an actual threat were real. Have you ever had a nightmare where you woke up in a sweat? Was your heart pounding out of your chest? It seemed awfully real, didn't it? That's because, as far as your subconscious mind was concerned, that experience *was* real. As a result, it generated all the physiological responses that are congruent with that perception of reality.

Reality is really a matter of perception. We perceive life through our five-sensory system. We see, we hear, we smell, we taste, and we feel. Where do we feel our feelings? In the body. But strong emotions can be overwhelming for a Child because the emotional centers of the brain aren't fully developed yet. And the younger the child is, the more body-centered it is. When something feels too overwhelming – that's trauma.

Those first impressions, whatever they happened to be, formed the basis of thoughts and decisions. The ones that stuck became beliefs. Beliefs decide what we're going to get in life. What's generating the symptoms in the client's adult life, whether they be unwanted thoughts, or feelings, or behaviors, are coming out of the thoughts, and feelings, and learned responses of the Child they once were.

Remember, these will be based on decisions that have to do with "who I am", "how I have to be in order to get my needs met", "how life works", and "what I deserve in life". These are the things that make up a person's belief system. But just because you believe something doesn't make it true. It's just that, until about age three, a child's perception of the world around it is predominantly egocentric.

What this means is that whatever is happening in a situation is perceived by the Child as an extension of him/herself. For example, if Mommy and Daddy are fighting, it is not unreasonable for the child to think, "I did that."

If Mommy is preoccupied, not paying attention to the Child, it's perfectly logical for the Child to think, "I'm not wanted." The Child will then conclude that she's responsible. She'll think, "It's my fault that Mommy and Daddy are fighting," or "There's something wrong with me that I'm not wanted."

I'm sure you can appreciate how having a belief like that could seed a lifelong problem. Even though it's not based on fact, or truth, or reason, or logic, as far as the subconscious mind is concerned, that's how it is. And it will generate uncomfortable feelings that are congruent with the belief – in this case, fear.

The fact of the matter is that parents are responsible for the well-being of their children. They're the Grownups. The child is innocent. Whatever is going on in the child's environment is never the child's fault. There's nothing wrong with the Child. But this is the logic of the subconscious mind. And it's because the subconscious is the Child mind. Reason and logic are characteristics of the conscious mind. The subconscious mind has its own reasons that don't always make sense to the conscious mind.

This is why we can come up with all the reasons why we should change our thinking or our behavior and then fail to do so. It's because the subconscious mind is running the show based on our experiences growing up. This has nothing to do with adult logic. It's the logic of the conscious mind *of the child* - at whatever age those decisions were being made.

Research shows that our current knowledge and understanding influences how we remember past events. Every time we recall an incident from the past, it changes the memory. This quality of mind is what makes regression hypnotherapy so effective. But the fundamental purpose of regression-to-cause hypnosis is not to verify facts. It's to uncover the feelings that got trapped in painful past events so that you can transform how the client feels. This involves a process of guiding a person back into past events to review and re-evaluate the perceptions of the Child they once were. They can then reality-check those things for truth and accuracy using the benefit of Adult consciousness.

Remember, as far as the subconscious mind is concerned, the feeling is what's real. When you change how an event feels, the client is free to make newer, better decisions for themselves, their relationships, and their life in general. This is how you can transform lives for the better.

When a client asks you, "Did that really happen?" or "Was that event real?" ask them, "Was the *feeling* real?" That's all we're interested in. Then ask, "How do you know it was real?" because the answer is always the same. The client will say, "Because I could feel it." *That's* what tells us something is real and true. We can feel it.

Next, ask the client, "How do you feel *now?*" because if they've released all or some of the feeling, they're going to be feeling better. They'll be feeling more calm, or more peaceful, or even happy because they're feeling better about themselves.

That's when you can ask, "What's more important . . . that we validate the facts about what happened? Or that you feel better?" Immediately add, "Realize we're not here to do forensics. We're not here to establish the facts. What was revealed through the process are just the facts as your subconscious mind has it. That's based in the perceptions of the Child you once were. You've seen for yourself how children can misinterpret things. But your feelings will never lie to you. True or false - the feelings were real. (True.) That's all that matters because *the goal is to get you healed*. And to do that, your subconscious mind just needs to understand that you're not a Child, anymore. That's what will allow you to heal and feel better." Then nod knowingly and say, "And you *do* feel better, don't you?"

Set Up for the Next Session

When a client emerges from a regression session, they're still processing at both a conscious and subconscious level. But they may not realize this. They may even feel a little discombobulated because they're not fully emerged yet. They're still in hypnosis. This means that they're still highly suggestible.

You can use these valuable few moments to continue the healing process, reinforce all changes, and set up for the next session by offering three suggestions.

1. **"Change is occurring. It has already begun."**

First, let the client know that change is happening beneath the surface. The subconscious mind now has the information it needs to begin making those changes. This process is occurring beneath the surface. And *it will continue* after the client leaves your office.

2. **"The subconscious mind will work on the issue between sessions."**

Hypnotherapy is a learning process. All the insights and realizations and discoveries that occurred in the session are going to be worked on and integrated at a deeper level of consciousness to become more fully a part of the client.

This is because the subconscious mind's job is to find answers to questions and solutions to problems. It does this 24/7, whether we're aware of it or not. It's going to be working behind the scenes, sorting through everything that happened during the session. Because it's going to continue to work on creating that change the client wants, the client may experience vivid or interesting dreams following a session.

Dreams are the subconscious mind at work. When we sleep, the mind and body work together for the purposes of healing. As we sleep, the body performs repair functions at a physical level while the subconscious mind works on psychological healing by sorting through all the unresolved emotional debris of the day. This is when learning is consolidated.

3. "Feelings and memories can arise between sessions."

Because the subconscious mind doesn't sleep, insights may bubble up to the surface while they're awake. They may have memories or *feelings* coming to awareness. This is completely normal. It's a by-product of stirring things up during the session. Feelings are one of the ways that the subconscious mind communicates with the conscious mind. For this reason, you want the client to *be more aware* of their feelings between sessions.

If they become aware of an emotion coming up to the surface, you want them to notice what happened to cause them to feel that way. That way, they can give you a report when they come back in for their *next* session. This will tell you what their subconscious mind *feels* is most important.

Now, what have you just done?

First, you have just made the client responsible for the results. It takes consciousness to change consciousness. You have just instructed your clients to *be more conscious* of how they feel in everyday life. Feelings naturally arise and pass away throughout the day. But most people don't realize this because they're in the habit of avoiding their feelings. You're teaching the client to be more consciously aware of how they feel in daily life. That's smart.

Second, you've just set up for the next session by giving the client a little homework assignment that can give you the information you need to guide the process effectively. You're enlisting the client's own mind to tell you what needs to happen next. That's working with the client's subconscious mind. That's smart. Working *with* the subconscious mind is much easier than trying to tell it where to go. And it will get you better results every time.

Third, you have enlisted the client to be a partner in their own healing. You're asking them to participate even when they're not in your office. That's smart because all healing is self-healing. I only give clients homework when they're willing. But there is one assignment I give *every* client after every session, and that is to pay attention to their feelings between sessions.

Ignoring and denying feelings is a bad habit. And it's a big part of the client's problem. This is one concrete action the client can take between sessions that can significantly contribute to your success rate. And taking action in daily life empowers the client because they're no longer playing the role of the passive patient. They're taking charge of creating the change simply by being more aware.

Two-Minute Coaching Session

The 2-Minute Coaching Session is a debriefing technique I learned from Stephen Parkhill, the author of *Answer Cancer*. It's a technique that you can easily incorporate into every session that will help you to get better results. The 2-Minute Coaching Session is a set of instructions you deliver to the client before sending them out of your office. If you install these instructions in the first session, all you'll have to do in subsequent sessions is remind the client right after you emerge them each time.

These instructions set the client up to *expect* something to happen between sessions. In the first session, I always give these instructions while the client is still in hypnosis just before I emerge them. I then repeat the same instruction after emerging them. That way, both the conscious and subconscious mind receive the instructions.

> "Following a session there are three things that can happen. First, you may feel better. Second, you may feel worse. Third, you may experience some ups and downs."

If nothing changes ... nothing changes. There's got to be some kind of movement following a session. You just need the client to notice that movement.

Knowing what to watch for will help the client to recognize that something is happening. No matter what happens between sessions, as far as you're concerned, it's all good. It's simply information that will tell you what needs to happen next in the client's program.

Feeling Better? If the client comes back and says they felt better following the session – yay! You'll know that whatever you did in that session was effective. You made some headway. That's good.

What needs to happen next is to celebrate that success. Nothing breeds success like success. Reinforce those positive changes before moving on to the next piece of the puzzle.

Feeling Worse? If your client comes back and tells you that they felt worse, you'll know that you touched the "owie." This tells you that their subconscious mind wants this issue resolved. It's pushing stuff up to the surface for you to take care of. That's good. But the client needs to know that this can happen because that stuff is uncomfortable.

Even when the client feels great after they leave your office, they may not be able to hold onto those better feelings. If they lose the better feeling, that's a clear sign that you haven't resolved the whole problem yet. That's fine. It just means there's more work to be done.

If something happened to trigger the client, if they "lost it" or dived into a bucket of pain – yay! Now you know that that's the next issue that is calling for a resolution. This is what their subconscious mind feels is most important.

The next logical step would then be to follow "that feeling" back to when it got started and resolve it there. Simple, right?

Ups & Downs?

If the client experiences some ups and downs - that's life. I like to say, "Welcome to Planet Earth." Ups and downs in life are a fact of life. What you want to identify is whether something happened to trigger the client. If so, what happened? For example, if they left the last session feeling good, and then something happened to change that, what happened? Did they gradually lose the benefits, or did they get triggered?

If the client got triggered, what specific situation set them back on the emotional roller-coaster? This will give you a specific event to work with. A recent triggering event can act as a gateway to the past because it has a specific set of feelings associated with it. Just review the event to bring up a feeling, find the Bridge, and go to work.

Remember, the transformation doesn't occur in the hypnosis session. It happens after the client leaves the session. And a lot can happen between sessions. You need to prepare the client for the time between sessions because healing can take time.

Trust that their subconscious mind is going to be working behind the scenes, bringing all the pieces into alignment. But change tends to happen in increments rather than all at once. There can be setbacks and back-sliding on the road to permanent change. And it can take time for the client to accrue enough healing to be able to hold onto the healing.

It only takes a couple of minutes following a session to prepare your client up for the next session. Set them up before you send them home. Find out what happens between sessions. When the client comes back have them give you a report. You can then use whatever happened between sessions to gauge the client's progress while you continue to clean house.

"Feelings buried alive never die."
~ **Karol K. Truman**

CHAPTER 14:
Preliminary Check-In

Once you have guided a client through the Ready for Regression session you'll be all set. You'll have a client who is ready for the work of regression-to-cause hypnotherapy. Every subsequent up session will then begin the same way, with a brief check-in. Remember, healing doesn't happen in the session. It happens following a session. That's when post-hypnotic suggestions take effect. During the check-in, you need to find out what happened between sessions.

Lots of things are going on in your client's daily life. A lot of things will happen between sessions. Your preliminary check-in gives the client a few minutes to fully arrive before you begin the hypnosis while giving you a way to identify what the next step in the client's healing process might be.

Typically, here's what happens; during a regression session the client will experience some events from childhood. They'll gather up some resources and better feelings. They may even have a few insights. They'll leave your office feeling much better than when they came in. Then, life happens. They'll go back to life as usual, and they'll lose the good feelings. That's okay. The work's not done yet. It's just that something happened to trigger them. You need to find out what that was because this will give you a specific situation you can focus on to bring up the feeling for Affect Bridge. "That feeling" that got triggered has everything to do with the client's problem. This is the easiest way to find a Bridge for the regression work.

Affect Bridge is the backbone of regression hypnotherapy because the subconscious mind is the emotional mind. That fear, anger, or sadness is a signal beaming out from the event that caused it. It is the one thing that every SSE shares with the ISE. All events leading to unwanted symptoms are lined together emotionally. By following that energetic signal, you can locate the earliest event and resolve the problem where it got started.

Because you are working with the native language of the subconscious mind, Affect Bridge is a very natural process that is easy to facilitate, once the client is ready for regression. All that's required is a strong emotion. You need a strong Bridge to make it all the way back to the ISE. Resolving the feeling where it got started will restore much-needed energy to the mind-body system.

While it's possible to Bridge back on a thought (Cognitive Bridge) or a physical sensation (Somatic Bridge), the most direct path to the root of the problem is to follow an emotion (Affect Bridge). But if you can connect a thought *and* an emotion *and* a sensation in the body, you'll have a powerful Bridge capable of zeroing in on the ISE bullseye. For example, the client reports (a) the thought "I'm not good enough," which (b) makes her feel the emotion of fear, which expresses as (c) a tight knot in her stomach, is a very specific signal you can follow.

The more specific you can be, the better, because you're looking for a specific event. If you can target the specific thought-feeling-sensation pattern, you'll have a very specific path leading back to the roots of "that feeling."

Did you notice how this combines all three Bridges? Cognitive Bridge is the thought, "I'm not good enough." Somatic Bridge is the physical sensation of a tight knot in the gut. Affect Bridge follows the specific fear that has everything to do with "that thought" and "that feeling." This gives you a very targeted approach.

Same, Better, or Worse?

If your client says that they've been feeling **better** since their first session, that's great. Affirm that they're moving in the right direction. Maybe they're sleeping better or feeling more hopeful. This tells you that something shifted in the previous session and the client was able to hold onto that change. Yay! Here's where you can remind your client that healing is a process and that the fact that they're feeling better indicates that progress has been made toward their goal. Then, remind the client of their goal which is to get a complete resolution to the problem. That's when they'll be free of the symptoms.

If your client reports that they felt the **same**, dig down deeper. How did they feel immediately following the last session? If they were feeling better, when did that change? If they were feeling upset, what specifically was revealed in that session to cause that "upset" feeling? What emotion might that "upset" feeling be?

The objective is to find the specific emotion. This will give you a Bridge you can follow.

If your client tells you that they felt **worse** following the session, don't take it personally. Recognize that you stirred something up in the previous session and the client's subconscious mind has been ruminating on it ever since. This is good news! Affirm that their subconscious mind is letting you know that it wants this problem resolved.

While it may not have felt good, the feeling you're after, that can help you to gain access to the cause of the underlying problem, is there right beneath the surface. All you need to do is poke a stick at it to bring up the feeling.

Poke a Stick Technique

The Poke-a-Stick Technique is a five-step process you can use to bring up a feeling that can be used to Bridge back to the causal event.

1. Tell the Story

First, invite the client to tell you the story about what happened to trigger them. Just talking about a triggering experience will provoke the feeling to come to the surface. All you need to do is watch for it to happen.

Wait and watch as the emotions start coming to the surface. For example, tears, physical tension, changes in tonality, etc. If the feeling is already there on the surface, talking about it will help to increase the client's focus, allowing more of the feeling to come to awareness.

2. Locate the Feeling in the Body

Once you have found the feeling, ask the client to locate the feeling in the body by asking, "Where in the body do you feel that (fear)?

Remember, what you're looking for is an actual emotion. Emotions are targeted feelings which are expressed in the torso region of the body - primarily in the throat, the chest, and the gut. What emotion might that be?

3. Take a SUD

Once you have located the feeling in the body, test the intensity of that feeling by eliciting a Subjective Unit of Distress (SUD). To take a SUD, ask the client to focus on the feeling in their body. Then ask, "On a scale of one to ten, where ten is the strongest it's ever been, how *strong* is that feeling in your (gut) right now?" Ideally, you want it to be a ten. But if it's a seven or higher you have enough intensity for Affect Bridge.

If it's a twelve you don't even need a formal induction. The stronger the emotion, the deeper the client is going into the subconscious mind. This means you already have deep hypnosis. This is another time-saving technique you can use by piggy-backing your induction off the preliminary uncovering procedure. Just confirm that you have permission to proceed with the hypnosis.

You can then use the hand-drop induction that you conditioned the client for during the first session. This will formalize the process and reinforce the trigger.

Once you have deepened the client into hypnosis, have the client focus on the feeling. Make sure they're still feeling it. Then, take another SUD.

If they lost the feeling, just have them tell you the story again, while keeping their focus on what's happening in the body. This will bring up the feeling again.

4. **Amplify**

If the SUD is less than ten, get the client's permission to turn up the volume on that feeling. Tell them, "We need that feeling to be *at least* a ten. Would you be willing to let it come up to a ten understanding that I'll take care of it?" With the client's permission, you can then amplify the feeling with an increasing count.

I like to use autosuggestion for this because it helps to increase the client's focus. But the traditional approach is simple direct suggestion. It goes something like this… "In a moment, I'm going to count from one to three. As I do, let that feeling come up powerfully within you, understanding that … that feeling is allowed to be there. And your permission to allow that feeling … to be felt and released … is what allows you to heal."

Tell the client what needs to happen, give them a good reason for allowing it to happen, then proceed with the count. "One, there's the feeling. Two, coming up powerfully within you. You *feel the feeling*." And so on.

As you count up, observe the client's responses to your suggestions. Adjust your tonality so that it is congruent with the client's responses.

Alternatively, you can start the count at whatever the client's SUD level was and count upwards from there. For example, "There's the feeling. It's a seven. You can feel it in your chest. It's that tight, uncomfortable feeling. Coming up to an eight, now. You feel the feeling."

Continue the count until you get to ten. Then, take another SUD.

5. Take another SUD

When you get to ten, verify that the client is following your instructions by saying, "On a scale of one to ten, how strong is that feeling?"

Remember, you need a strong Bridge to locate the causal event. Once you've got the SUD level up to ten, immediately follow the feeling back to where it got started. All you need to do is start the count-back to an earlier event. For example: "Ten … going back in time. Nine, to a scene, situation, or event of significant to that feeling …" And so on.

When the client lands in a scene from the past you need to work quickly to uncover where their mind has taken them. Don't give the client any time to think. Remember, first impression! The first three uncovering questions are designed to help the client to step into the event more fully. This will give you access to the details with respect to the cause of "that feeling."

Poke a Stick Technique

1. **Tell the story** to bring up the feeling. What happened to trigger the client?
2. **Locate the feeling** in the body. Throat? Chest? Gut? What emotion might that be?
3. **Take a SUD.** On a scale of one to ten, how strong is "that feeling"?
4. Less than ten: Amplify with an increasing count.
5. Ten or more: Bridge back and begin the uncovering procedure.

Provoke the Feeling Patter[53]

There's a feeling inside that you just don't like. That feeling has everything to do with the reason you're here. As I speak, that feeling is coming to the surface. Let that happen. This is the perfect place for that realizing that you've tried running from it, you've tried stuffing it down, putting a lid on it, numbing and swallowing it away … THIS TIME you're going to face it. As I speak that feeling is allowed to come up powerfully within you …

Quickly perform the TEST. Then continue with Amplification Patter.

THE TEST - True or false, you *feel the feeling?*

True	False
Where do you feel that feeling in your body?	*Proceed to reversal statements*
If that feeling was an emotion, what emotion might it be?	
On a scale of one to ten, where ten is *the worst that feeling has ever been* how *strong* is that feeling in your (throat/chest/gut)?	
If the feeling is ten or more, go directly to Affect Bridge.	

---

[53] Stephen Parkhill

Provoke the Feeling Autosuggestion Technique

"Repeat after me …. There's a feeling inside that I just don't like (wait for client to repeat)/ I've tried running from it…. (wait for client to repeat)/ I've tried shoving it down …(wait for client to repeat)/ Putting a lid on it … (wait for client to repeat) /Numbing and swallowing it away … (wait for client to repeat)/ THIS TIME I'm going to face it (wait for client to repeat). /As I speak that feeling is coming up inside of me …"

Quickly perform a SUD test. Then continue with Amplification Patter or Bridge back.

Amplification Patter

Good. As I count from 1 to 3 (or 7 to 10), let that feeling come up powerfully within you, understanding that … that feeling is allowed to be there. And your permission to allow that feeling … to be felt and released … is what allows you to heal. Understand?

ONE – There's the feeling. It's that feeling inside that you just don't like. You can feel it in your body. It doesn't feel good.

TWO – coming up powerfully within you, now, bubbling up to the surface, you feel the feeling. And on the next count, there's the feeling, as strong as you've ever known it before …

THREE – There's the feeling. Say, "I feel" and put an ending on it." (*Find out what emotion they're feeling.*)

Go to Affect Bridge.

Affect Bridge Patter

Good! There's the feeling! I'm going to count from 5 down to 1. On the count of 1 your mind has you back in an *earlier* scene, situation or event that has everything to do with *that feeling* …

Five – Going back in time

Four – To a scene, situation or event of significance to *that feeling*

Three – Arms and legs may be growing *smaller* now as your mind takes you *further and further* back

Two – Moving right *into* that event of significance. The scene grows vivid, real, and clear. And on the next count, *there you are*, as real as the first time.

And ONE – There you are. Say, "Here I am (wait for client to repeat)/ And I feel (put an ending on it) (wait for client to repeat)

Continue with Uncovering Procedure

Autosuggestion Reversal Statements

If the client is resistant to allowing the feeling to come up, you can use these reversal statements with or without tapping.

Repeat after me …. Even though **it's not safe** to feel this feeling (wait for client to repeat)/ I choose to let it come up strong within me (wait for client to repeat)/so I can heal …(wait for client to repeat)/because I deeply and completely accept myself (wait for client to repeat)/and if I can feel it, I can heal. (wait for client to repeat).

And even though **it's not safe** to feel this feeling (wait for client to repeat)/ I let myself go where I need to go(wait for client to repeat)/and see what I need to see (wait for client to repeat)/and hear what I need to hear (wait for client to repeat)/and feel what I need to feel (wait for client to repeat)/ so I can heal …(wait for client to repeat).

And even though **it's not safe** to feel this feeling (wait for client to repeat)/ I do what I need to do to heal (wait for client to repeat)/ And even though **I don't WANT to** feel this feeling (wait for client to repeat)/ I can feel it (wait for client to repeat)/ I can feel it in my body (wait for client to repeat).

Conduct the Test.

THE TEST

That feeling is allowed to be there. *True or false*, you feel the feeling?

True:

- Where in your body do you feel that feeling?
- How strong is that feeling?
- On a scale of one to ten, where ten is the worst that its ever been . . . how strong is it?

If the feeling is 10 or more, go directly to Affect Bridge.

False:

The client is unwilling to allow the feeling to come up. This means you have not established the Contract. You can't do it for the client. They must be willing to let the feeling come up. Emerge the client and have a talk with them. Do what you need to do to establish the contract.

CHAPTER 15:
Get Lasting Results

Everything we work with in regression therapy has to do with some kind of trauma. Trauma is what happens to a person when two factors come together. First, the person is in a stress-response. As a result, their nervous system has gone on red alert and they're operating in fight or flight mode. When that happens, everything not essential to survival shuts down. For example, cognition shuts down because you don't need to *think* when you're in a situation of threat. You need to run! As a result, blood flow gets shunted away from the organs to the arms and the legs so that you can run away or defend yourself. The muscles get tense and tight. Blood pressure goes up, as does blood sugar levels, while things like digestion and sex drive shut down.

The second factor related to trauma is a state of helplessness. This is a common condition in childhood. Everybody has trauma. It's just a matter of degrees. You'll find that the decisions resulting from a traumatic experience are always related to a state of powerlessness. i.e. "There's nothing I can do." Events happening prior to age five will generalize this decision to form a part of the person's identity. "I AM powerless." "I AM helpless." "I AM unable to …"

Because we must all act in ways that are congruent with our beliefs, the person will then behave *as if* those things were true. If you believe that you're going to die every time you step inside an elevator, or drive over a bridge, or see a puppy dog, that becomes your truth. Your body is going to generate a response that is congruent with that belief. And you'll re-experience the original trauma. *That's* retraumatizing.

It's like a hamster stuck on a wheel. There's no way out. And every time something happens to act as a reminder of the original event, the wheel spins around for a replay. The whole pattern gets reinforced, and the problem gets a little stronger.

Regression allows the client to revisit a traumatic experience for the purposes of completing the process of digesting that experience. A small t trauma, or even a big T trauma, can be transformed into a learning experience that will empower your clients. You can help your clients un-learn beliefs that were formed when they were too young, and under too much pressure, to be able to think clearly. You can replace those beliefs with newer, better beliefs that will support them in living a healthy, happy, more productive life.

The goal of regression to cause hypnotherapy is to locate the causal event and clear the underlying pattern where it got started by releasing the emotional charge around the event. That's what's holding the whole pattern in place. But what if the client dives into a big bucket of pain and abreacts? What if the subconscious mind takes you back into a subsequent event that has a lot of emotional pressure in it?

Do you always need to locate the ISE?

The goal is to get the causal event. But anything you can do to calm down the energy system, even if it's a little, will help the client to feel more confident. Releasing some of the emotional charge will allow the stress-response to stop, and the client will start to relax. As a result, they'll start to feel better right away. This will increase their faith in the process, giving you a more cooperative client when it comes time for them to face all the undigested psychological debris that got trapped in past events.

Guiding the client out of a stress-response will allow them to think more clearly. This will help you to uncover all the aspects that are contributing to the client's issue. As they start to make sense of what happened, the client will be better able to inform their Inner Child. As the Inner Child realizes that the event is over, the subconscious mind will begin the process of moving that experience into the past as a completed memory. Once this starts to happen, it's just a matter of generalizing all the changes.

The subconscious mind does this automatically, but you can encourage this natural process by guiding the subconscious mind to connect *that* event to "all the times and all the ways" that the client ever felt that way, or thought that thought, or reacted in that way. The subconscious will then apply all changes to those events as well. This means that the client won't need months or years of therapy to achieve a complete resolution to their presenting problem.

The Backwash Effect

Because the subconscious mind naturally generalizes all learning, clearing a high-intensity *subsequent* event can have a "backwash" effect into the ISE. You just need to discharge the energy that's trapped in the high intensity event. Then, all the changes that occur in the SSE can flow back into the ISE. In some cases, it can even clear the ISE. Nice, right?

While emotional intensity can certainly give you a strong bridge back to the ISE, Bridging back further isn't always your best strategy. Sometimes it's just better to stay put and release some of the energy trapped in that event.

Remember, Rule #1 is to work *with* the subconscious mind. When the subconscious mind dives into an event with emotional intensity, realize it is showing you that event for a reason. It's because there's significant pain and pressure trapped in the event and the subconscious wants some relief. You do not want to ignore that. Yes, it's probably not the ISE. You're probably just dealing with a subsequent event. But the subconscious mind has just shown you something very important. It has shown you the "owie." Sometimes the smartest thing you can do is to stay put and process that event.

While the ISE is the weakest link in the chain of events leading to the surfacing of symptoms, as far as the subconscious mind is concerned the ISE is of secondary importance. This is where the pain and the pressure are!

If you land in an event with a big emotional charge trapped inside, roll up your shirt sleeves and get to work. You're right where you need to be. There's no need to go looking for the ISE, just yet. *This* is where the work needs to be done. You don't need to release everything. Just release enough of the internal pressure to restore a sense of safety.

If you're bumping into strong resistance, releasing some of the internal pressure trapped inside can clear a path to the causal event while giving you a client who can think. You'll need that when it comes time to do the hypnoanalytical work at the ISE. They don't teach you this in hypnosis school, but the linear timeline model is only useful when it comes to mapping[54] out your sessions. It's not how the subconscious mind keeps track of things. Because the subconscious mind is non-linear, it's possible to pull the plug on the whole problem without ever locating the ISE.

Thought-Cause Alignment

The root cause always comes down to a thought, or a cluster of thoughts. Thoughts become beliefs and beliefs decide what we're going to get in life. It's not "what happened" that's the problem. The problem has to do with how the situation was interpreted *at that time*. This is why we bring the client's adult consciousness back into the ISE. It's to allow the client to review and re-evaluate what happened from a more mature point of view.

Left unchallenged, decisions made in childhood can rule a person in adult life. This is because thoughts generate emotions. When a feeling gets trapped inside, it has nowhere to go. As a result, the pressure starts to build up inside, eventually finding a way to express as symptoms – physically, mentally, and emotionally. The feeling, however, is not the problem. Feelings are always there for a reason and serve a positive purpose. Feelings and emotions are meant to motivate us to take action to meet important needs.

E-motion means Energy in Motion. When you're Bridging back, the feeling is showing you where there's a block to that movement. There was an unmet need, a lack of something that was needed. But what caused the feeling has to do with a decision of mind. That's what a thought is. It's a decision about self, others, and life. *That's* the underlying problem. The thought will tell you *specifically* what the

---

[54] For Session Mapping see The Devil's Therapy: *Hypnosis Practitioner's Essential Guide to Effective Regression Hypnotherapy*

problem is because it has everything to do with how the client is making sense of what's happening in that event. It's the meaning they're giving to those things.

It's not what happened. It's not the feeling. It's the decisions that were made based on those things. That's the problem. If you can help the client discover this for themselves, and how that decision resulted in the symptoms, they'll realize they've been doing it to themselves in their mind. When the client realizes that the problem they came to see you about came out of the thoughts and feelings of a Child, it puts them back into choice. Now they can choose. This is the threshold of change.

Threshold of Change

When the client realizes that they're not a Child anymore, that they're a grownup capable of choosing whether they want to hold onto that old pattern, or just let it go, that's forgiveness. This decision, to let go of the problem, happens the moment the client understands that it's not their fault, that stuff happened when they were just a child, that they were doing their best to make sense of things, but they were too young. They lacked maturity. There was no one there to support them. They didn't have the resources. They were feeling overwhelmed and making decisions that would impact on them for the rest of their life.

That's the insight you're after. They were making decisions about themselves, and what to expect from others, and from life. *That's* what caused the problem. That's the realization. The minute the client realizes this they can let go of the whole problem. The moment the client realizes that the *real* problem had everything to do the perceptions, and thoughts, and feelings of the Child they once were, they can change it.

Healing can happen in a heartbeat. It can happen in *any* event, at any time. What takes time is bringing the client to the point where they're willing to allow healing to happen. Healing happens the moment the client is willing to let go of the problem. This is why there's no such thing as a one-size-fits-all therapy that works all the time, for every person. You need to find what fits for the client.

All that's required is a change of mind. That's the healing. When the client comes to peace, their subconscious mind will realize that they're not a Child, anymore, and turn over control to adult consciousness. As a grownup, the client can handle things better. The subconscious mind needs to know this.

The client can take care of themselves, now, and they can make better decisions for themselves than they did as a child. They can come up with strategies, now, and in the future, to take care of their most important needs. When the subconscious mind *gets* this, that they're not a child, anymore, the whole problem-pattern becomes irrelevant. It no longer serves any purpose, which makes it safe to let it go. That puts an end to the whole problem. Nice, right?

So, do you need to find the ISE? Not really. It's just easier because the ISE is the event with the least emotional charge trapped inside. It's more important that you work with the subconscious mind. Trust it to show you where you need to go.

If it lands in a highly charged event, recognize that it's showing the "owie." That's the pattern that is calling for resolution.

If you stay there, and release some of the energy of that event, the client will start to relax. They'll come to clarity in some regard. This will give you a more insightful client. And because of the natural tendency of the subconscious mind is to generalize all change, it's possible to pull the plug on the whole pattern, the whole problem, without ever having to find the ISE.

Follow Up

Even when your client emerges following a session, feeling like a new person, you won't know, for certain, whether the problem has been completely resolved. You won't know whether you got everything, whether the results are going to stick, or for how long. To get complete healing of an issue you need to take care of all the aspects that are contributing to it.

The only way to know for sure that you have got everything is to test your results. Testing is a way to bring to light any hidden aspects. This takes the guesswork out of the equation by giving you the information you need to guide the healing process effectively and ensure a lasting result.

There are two ways you can test outcomes - during the client's session, and between sessions. The tests you use during a session are just preliminary tests. They're helpful because they give you a way to gauge the client's expectations and responses. But they won't tell you whether the issue has been completely resolved.

The only *true* test of the results is in the client's daily life. This is because the client's daily environment is a support system for the problem.

Whatever is supporting the problem has to do with the status quo in the client's life. There might be a problem in the family system. It might have something to do with their primary relationship. It might be in the workplace. There could be saboteurs the client is not even aware of. But when the issue is not yet resolved, the client is still vulnerable to being triggered in their daily life.

This is why regression hypnotherapy is not a single session approach. It's because the *real* transformation doesn't happen in the session room. It happens *after* the client leaves your session. That's where post-hypnotic suggestions are going to take effect - or not.

If all you do is see a client for a single session, you'll never know. You'll never know, for sure, whether the problem was resolved for good. If there's a recurrence of symptoms, or things get worse, you may never hear about it. The client could just assume that the hypnosis didn't work – which is a shame. Getting the problem resolved for good could just be a matter of resolving that one last thing.

If your goal is to get lasting results, the single session approach can rob you of your success. It doesn't give you the time you need to uncover everything that's contributing to the problem. And it doesn't allow you to thoroughly test the results.

The longer the client's problem has been around, the deeper the roots are going to be. The deeper the roots, the more time it takes to thoroughly address all the aspects that are generating symptoms.

It's simply unrealistic to expect a one-session miracle every time. Even if you are successful at getting that one-session miracle, you won't know for certain whether the client is going to be able to hold onto the changes. You need to test the results under real-life conditions. That's where the rubber meets the road.

Testing in Hypnosis

Mental Rehearsal and Future Pacing are preliminary testing techniques you use while the client is in hypnosis. Following a session, you can use them to uncover specific aspects that are still calling for resolution, and to test the client's expectations and responses to situations in daily life.

Mental Rehearsal

Mental Rehearsal is a preliminary technique you can use to give the client the experience of being successful. It helps to set the stage for actual success because, when the client passes the preliminary test, it's a rehearsal for being successful in an actual situation. When the client passes the *real* test in their daily life, it has a compounding effect and provides proof that change has truly happened.

Mental Rehearsal is a process of guiding the client to imagine specific situations that, in the past, have been challenging. If the client bumps into a problem during the preliminary testing, you'll know the problem hasn't yet been resolved. In this case, there's no need to conduct a test in waking life because you've still got work to do. But if the client comes through the *preliminary* testing with flying colors, the next step would be to test things out in their daily life.

Before suggesting that the client take any action in daily life, test the results in hypnosis. If the client can feel confident in that situation in the privacy of their own mind without getting triggered, chances are they'll be able to actualize that confidence in daily life. This is when you could come up with an appropriate homework assignment to test the results in the client's daily life. For example, a weight loss client imagines going out for dinner at a restaurant. He imagines confidently making healthy food choices. He feels the pride of success. His homework assignment is then to test the results in daily life by going out to a restaurant. Whatever happens will give you the next step in the client's healing program.

A client with a fear of public speaking imagines giving a presentation in front of a group of people. She imagines feeling calm and confident. She feels surprised at how clearly that she is now able to deliver the information. When she finishes speaking, she is met with rounds of applause. She feels the approval of her audience. This fills her with feelings of accomplishment. Her homework assignment then becomes to test the results in an actual speaking situation. What happens?

A smoker imagines being a non-smoker while in the company of a group of smokers. He discovers that he has no desire to light up. In fact, he feels sorry for the smokers who are slaves to an expensive habit. He realizes he has overcome the tyranny of tobacco. The freedom he feels is exhilarating. His homework assignment is then to put himself in a situation where there are smokers and notice how he feels.

When he comes back for the next session, he can then give you a report. This will tell you whether the issue is completely resolved, giving you the next step in the client's process.

Mental Rehearsal can be a guided imagery exercise. But where it's most powerful is when you use it in an interactive way. That's when it becomes a test.

To use Mental Rehearsal as a test, you guide the client to imagine the situation as if it were an actual event. Then, use the basic uncovering procedure of regression hypnosis to test the client's responses in that event.

Daytime or nighttime? Inside or outside? Alone or with someone? What's happening? How does that make you feel? The goal is to give the client an *internal* experience of success and *transfer* that experience into real-life situations.

When the client can move through the imagined event effortlessly, they have successfully passed the test. Now they have an experience of being successful. This creates positive mental expectancy which can then be transferred into real-life situations.

An experience of success during an imagined event can help to increase the client's confidence, allowing them to take empowered action in daily life. But sometimes, through the exercise, you'll discover a few "dust bunnies." Dust bunnies are residual aspects connected to the client's pattern. Because they're small, they often respond well to surface techniques such as tapping or direct suggestion.

Other times, you'll uncover a deeper-rooted issue that requires more work. The subconscious mind may reveal a related issue that you won't know about until you test. To get a complete resolution to the client's problem, you need to take care of these things.

If the client bumps into a problem in an imagined situation, Mental Rehearsal functions as an uncovering technique revealing something that is still unresolved. This then becomes the next step in the client's healing process. For example, your weight loss client may feel confident about making the healthy choice *until* he finds his favorite food on the buffet cart. The client who imagines giving a presentation may feel calm and confident stepping up to the podium. But then she has a thought that triggers fear. The smoker imagines stepping into a group of power-puffers and has no desire for a cigarette *until* he takes a sip of his coffee.

In each of these cases you have uncovered a block to the client's success. The next step in the client's process then becomes resolving that specific block. In the next session you can use the Poke a Stick Technique to identify the thought-feeling-sensation pattern to bring up a targeted Bridge to the event responsible for forming that protective subconscious block. You can then resolve those aspects *before* conducting any tests in the client's outer life in daily life.

Future Pacing

Future Pacing is a variation of the Mental Rehearsal technique that gives you a way to test the results by projecting the client forward along their timeline. This allows you to have a look at your client's expectations for the future. Whatever happens during Future Pacing will show you where your client believes they're headed. It's a snapshot of what they expect.

The future situation you guide the client into might be unplanned. Or it might be an event that they're anticipating. For example, it might be an upcoming event like giving a presentation, getting married, or going for bloodwork. Or it might be more of a generic situation like putting on your shoes and going for a walk. Or bumping into their ex-husband and his new wife.

This technique gives you a way to uncover any unresolved fears about the future and take care of them before the client must face those situations in real life. For example, let's say that your client has a fear of needles. You do the regression and emotional release work, and when you rewind and replay the ISE, the client reports feeling calm and relaxed. Yay!

After growing the Child up, you invite the client to imagine moving forward along her timeline to a situation or date in the future when she's going for her first chemotherapy treatment or blood work. During the uncovering procedure, the client feels surprised to discover how calm and relaxed she feels. In fact, she's amazed to find that the old panicky feeling is gone. But then something happens . . . She starts to feel some anxiety. Further uncovering reveals that there's something you missed. It might be the smell of the antiseptic. It might be hospital sounds. It might be a thought that comes to mind.

But now you know! This is a trigger. Now you can resolve it.

Future Pacing is a great test because it shows you the client's expectations for the future. It shows you if there are any aspects that might have been missed during the regression work. This will get you a better result.

When a client can imagine themselves responding differently to situations that, in the past, were impossible to cope with, they get to experience success. This changes how they see themselves. It changes how they feel. And it changes their expectations with respect to future situations.

It can come as a bit of a revelation for a client to realize they're moving effortlessly through a situation that, in the past, was scary or challenging or frustrating or just impossible to deal with. This can generate insights which can then be employed to formulate suggestions to wrap up your session powerfully because the client is realizing that something has happened.

What's happened is that they've changed!

The world hasn't changed. The people around them haven't changed. Situations in daily life haven't changed. What has changed is *the client*. That's the insight you're looking for! They're not the same person they once were. As a result, they don't need to hold onto the problem anymore.

When a client comes to this realization, it becomes a suggestion that you really want to drive home because now it's true. This isn't just something you're telling the client. You're not just reading from a script. This is a suggestion that comes from the client, based on their internal experience. This makes for a powerful suggestion.

You don't need to try to convince the client of anything. All you need to do is feed it back to them. *How* have they changed? How do they *know* that it's true that they've changed? It's like that scene in *A Christmas Carol* where Scrooge wakes up and realizes, "I'm not the man I was!"

Testing in Daily Life

You need to schedule at least one follow-up session so that you can test the client's responses between sessions. The easiest way to test the results in the client's daily life is to give the client a homework assignment. When they come back in for the next session, the client's feedback will tell you whether the issue has been fully resolved.

A homework assignment needs to be based on the client's Therapeutic Goal and, ideally, it should come out of whatever happened during the session. For example, let's say that you're confident that your client's fear of closed-in places has been resolved because you can't find any trace of the old fear. But you won't know for sure if the problem is resolved until the client finds themselves in a tight place in real life.

This is something you would need to test in the client's daily life because, to ensure a complete resolution of the problem, you need to take care of all the contributing aspects. In this case, all you would need to do is come up with a homework assignment that would put the client into a situation which, in the past, caused them to feel that fear.

If the issue is truly resolved, the client will be able to get through that experience without a hitch. Having this experience of success in real life becomes a powerful convincer. This will help to reinforce all the benefits of change.

If something is still calling for resolution, you're going to find out. The client's feedback will tell you what needs to happen next to take care of it. Simple, right?

The purpose of a homework assignment is not to assign a task. It's not about requiring the client to perform some action. That can just set them up for failure which will then generate guilt. That's not helpful. The purpose of homework is simply to test outcomes. You need to make this clear to the client. The time between sessions will let you know when the issue has been resolved.

Remember, people don't pay for hypnosis, they pay for results. Testing is about being thorough and making sure the client is getting what they paid for. It's about getting the feedback you need to ensure a lasting result.

If the client doesn't take the agreed-upon action, that's not a problem. It just means that there are still aspects of the problem that haven't been addressed. That's useful information. There could be a deeper layer. Or there could be other events feeding into the problem.

A homework assignment shouldn't require any willpower. All that's required is the client's willingness to test their responses in daily life. You need 100% conscious consent. If your client shows any hesitancy, you're asking too much of them. It's simply too soon for them to take that particular action. Adjust the assignment until you find the sweet spot.

The client should feel confident in their ability to be successful. If you ask too much, too soon, what often happens is that the client will "forget" their homework assignment. That's resistance, plain and simple. But when this happens, they'll see it as a failure. They'll decide that *they* failed. Or the hypnosis failed. In either case, it's not helpful.

Before you assign any homework, make sure the client is 100% willing to commit to taking action. A client who is willing to do homework is willing to participate in their own healing.

When a client is willing to do their own work between sessions, you're going to get better results because your client is not expecting you to do all the work. They are highly motivated to create the changes they want. This can help to accelerate the healing process.

When the issue has been completely resolved the client will no longer experience resistance to taking appropriate action. And as old, unhealthy responses dissolve away, situations that bothered them in the past will no longer have the power to trigger them.

Emotional Responses

When you're dealing with an issue that involves emotional responses to situations in life, it's easy to come up with a test. Ask the client, "What would be a way to test the results?" They'll tell you. For example, I had a client with claustrophobia. I asked her how she could know *for certain* that the problem was totally gone. She gave me a list of situations that, in the past, had triggered a panic attack. These were the situations that made up this client's Conditions for Change which became ways for us to test the results.

The client knew that, when she could allow herself to experience these situations without being triggered, she would be free from the problem. For example, one of these situations was being able to sit in the back seat of a car. The sense of having "no way out" would bring on the panic. Following what proved to be her final session, I decided to test the results right away.

We went outside to my car - a two-door sports car with a *very* claustrophobic back seat. I asked the client how she felt about sitting in the back seat of my car. She said that normally she could never even get into the backseat of a car. Not even a taxicab! But she agreed to test her responses.

The client was willing to climb into the back seat, but *only* if I agreed to leave the front seat down and the door open. When she settled into the back seat, I asked her, "How do you feel?" She looked surprised. "Nothing!" she said.

Next, I put the front seat up, trapping her in the back seat with no way out. I tested again. "How do you feel?"

Still nothing. So, I got into the driver's seat and closed the door. "How do you feel, now?"

Still no problem. I then started the car and drove her around the block. As we were returning, I looked in the rear-view mirror to see how she was doing. The client's hands were raised in a victory cheer. Yay! The client knew she was free. She was convinced. This freed her to finally take a vacation during which she passed all her tests. She rode on an elevator, an escalator, an airplane and felt comfortable staying in a hotel. These were the conditions that had been out-of-bounds for her.

Best of all, when her co-workers challenged her, saying they couldn't believe that her fear of closed-in spaces was gone, she let herself be put in a closet with the door closed to prove that she no longer had the problem.

Behavioral Changes

Let's say that your client had a breakthrough during the session, and suddenly realized that she'd been thinking, or feeling, or acting in ways she didn't like because of certain factors. That realization can form the basis of a newer, better decision.

Remember, decisions become beliefs, and our beliefs decide what we're going to get in life. Whatever that newer, better decision happens to be can then be used as an assignment to take specific action.

What action might be called for? Ask the client! Then use it to formulate a homework assignment to test the results.

If your client has multiple behavioral changes on their list of Conditions for Change, you can establish them as mini-goals and use them to test the results. For example, throwing out the stash of candy bars or cigarettes. When the client successfully takes action to achieve this goal, they experience success.

Homework

Nothing breeds success like success! When you're working on a major or long-term goal, a series of short-term goals can make the bigger goal seem less daunting. It's much easier to create one small change and then add another change to it. This allows the client to experience success incrementally, which can encourage other changes to happen much more quickly and easily.

These milestones can then be used as opportunities to celebrate success, helping to increase motivation and confidence in the process. It also keeps the clients in the game long enough to get those bigger wins that they're after. For example, I had a client with an extreme fear of snakes. She avoided any place where she might potentially come across a snake. She couldn't go anywhere in nature because there could be snakes. Preliminary tests showed that she could safely move through an *imagined* scenario without getting triggered.

Once the client could move through the *imagined* scenario without any fear, the next logical step was to test her responses out in real life. Fortunately, this client was very enthusiastic about testing herself. She needed to know that her debilitating fear was no longer a problem. As a result, she was 100% willing to commit to taking action.

One such scenario involved taking her dog to the dog park. The dog park was a trail that goes through a wooded area where there was lots of tall grass and bush. And snakes. Her homework assignment was to take her dog for a walk in the park and notice how she was feeling. If anything happened to trigger her – any thoughts or feelings – she was to make note so that she could give me a full report for the next session. Simple, right?

It needs to be simple. It needs to be something that the client should be able to do without a hitch because, if the client can get through the homework assignment without running into resistance, that's a win. The next step would then be to celebrate success.

Even if there's still work to be done, perform a mini wrap up review to reinforce all the positive changes. This will make it easier to allow more change to happen.

If the client bumped into a problem or got triggered, that would still be a win because they were willing to take action. That took courage. Whatever triggered the client would be the next piece to work on.

When you test your results, you always know what to do next. Even when there's still work to be done, an increment of success gives the client proof that change is happening. They're making progress and moving in the right direction. This increases confidence in the process. That's a win-win.

No matter what happens between sessions, the client's feedback will give you the information you need to guide the next step in the healing process. If you get a complete resolution, yay! Celebrate success. If you get partial relief, that's a measure of success you can build on.

Partial success isn't a failure. It's just information that can help and guide you to get a real and lasting result. Celebrate that increment of change as a win. Then, find out what's left. This will give you the next step toward complete resolution.

If there's no change, you need to dig a little deeper. Find the resistance to making that change and neutralize it.

When the problem is completely resolved, internal resistance will be gone, and the client will find it easy to take action or feel safe in the specific situations that were calling for change.

Trust the process. When the internal shift is sufficient to bring the client into alignment with their external goal, they'll be able to hold onto the changes and the results will last. That's the healing. It happens between sessions because that's when suggestions for change get integrated at a subconscious level of mind. It's also where those suggestions get road-tested under real-life conditions.

The Artist's Way

I never assigned homework unless a client is willing. If the client isn't interested, that's fine. Insisting that they do homework between sessions will only set them up for failure. That won't help. But if you have a client who is willing to keep a journal, *The Artist's Way* can help to accelerate their healing. I cannot recommend this enough. You can use it with clients. You can use it yourself. And it really works! It will help you to get more clarity in your life.

The Artist's Way is a 13-week self-study, self-healing, self-empowerment program created by Julia Cameron who, at the time, was working as a screenwriter in Hollywood which, by all accounts, is Crazy Town. Cameron was just looking for a way to get clear and stay clear in a crazy business just so she could function. What she discovered is that the best way to stay sane in an insane world is to do your own inner work.

The Artists Way was a process Cameron developed to support her in doing just that. What she wasn't prepared for was how her life's work would become teaching *The Artist's Way* to others.

Anyone can do it. All it requires is a willingness to put pen to paper. But what makes this an ideal homework assignment for hypnosis clients is that it works with the subconscious mind.

Hypnotherapy sessions naturally stir up subconscious material which can bubble up to the surface between sessions. *The Artist's Way* can support the healing process because it gives the client a way to release emotional debris between sessions.

I first discovered the *Artist's Way* in 1993. At that time, I owned a bookstore. My customers were always recommending books for us to carry. When a customer recommended *The Artist's Way*, I asked her to tell me what was so great about it. She said, "*It saved my life.*" At the time I thought this could be said about a great many books. In fact, I often joke that "my life has been greatly affected by all the books I have *not* read."

But after hearing this woman's story, I was intrigued enough to order a copy to review. When the book arrived, it ended up on a bookshelf with the rest of the new stock. And I forgot all about it. That is, until another customer came in and asked me the same question. "Have you done *The Artist's Way*?"

When I asked her why I should do it, she said, "*It changed my life.*" That's when I got goosebumps. I already had too many books to read. (I still do!) But I decided to take the book off the shelf and give it a go. After a couple of weeks, I was filling the front window of the bookstore with *cases* of *The Artist's Way*.

It's important to understand that this is not merely a book. It's something you "do." "Doing" the Artist's Way is really a process of "undoing." The same could be said of regression-to-cause hypnosis.

It's not about putting stuff in, it's about removing the blocks that cause a person to think, and feel, and act in ways they don't like so that they can live a more fulfilling life.

Julia Cameron describes *The Artists Way* as a process of exorcising the judgments that prevent you from living a creative life. The way she did this was to use two basic tools - Morning Pages and the Artist's Date. The Artist's Date is a weekly date you make with yourself to spend time with your creative self. This is the Part of you that is the Creative Child.

Notice how this is congruent with the Inner Child Work of regression hypnosis? You're making a commitment to spend time with your Inner Child. This makes it practice of self-healing because you're giving attention to an important Part of you – one that has been starving for attention. The Artist Date is about honoring this Part and finding ways to feed it.

Morning Pages is about writing three pages first thing, every morning. Morning + Pages. For clients who like to journal, Morning Pages is a welcome homework assignment. For those who are willing to give it a try, it's relatively undemanding. It's only three pages. But Morning Pages can pay big dividends.

All that's required is to show up to the page and write – stream of consciousness – every morning. Think of it as a Brain Dump. It doesn't require any skill. It's not an exercise in creative writing. It's simply a process of noticing whatever comes to mind and putting it on the page.

This is a daily practice. It must be handwritten. Some people ask if they can type or text their pages. But you won't get the same benefits as you will writing long-hand because typing is using the wrong part of the brain. When you write by hand, you're tapping into the subconscious level of mind where all our feelings and memories are stored. That's where all the negativity is buried. It will find its way into your Morning Pages – if you just go with your first impressions.

When I first started doing the practice of Morning Pages, I discovered that what lands on the page ain't pretty. At least, not to begin. It's not meant to be. The client needs to know this because what ends up on the page tends to be pretty negative stuff; like worries and concerns and resentments and blame. The client needs to understand that this is a process of giving the negativity a place to go. Sound familiar?

The page is a place to put all that stuff so that you don't have to carry it out into their day. What goes onto the page tends to be negative at first. It's like a psychic landfill for all your kvetching and whining and complaining. You might even wonder where it's all coming from. But if you keep writing, you'll find a deeper layer.

You'll find that there's sorrow and grief in there. You'll begin to discover how much of yourself has been stuffed down inside. What's been missing is a connection to your Creative Self.

Your Creative Self is a Child. As you clear away the layers of accumulated emotional debris, and negativity, this Part of you gets stronger. And it starts to show up in your pages.

I tell clients, "Think of the page as a toilet." It's simply a place to get it all out. And when you're done, what do you do?

You FLUSH, right? You're not going to spend any time peering into the bowl after the fact. Just get it out and you're done. There's no need to go back and re-read what you've just written. Whatever goes on the page is emotional trash. The important thing is to get it out. The page gives you a place to do that, so that you won't have to carry it out into your day. But here's the thing . . .

This matches the processes we use in regression-to-cause hypnosis. Go with the first impression. Don't think – feel. If it doesn't feel good – give it a place to go and *get it out*. The way to get relief is to release the thoughts and feelings that are generating internal tension and pain.

Dumping emotional garbage on a daily basis can pay off very quickly. I started to notice right away that I was feeling better. I also noticed that, over time, there was less and less shite showing up on the page, and more and more creative stuff was starting to flow out of me and onto the page, instead. I soon discovered that releasing emotional trash creates space for your Creative Self to express.

In fact, this daily practice led me to write seven books about regression to cause therapeutic hypnosis.

Like a hypnotherapy session, Morning pages give you a safe place to be yourself. It gives you a place to speak your "truth" without judgment and gives you a way to allow your innermost self to be heard.

I've been doing Morning Pages for over twenty years. From time to time, I wander away from it. I think, "I'm too busy, I haven't got time." But it doesn't take long for the pressure to build. Then I go back to the pages to get some relief because Morning Pages help to keep me sane in an insane world.

For me, the page is a place to go to get some clarity. It's often a place to record my dreams[55]. I have been paying serious attention to my dreams since 1988. As a result, I wake up most mornings with a dream. In fact, the thing that helped me to make sense of regression hypnosis was paying attention to dreams.

Dreams are direct communication from the subconscious mind. They show you what your subconscious mind is working on, what it feels is important. That's useful information for any hypnosis practitioner. Dreams can provide answers to questions and solutions to problems. They can reveal gifts and talents that you're not even aware of. They can point you in the direction of your life purpose, if you give them your attention. Giving attention to your dreams is paying attention to what your subconscious mind has to say.

Hypnotherapy naturally stirs up subconscious material between sessions. Morning Pages give the client a place to put that stuff. It also gives them a written record of their healing journey with you, making it a great homework assignment for many clients.

The Artist's Way also gives *you* a way to do your own self-healing work on a daily basis. The pages give *you* a place to process your thoughts and feelings. Morning pages can help you to get clear and stay clear by giving you a place to process your own stuff. Believe me, just getting it OUT will help you to feel better.

When you're working with clients, you're not just processing your own stuff. Your subconscious mind is also working on their stuff because you're focused on finding strategies that can help you to guide your clients to their healing. Sometimes, other people's emotional stuff gets

---

[55] Learn more in Dream Healing Practitioner Guidebook: *A Healer's Guide to Uncovering the Secret Messages of Your Dreams.*

on you. Your subconscious mind is going to be working behind the scenes to find the answers you need, and it will show up in your pages. When you dump thought and emotional debris onto the blank page – whether it's yours or somebody else's - it creates space in your mind. That's space for good stuff to flow back in.

Self-Hypnosis

Most people practice self-hypnosis for the benefits of stress relief because it employs both physical and mental relaxation. But it can also help to improve sleep, increase energy, improve mental clarity and memory, enhance immune function, and increase general wellbeing, both physically and emotionally.

When we enter into a state of hypnosis, we cross through an invisible barrier called the Critical Faculty. The Critical Faculty has been described as a semi-permeable barrier that sits between the conscious and subconscious levels of mind. Its function is to keep us consistent with our beliefs. The way it does this is by reality-checking information that's coming in against what we already know to be true. (This prevents us from acting and feeling like a crazy person.) Unfortunately, for many people, the Critical Faculty is working overtime.

My experience of the Critical Faculty is like watching a train passing by. The conscious mind is aware of the cars passing by. Each car is a thought. As the train passes by, thoughts pass by. The trick is to keep your focus on the gap between cars. But your attention tends to get drawn to the thoughts.

Next thing you know, you're following the train of thoughts. Now you're thinking. And thinking will prevent you from entering a state of hypnosis.

If you can maintain focus on the gap, what happens is that you'll find yourself on the other side of the tracks. The train of thoughts will still be there, but they'll take a place in the background. They simply won't hold any interest for you. That's when you're in hypnosis. As a result, you experience a calmer, more peaceful state of mind, which is lovely. But here's the problem.

Many of your clients will welcome the opportunity to learn self-hypnosis. They will appreciate having a tool that they can use on their own for the rest of their life! But many of your clients have minds that are so busy and chaotic that it's more like a train wreck! This will make it very difficult for them to keep their attention focused long enough to enter the state of hypnosis. This will generate resistance to practicing self-hypnosis.

The key to a successful self-hypnosis practice is to make it a daily habit. If your practice is sporadic, you're going to have problems because, as far as your Critical Faculty is concerned, you're *not* a person who practices self-hypnosis. That's why, when you sit down, close your eyes, and try to relax, it starts to kick up a stink.

If you have a lot of mental activity going on, you're normal. We all have busy lives, and this contributes to overly busy minds. But just a few minutes a day can change that. Whatever techniques you find helpful, the key is to make your self-hypnosis practice a habit. When it becomes a habit, you won't have to think about it anymore.

The easiest way to establish a habit is to schedule your practice at the same time every day. Most people recommend morning and evening practice, but I found that mid-afternoon can be a good time to practice because most of us experience a dip in energy around this time.

Taking advantage of the mid-afternoon slump to take a break and practice self-hypnosis for a few minutes can make it much easier to slide into the state of hypnosis because your body-mind system is ready for a rest.

Instead of grabbing a coffee and a sugary snack to boost your energy, why not give yourself a little 15–20-minute Power Break? This will give you all the benefits of taking a nap without any grogginess, and you'll save yourself from the crash that comes after a sugar high.

It's been said that it takes 21-days to create a new habit, but that's not actually true. The 21-day theory is a concept that came out of Maxwell Maltz's book, Psycho-Cybernetics and was based on observations Maltz made with some of his clients. But research shows that habit change is a highly individualized process. It might take seven days, or twenty-one days, or it could take 221 days. It all depends. You just have to persist until you achieve the results that you're after. The same is true when you're working with clients. But try this. Make a commitment to sixty days. Set aside a specific time, every day, to show up for your self-hypnosis practice.

In other words, schedule it. Make an appointment with yourself. This lets your subconscious mind know that it's important to you. Then, keep your appointment. This is important because you're making a promise to your innermost self to spend time with it. You don't want to let yourself down!

Many people find it difficult getting into or staying in hypnosis when they're practicing on their own. This has to do with something Buddhists call "Monkey Mind." Picture a tree full of agitated monkeys and you'll get the idea. That's what the conscious, thinking mind is like. It's active. As soon as you close your eyes, you become more aware of just how chaotic your mind is. Thoughts are bouncing all over the place. You're thinking about things that have happened during the day, and things that are about to happen, and all that mental busyness will prevent you from entering the state of hypnosis. This is why rapid inductions are more effective for analytical types. They have very busy minds, and their thought processes are very quick. They tend to function at hyper-speed.

This is also true of highly anxious people. They can't seem to relax. The problem is that relaxation hypnosis relies on slowing down brain-wave activity. These folks can't let their mind relax long enough to enter hypnosis. A rapid induction works best because it bypasses all the mental yammer-yammer. It gets them into hypnosis quickly so that you can go to work.

But with self-hypnosis a rapid induction isn't an option. You're stuck with a relaxation-style induction process. And it's very difficult to get all those chattering thoughts to settle down long enough to access the state. So, what do you do?

If you find that Monkey Mind is preventing you from entering a state of hypnosis, the following seven tips can help to settle things down and make it easier to relax into a state of hypnosis.

1. Tap

Tapping has been shown to calm the amygdala of the brain. The amygdala is the alarm center of the brain that generates a stress-response. A few minutes of tapping can help to calm down the mind and body, making it easier to let yourself go into hypnosis. Instead of trying to stop all the yammer-yammering going on – tap on it.

Tap on any worries or concerns. Tap on your to-do list. Tap on all the have-tos and not-enoughs. Tapping on all the distractions will help to settle the mental busyness, allowing you to set it off to one side. The monkeys will still be there, bouncing around, but they'll find a place in the background allowing you to relax into hypnosis.

2. Brain Dumping

Grab a pen and write down all those busy thoughts. Give them a place to go. Whatever comes into your head, put it on the page. Giving those thoughts a place to go will help you to set them aside, allowing you to feel ready to allow hypnosis to happen.

3. Make a List

This is a variation on the brain dump. If you've got a lot of stuff to think about, make a list. Then, take your list and put everything in order of priority. Organizing all the tasks and things to do will help to get them off your mind so that you can relax into hypnosis.

4. Listen

An audio recording with lots of deepening suggestions can help you to maintain your focus long enough to slip into hypnosis. I found that a 15-minute recording is perfect. At the end of the recording, give the suggestion to either continue going deeper or to count yourself back up. That way, if you want to extend your hypnosis session, you can just keep-going-deeper . . .

5. Breathe

Formalize the induction with a little ritual to let the mind and body know that it's time to go into hypnosis. For example, take a nice, deep, relaxing breath in . . . Then, at the top of the in-breath, hold the breath for a moment. Build up a little tension in the chest area. When you exhale, relaxation will naturally follow, helping you to relax into hypnosis.

6. Count Down

We routinely use a deepening count in hypnosis sessions. The repetition can help you to access deeper states. To increase your focused attention, combine it with imagery. For example, you can imagine each number on a whiteboard, or on the screen of your mind. You can then mentally relax the number out of your mind by erasing it. As you erase each number, give yourself the suggestion to "go deeper."

A variation on this is to imagine numbers written in the sand of a beach. Add the sound of the waves coming in and going out and it becomes hypnotic! As a wave comes in, it dissolves the number. As it goes out, it takes the number with it, and you go deeper.

Alternatively, you can imagine a set of stairs, or an elevator, or you can simply count. Try using three counts of ten down to one. For the first two counts, incorporate intermittent suggestions for going deeper. For the third count, leave a gap of silence between each count with a progressively longer pause between each count. This helps to slow the mind down as it follows each count.

7. Saturate the Mind

Before you begin your hypnosis practice, formulate a clear suggestion for the change you want to make. Spend a few minutes with pen and paper and write down all the details you can think of. What do you want? What does it look like to have achieved this change? What action do you need to take to realize this change? What are the rewards? Who do you get to enjoy them with? What else?

The idea is to saturate your mind with a single idea. Then, as you drift across the threshold into hypnosis, those suggestions will drop down into the subconscious level of mind. All you need to do is keep going deeper, and the suggestions will go with you.

Keep the Contract Open

In his book, *Joy's Way*, Dr. Brugh Joy shares an axiom for healing.

1. Make no assumptions
2. Make no judgments
3. Delete the need to understand

This is good advice for a healer. Don't assume. TEST. Prove that the results will stand up in real life. There can be multiple aspects and multiple events contributing to the client's problem but not all of them are necessarily going to be brought to light in sessions.

This is why we must test. The fact is: you might not get it all the first time. Or the second time. Or, in some cases, not even the tenth time. This is because the subconscious mind will only show you what it feels is relevant at the time.

If something isn't currently an issue for the client, it may not come up in session. It might not be an issue until the client bumps into a specific trigger. That might not happen for weeks, months or even years.

Life is always going to be throwing tests out in front of the client. You need to be diligent about testing the results both in the session and between sessions. Even when the client can move through an imagined event without getting triggered, and you're confident that the client is good to go - *never assume*. Keep the Contract open.

The basis of the Contract is the therapeutic relationship. When you're wrapping up a program, let the client know that you're always there for them. Tell them, "Time will tell." Let them know that if they ever have a problem, all they need to do is pick up the phone and call you. That way, if the client bumps into an unexpected problem they'll know to come back to see you, and you'll take care of it.

You need to keep the door open for the client so that they'll feel good about coming back in if the need arises. Stuff can happen when a client goes back to daily life. It's often stuff that you have no way of anticipating. For example, let's say Uncle Charlie is a problem. But you don't know this because Uncle Charlie has never shown up in a session. That's because your client hasn't seen Uncle Charlie for the past thirty years.

You'll get clients who will tell you that a certain person used to be a problem. But they went to counseling. They forgave that person. They're convinced that they're fine now. And they *are* - until six months later when they bump into Uncle Charlie at the family reunion. That's when they get triggered.

You keep the Contract open so that, if there happens to be a recurrence of symptoms, or the client gets triggered, they won't judge. They won't judge themselves and they won't judge the hypnosis. They'll know to come back in and get the rest of the problem resolved.

It's not that the hypnosis didn't work. It's not that you didn't do your job right. It's just how the mind works. The subconscious mind is only going to show you what is relevant and what it feels the client is ready for. And it is *very specific* when it comes to triggers.

If situations arise (as they will) and the client *doesn't* get triggered – yay! This tells you they're on a new path. In time, your client will embody a more empowered identity of someone who is now in charge of their life. That's the goal.

If they bump into something that doesn't feel good, they're not clear yet. That's okay. That's the purpose of testing. Keeping the contract open is testing the results in an ongoing way. It's about being professional and ensuring that you have got everything, that you're not sending clients home half-baked. Even when you're confident the client is good to go - make no assumptions. Keep the contract open. Test your results.

You have *preliminary* tests you can use to uncover any unresolved aspects while the client is still in hypnosis. And you have ways to test the results in the client's daily life between sessions. But you still don't know whether the issue is completely resolved. You can't.

What you *can* do is prepare the client. That way, if something happens in daily life to act as a trigger, it's nobody's fault. You just need to find out what the problem is so that you can pull the plug on it. To do that, the client needs to feel good about picking up the phone to call you.

Time will tell. So, make no judgements, make no assumptions, and delete the need to understand. You don't have all the answers. It's not up to you to have all the answers. The answers are in the mind of the client. And you can only work with what the client gives you. .

CHAPTER 16:
Healing Trauma

Post-Traumatic Stress (PTS) used to be considered the after-effect of a terrifying ordeal such as rape, carjacking, armed robbery, and war, etc. However, new research is showing that trauma is in the mind of the perceiver rather than the event itself. Neurologist, Dr. Robert Scaer defines trauma as "an extreme form of stress, one that has assumed life-threatening proportions."[56]

Any situation which represents a life-threat will elicit a fight/flight response. When combined with a state of helplessness (where it is not possible to fight or flee), it results in a freeze/immobility response. Surgical interventions, receiving a diagnosis, undergoing medical tests, even being involved in a fender-bender, can be perceived as traumatic and result in the Freeze response. When the Freeze response occurs, the event gets locked into the body.

Every problem is the result of a life experience. Feelings and emotions are responses to actual life experiences. They are actual experiences and responses that are felt in the body. Trauma has to do with an experience of facing a threat while in a state of helplessness. It doesn't

---

[56] Dr. Robert Scaer, The Body Bears the Burden, 2001

have to be an actual threat. The experience is real. It's just that how an event is remembered may not necessarily be factual. It's how what happened was *perceived* that's the problem - not the actual event. For example, I developed a real fear of needles that tracked back to getting booster shots as a baby. It wasn't the needle that scared me. It was Mom handing me over to the nurse, a stranger. I thought she was going to give me away. It wasn't a fear of needles. It wasn't even a fear of strangers. I thought I was being *abandoned*.

This is old-brain stuff. Every Child knows that it cannot survive on its own. Because a child is dependent on others for its survival, abandonment is a very real threat to survival *to a child*. The subconscious mind is the conscious mind *of the Child*. It lacks the ability to discriminate between real and imagined. And because the subconscious mind doesn't keep time the same way the conscious mind does, an unresolved experience continues to be viewed as a current event.

Subconsciously, it's happening still. As a result, the subconscious mind continues to ruminate, trying to come up with a solution, because the memory has not been brought to completion. It's not finished. But the subconscious mind can't resolve the problem because it only has the resources that were available at the age the event happened.

The younger the Child is, the more helpless they are, and the more likely they are to misinterpret things that are happening around them or to them. It doesn't matter whether the event was real or imagined. What matters is that the *feeling* is real. A person with a fear of spiders knows the plastic spider isn't a real threat. That's why they think they're crazy. But the feeling of fear is real. Very real.

To a small child, any situation where she feels pain, overwhelmed, vulnerable, unsafe, shocked, or unable to control what's happening is perceived as life-threatening. For example, hearing Mom and Dad fighting for the first time; overwhelming loneliness with no one present to comfort the child; witnessing a loved one being injured or harmed. Brent Baum[57], developer of *Holographic Memory Resolution*, suggests that trauma also includes any slap or blow to the head before the age of five.

Paula was considering relocating her business. She was feeling "tied down, held down" by the restraints of her workspace, but the substantial financial outlay required prevented her from taking any action. Paula sought relief from the internal pressure she was feeling in her stomach and chest. Through the regression, she discovered that this event was linked to irrational feelings of dread associated with speaking up for herself and disappointing others.

As Paul focused on "that feeling," she felt suffocated. Panic! A chill flooded throughout every part of her body. Bridging back on the feeling took us back to age two where Paula was about to undergo surgery to correct the heart defect she had been born with.

In the operating room, Little Paula was feeling the distress of being separated from her parents. Her little body felt drained and heavy. She did not understand what was happening. Nor did she recognize any of the people around her or anything they were saying.

Worse, Paula had been strapped down on the operating table to immobilize her, a routine practice with small children. She was unable to see because her eyes had been taped shut, and a tube was being

---

[57] Brent Baum, Healing Dimensions: Resolving Trauma in Body Mind and Spirit, 1997

forced down her throat, making it impossible for her to cry out. Picture this trapped, terrified child as she listens for some shred of comfort and safety - the sound of Mother's voice. She would not hear this voice amidst the strange and terrifying sounds of the operating room. Feelings of dread wracked her tiny body as the anesthetic began to take hold. Fighting sleep, she feared that she would never wake.

Following the post-session debriefing, Paula admitted having no conscious memories of this event. However, she had been told by family members that, until the age of two, she had spoken only her native language, Hungarian. Following the heart surgery, she stopped speaking it.

What to Watch For

1. **What's happening?** Whatever is happening gives you the perceptions of the Child at that time. They're not necessarily facts. Perceptions are five-sensory. What is the Child seeing, hearing, smelling, tasting, or touching? Watch for anchors!

2. **What about what's happening feels threatening?** How is the Child interpreting what's happening? What meaning is being given to various aspects? Is that true? If it's true, the Child needs to know that she gets to grow up. If it's not true, that's what needs to change. Watch for the specific thoughts regarding what's happening.

3. **What does the Child need?** Identify the unmet need. What's missing that the Child feels helpless or powerless?

Core Needs

The following three core needs correspond roughly to the Triune Brain Model which comprises the old brain or brain stem at the base of the skull, the mid-brain, and the new brain. Watch for what's needed because, once you have identified the unmet needs of the Child, you can help the client to find ways to satisfy those needs.

1. Avoid

The old brain is the survival brain. It's sometimes referred to as the reptilian brain because it doesn't think or feel. It just responds to stimulus through the nervous system of the body. The first core need is to avoid any threat to survival. What's needed? Safety.

Human beings are hardwired to avoid any perceived threat. To this end, the brain stores negative impressions over positive ones. Even a fleeting negative impression will get recorded for future reference for purposes of survival. For example, if you ate the berries and they made you sick, you're going to remember that and know how to avoid them next time.

The need to avoid any perceived threat is based on old brain, survival-based needs. The younger the Child, the more "reptilian" the response. Simply being left alone in a crib can be perceived as abandonment. Because children cannot survive on their own, the perception of abandonment poses a serious threat to survival. The same goes for rejection. Rejection is perceived as abandonment. It's a survival fear!

The subconscious mind's Prime Directive is to protect but it does not make a distinction between real and imagined. The fact that nothing bad happened isn't relevant to the reptilian brain. It's reactive, not proactive. If you come across a snake in the garden, you'll learn to be on the alert for snakes in future. If it turns out to be a garden hose, it's better to stay safe than be sorry.

Being denied something that feels important, or being isolated from family, is perceived as a threat to survival. For example, the child loses his security blanket or beloved Teddy Bear; being hospitalized means being separated from sources of safety and security.

Any situation that confuses the Child is interpreted as a threat to survival. If you are not able to figure out how the world works, you do not know how to respond to what's happening around you. Confusion can often be a sign of a perceived a threat to survival!

2. **Achieve**

The mid-brain is the emotional brain or mammalian brain. This part of the brain is the reward center of the brain. Human beings naturally seek pleasure and avoid pain. The feeling of satisfaction that comes from achievement gives us pleasure.

Any block to our ability to fulfill this basic, human need, or to enjoy the rewards of our accomplishments, will result in feelings of frustration and dissatisfaction. And not having enough resources to satisfy one's need to achieve can generate anxiety. What's needed? Resource states.

In regression sessions you can utilize experiences of pleasure and enjoyment to anchor resource states. You can also create new resource states by transforming blocks into sources of empowerment through the healing process.

Gallup conducted a survey which identified that the most rewarding area of life is work. That's where most people experience the rewards of achievement.

Memories of achievement provide positive feeling states. For example, winning the race in grade school, or overcoming/enduring a challenging situation.

Recalling favorite things will evoke pleasurable feelings. For example, "Something I love . . ." An experience of gratitude will flood the body with feel-good hormones. For example, the physical pleasure of witnessing a sunset, the grandeur of purple mountain peaks, holding a newborn in your arms.

3. Attach

#2 on Gallup's list of most rewarding areas of life had to do with social connection. Human beings have a basic human need for love and belonging. This has to do with our need to attach. Attachment is associated with the most modern development in the brain that makes us human.

This is the primate or human part of the brain and has to do with our need for love and belonging. What's needed? To be seen, accepted, and appreciated for being.

Insufficient bonding with Mom following birth can generate anxiety. What the Child needed was to be held, make eye contact with Mom, and hear words of endearment. You can provide this!

Incomplete or missing bonding in childhood can result in shame[58]. How a Child is parented affects her ability to trust in the world and sets the tone for relationship issues later in life.

---

[58] Brene Brown defines shame as the fear of not being worthy of connection and belonging, stemming from the belief that one is not enough and will be rejected for

Emotionally distant parents, caregivers, or siblings who are hostile or rejecting are devastating for a Child because the Child doesn't know how to make sense of their behavior.

If you have a client who was an "afterthought," pay close attention to their relationships with siblings. A significant age gap could point to unresolved resentments, bullying, and/or punishing behaviors.

Providing experiences of loving touch, recognition, and appreciation changes the client's internal experience of self.

Tapping Techniques

Emotional Freedom Technique (EFT) theory views every emotional problem as a disruption in the energy system. It's a ZZT! to the nervous system that locks the emotional energy of an event into memory. ZZT! is a great description because it actually feels like an electrical shock. The problem is that young children can interpret seemingly inconsequential things as a threat to survival.

When you're two feet tall, everything around you seems bigger than you. Grownups are giants to a young child. This makes any perceived threat much larger than it actually is. The bigger the perceived threat the bigger the ZZT! The bigger the ZZT! the more energy disruption there is. The initial perception of threat will generate uncomfortable sensations in the body. i.e., tension or nervous energy. The feeling of tension will then result in a decision about what's happening. The specific thought will then generate an appropriate response in the form of an emotion.

---

their weakness. Brown's work on shame resilience theory suggestions that building resilience to shame involves confronting it directly and speaking about it openly.

Remember, behind every emotion there's always a thought. Emotion is the motivating energy of the mind. The specific emotion, whether fear, anger, sadness, or something else, will indicate what meaning was being given to the situation at that time. That's the thought. Fear, for example, gets us up and moving to avoid a threat.

All negative emotions are rooted in fear. The emotion might be sadness, or anger, or something else but underneath it all, there's going to be a fear. It's there because the Child feels helpless in the face of a threat. Fear is the subconscious mind stepping in to protect.

EFT or tapping[59] is a very effective tool for quickly bringing down the emotional charge very quickly. There's good evidence showing that stimulating the meridian points by touching or tapping helps to calm the energy system of the body.

If you don't yet know tapping, you can use autosuggestion to validate and then neutralize the painful perceptions. This gives you a very versatile tool that you can adapt to the needs of each client. The following are some of the many uses for tapping in regression sessions.

1. Preliminary Technique

You can use tapping as a preliminary technique. For example, some clients have doubts or concerns about hypnosis. If the client is feeling a little apprehensive, you can use tapping to neutralize their fear. If the client is feeling overwhelmed, or confused, or frustrated, you can help them reduce the overall volume of pressure. This will help them to relax about the process.

---

[59] Developed by Gary Craig

Releasing fear, doubt and frustration *before* you begin the hypnosis means the client won't be carrying those things into the hypnosis session. As a result, there's going to be less resistance to deal with.

2. Convincer

Tapping makes a great Convincer. It only takes a few minutes to teach a person how to tap. In just a few rounds you can show them just how quickly they can shift to a better feeling.

You don't have to release everything. Any shift toward the better can be used as *proof* that it's *possible* to feel better. By extension, the client's desired change is possible. As a result, instead of questioning you or the process, or worrying about what might happen, the client will be thanking you for helping them to get some relief and feeling more hopeful about the process.

3. Induction

Tapping is a natural hypnotic induction. Tapping combines focused attention and autosuggestion. That's hypnosis. Because the client is focusing and tapping and talking at the same time, this gives you a covert, Confusional Induction that can very quickly get the client into a hypnotic state. Try it! It's a very organic approach to inducing hypnosis.

4. Find a Bridge

Tapping can give you a Bridge. During a Tapping sequence, thoughts and feelings naturally bubble up to the surface of awareness. As soon as a client starts experiencing strong emotions, you have hypnosis. Any feeling is a Bridge to the past.

The stronger the feeling, the stronger the Bridge. Tapping can therefore be used as a launch-pad for regression hypnosis. Just bring up the feeling and count the client back into a scene from the past.

5. Spontaneous Regression

Tapping can elicit spontaneous regression. Because the mind works through association to form memories, as the client is focusing on thoughts, feelings, and sensations in the body, they're naturally going to start mentally connecting with earlier situations when they felt that way. This can lead to spontaneous regression. The best kind.

6. Release in an Event

You can use Tapping to clear an event from the past. Using tapping in a regression session allows you to quickly release the emotional charge that's been holding the problem in place. Tapping has been *proven* to be effective for resolving traumatic memory because it calms the amygdala.

The amygdala is the alarm center of the brain. It's responsible for generating the fight or flight response. If you turn off the alarm, the client will go back to feeling safe, and secure, calm and relaxed. That's when healing happens.

When you tap on feelings in a past event, one of the things you'll find is that there are often multiple layers of perceptions, thoughts and feelings. It's not just one thing. When you clear one layer, it gives you access to the next, deeper level. If you clear *all* the aspects contributing to a problem, you'll get complete healing.

This really is the key to getting real and lasting results. When you release the emotions that got trapped in an event and the client will feel relief immediately. This will then ripple throughout the mind-body system to generate change.

7. Homework

Tapping is a great way to empower your clients. You are literally giving them relief at their fingertips. Once you have taught your client how to tap, and you're confident that they're ready to use it on their own, you can assign it as homework (but only if they're willing.) A client who is willing to do homework between sessions gives you a much better client to work with simply because they are participating in their own healing. This can help to accelerate the healing and get a deeper level of healing.

8. For Yourself

Tapping gives you a way to do your own self-healing work. Self-healing work can teach you a great deal about regression hypnosis – from the inside. For example, you'll discover how tapping can induce a light state of hypnosis. There's no need for a formal induction process because you're literally "tapping into" the subconscious mind. You can discover for yourself how releasing the surface layers of an issue can free up deeper layers to be released. You'll learn how the mind naturally associates into earlier events and use it to self-regress.

You can discover how your thoughts and feelings are connected to events from the past, and how these things relate to an issue you're working on. Best of all, you can locate past events and resolve them using the same tools and techniques you use with clients. This will give you a deeper understanding of how your tools and techniques work.

All in all, tapping is a very useful tool to have. The idea is to adapt to the needs of the client. Introduce tapping when it's most relevant and use it to offer the client some relief. For example, you can teach it during the intake, educational pretalk, conditioning phase, or Ready for Regression phase. Or you can watch and wait for an abreaction and then use it to Bridge back to the event that cause "that feeling".

Like every tool, tapping requires skill to use effectively. If you're new to tapping, my advice is to first master the tools of regression hypnosis. Then, once you're confident in your abilities to facilitate regression-to-cause, incorporate it into your sessions with clients to achieve a deeper level of healing. If you already know how to do tapping, you'll discover that adding regression hypnosis to these techniques gives you a powerful system for resolving the root cause of the problem.

Many hypnosis practitioners started out with technique-based methods like NLP or EFT. What brought them into regression hypnosis was a desire to do healing work. When you consider that every problem is the result of a life experience, regression hypnosis just makes sense.

The first step to resolving a problem is to identify the experience that caused the problem in the first place. In the absence of an obvious, organic cause, the next step is to release the energy of the problem. That's what's holding the problem in place.

Releasing Tip:

If you can pair the thought with the feeling, you can process them together. This will give you a more complete releasing of the problem. For example, "The thought (I can't breathe) makes me feel (scared)." Or "The thought (I was bad) makes me feel (guilty and scared)." Or "The thought (that's not right!) makes me feel (angry)."

Pairing the thought and the feeling generates insight. Insight is the subconscious mind connecting the dots. Insight will allow more release to happen, and the client will start to experience a cascade of insights. The biggest insight is the 'OMG Moment.'

When the client realizes, "OMG! I've been doing it to myself," they are on the threshold of liberation. When the client realizes that the *thought* is the problem, that every time they say "that" to themselves, or think "that" thought they feel that feeling, the realization restores their power of choice.

NOW they are free to make a new decision.

Abreactions

When your client lands in an event and bumps into more intensity than they can handle, what do you do? Do. Not. Freak. Out. If the client is freaking out your freaking out isn't going to help. A person in hypnosis is hyper-aware. If you're freaking out, the client is going to feel it, and it will only make things worse. Stay calm.

Remember, this is why the client came to see you. Even the most horrific circumstances can be faced, processed safely, and brought to resolution. It's just that their mind has brought them into a situation that has a little more energy than they were prepared for. The good news is that it has everything to do with their issue. Stay calm. Take charge. Manage the energy by releasing some of the intensity.

Meridian Tapping Technique Basic Formula

1. **Find it.** As you think about the problem, tune into your body. Notice where you feel discomfort or distress.

2. **Feel it.** Stay focused on the body as you think about the problem. What does that discomfort feel like? Be as specific as possible. E.g. "This tight knot in my gut." "This scared feeling in my throat."

3. **Heal it.** Tap with your fingers lightly. Use the same pressure you would use if you were tapping on the arm of the chair. While tapping on the Karate Chop Point repeat the *Basic Self-Acceptance Phrase* three times. Tap through the *Tapping Sequence.* At each point repeat the Reminder Phrase to help you stay focused on the feeling.

4. **Seal it.** Take a deep breath and exhale. Acknowledge any change. Congratulations! You got your energy moving!

Basic Self-Acceptance Phrase: Tap on Karate Chop (KC) or rub the Sore Spot (SS) and repeat 3 times:

"Even though I have this (negative perception/feeling) ... I deeply and completely accept myself anyway."

Reminder Phrase: Tap on each point 5 – 7 times each while repeating the Reminder Phrase.

"This _____ (feeling)"

Tapping Sequence:

- Inside of eyebrow (IE)
- Side of eye (SE)
- Under eye (UE)
- Under nose (UN)
- Under lip (UL)
- Collar bone (CB)
- Breastbone/Thymus
- Thumbnail
- Index finger
- Middle finger
- Pinkie
- Karate Chop (KC)
- Other Points You Can Tap On:
- Under arm (UA)
- Top of Head (TH)
- Inside Wrists

If you still have some remaining discomfort, rate the intensity on a scale of 1-10 and compare it to where it was when you started.

To release what's left, you can modify the set-up phrase to: "Even though I still feel some of this _____, I deeply and completely accept myself." Then, change the reminder phrase as you tap the points to: *"This remaining _____"*.

To help release things more quickly *be more specific*.

Uncovering Tools

Think of the subconscious mind as a DVD player. Like a DVD player, it records events as memories. It also has a "play" button. When events in daily life trigger memories and feelings from the past, something happened to push the "play" button. The subconscious mind has some other buttons that you can use to control things in an event during regression. They are the "stop" button, the "pause" button, the "rewind" button, and the "fast forward" button. These four buttons give you total control over what's happening in an event.

The Stop Button

The main problem with traumatic memories is that too much was happening too quickly. The client wasn't ready for it, it took them by surprise, and they didn't have the resources they needed to handle what was happening. Maybe there was no one there to support them and help them to make sense of things. Because they didn't know that they would get through it okay, their subconscious mind has been ruminating on that situation ever since. It just never ends. It keeps playing in a loop which compounds the problem.

If the client goes into overwhelm, give the suggestion, "Everything stops!" Speak with authority. Stopping the scene is like hitting "freeze frame." This allows you to keep the client in the event while providing safety.

The Pause Button

Sometimes the client will try to race through what's happening. When that happens, they'll skip over all the important details. The problem is that they're trying to avoid the trapped energy – perceptions, thoughts, feelings – that are calling for resolution. If the client is trying to move forward too quickly, "pause" the event. Then "play" the event frame by frame. Slowing things down will prevent the client from getting into a state of overwhelm by allowing them to process smaller chunks of awareness.

The Rewind Button

Often the client knows what's going to happen. The Child might not have seen it coming but the Grownup does! Grownup's anxiety will feed into the fear of the Child. This means there's much more intensity than there needs to be.

If there's anticipatory fear feeding into the event, "rewind" to right before any of the intensity came on. Stop right there and have a talk with Grownup. Then, guide Grownup to prepare the Child for what's going to happen.

If you need to uncover more detail, "rewind and replay" to discover what you missed the first time through. You can also use the "rewind and replay" command to test and make sure that the ISE is clear.

The Fast Forward Button

If it seems like it's too much, "fast forward" to after the event. Then, clear everything in retrospect by using past-tense language. Research shows that providing support immediately following a traumatic experience allows the person to process their thoughts and feelings. Releasing the emotional charge means that there will be no lasting effects. Release the charge and it's over.

Titrating

The uncovering process in an event that has a lot of trapped emotions in it can be overwhelming for the client *and you*. A lot can be happening as the client tries to report all the thoughts and feelings arising in response to what's happening. Rule of thumb: if it feels like it's too much, it probably is. The solution is to think in terms of increments of change.

Chunking things down into manageable bites will make it easier to process. Segmenting an event, so that you can deal with one piece at a time, is called "titrating."

An event is a story. It has a beginning, middle, and end. The beginning is whatever happened before the upset. (This is one of the tests for the ISE. Before anything bad happened, the Child was feeling okay, safe, happy. Then something happened to change that.)

The end is whatever happened immediately following the event.

The middle is where all the drama plays out. This is where you uncover all the key elements and sources of disruption that caused the internal conflict. To thoroughly clear an event, you need to address all three parts of the story. It always begins with a surprise or a shock. Release the shock and confusion of that.

There is always a peak or a critical moment to an event that causes disruption. The client would call this "the worst part." Think of it as the turning point in the story.

Everything has been building up to this moment. It's like the crest of a hill or the top of a bell-curve. It could be anything. Something said, something done. It could be the fact that something was missing or that it felt like "too much." It could have to do with someone who was there or wasn't there. Releasing the emotional intensity of "the worst part" will allow the nervous system to relax and reset. The client will feel a sense of relief as the stress response releases. When that happens, they'll have more clarity with which to evaluate the situation. (That's what was missing the first time!)

Finally, clear the thoughts and feelings associated with how the event ended. Remember, it's not always necessary to relive the event. What's important is that the subconscious realizes that the event is over. Processing the end of the event can effectively drain off a lot of the emotional charge, making it easier to deal with all the details. You can then go to *before* the event to prepare the Child for what's going to happen. Then run the event to test for any residual aspects.

There's no right or wrong way. Just find what works best for the client and make it safe for them to go there. Remember, it's just a story. It's how the memory got stored and it's all based on the perceptions of the client at the age they were when it happened. Memories are not static; they change over time. Triggering events add to the internal pressure by reinforcing the unresolved aspects. Releasing reduces the internal pressure, allowing learning to occur, thus changing the overall pattern.

Myoclonic Shaking

Myoclonic Shaking is something every hypnotherapist should know how to recognize and how to handle. Unfortunately, they don't teach this stuff in hypnosis school. It's important that you know about this because, sooner or later, it's going to happen in one of your sessions and it can be quite frightening for some clients. You need to be able to respond to it calmly and guide the client confidently when it happens.

Myoclonus refers to muscle twitches. Most people experience this as they're falling asleep. The arms and legs jerk involuntarily as you're falling asleep. It's the body's way of releasing energy from the nervous system. It can happen with varying degrees of intensity, and it can happen in a session, taking the form of involuntary twitching, quivering, quaking and shaking.

I first learned about Myoclonic Shaking in the early 90's while reading a book called *Paradox and Healing*[60]. But it was not until I started practicing hypnotherapy that I witnessed it first-hand. The book was written by two MD's (Greenwood and Nunn) who were using acupuncture to treat chronic pain patients.

What the doctors observed with these patients, particularly those with whiplash, were three phenomena which were linked to blocked emotional charge.

1. Emotional releases such as crying or laughing.
2. Myoclonic shaking. i.e., vibratory muscle movements that can mimic an epileptic seizure.
3. Regression. i.e., spontaneous reliving of a previous traumatic event responsible for the chronic pain syndrome being treated.

They also noted that when these three things happened together, there was a physical, emotional, and mental expression of blocked energy. This represented a "healing crisis" or "transformation" of the psyche. A dramatic reduction in pain followed immediately.

The two doctors theorized that the standard practice of suppressing these states with tranquillizers and muscle relaxants actually served to *block* the body's natural healing response. The underlying problem had

---

[60] Dr. Peter Greenwood and Dr. Peter Nunn, Paradox and Healing, 1992

to do with a Freeze Response that had locked the energy of a traumatic experience into the nervous system of the body. They also recognized that the healing process they observed was naturally occurring.

According to Dr. Robert Scaer[61] all mammals do this. When faced with a threat the nervous system goes into red alert. This is called The Stress Response. Then, when the threat has passed, the body naturally discharges the energy of the event.

Myoclonic shaking is nature's way of discharging the energy to extinguish the trauma. For example, if a hawk swoops down and catches a bunny, the bunny is helpless. There's nothing it can do. Chances are pretty good that it's about to be lunch. The bunny can't fight, it can't flee, so the body goes into a Freeze Response.

But if the hawk fumbles, and the bunny manages to escape, something very interesting happens. The bunny will remain limp. It will lie still and rest quietly. Then, after a while the body will start to quake. This quaking will gradually become more intense. The movements will get larger. What's happening is the body is releasing energy from the nervous system. It's discharging the trauma. For example, if the legs start jerking that's the body completing the movement of running. It's discharging the energy that didn't get released because the bunny couldn't take action to run away.

I experienced this first-hand when my cat, Mike, caught a baby Marten[62]. Fortunately, I managed to rescue the critter before it became lunch, but not before it was traumatized into a total Freeze Response.

---

[61] Robert C. Scaer, MD, The Body Bears the Burden: Trauma, Dissociation, and Disease, 2001
[62] A marten is a weasel-like animal which is incredibly cute and, unfortunately, endangered in my neck of the woods.

As I held this tiny ferret-like creature in my hand, it appeared to be dead. But when I looked closer, I could see that it was still breathing. I continued to hold it in the palm of my hand and watched.

After a while its tiny body started to quake. I could feel the energy in my hand as it rippled down the creature's body from the top of its head to its legs and feet. The energy had a wave action to it. This process lasted for about ten minutes. (My guess is that the process of releasing matches the duration of the freeze response.)

Once it had finished releasing the trauma, the Marten was laying very still, resting, so I set it into a box to see if it might recover. I didn't expect that it would live. Every 20 minutes or so I would check in on it. And each time it was just lying still. It hadn't moved an inch.

About an hour later, I checked again. To my surprise the Marten was energized. It was running around, jumping, and trying to get out of the box. I immediately delivered the Marten to a veterinarian who, coincidentally, had recently written a paper about this endangered species. I'm happy to report that the patient survived and was safely released back into the wild.

When we're not able to run or defend ourselves, there's a Freeze Response which locks the energy into the body. Dr. Scaer called this an event of "kindling." We call it sensitizing.

What sensitizes a person to subsequent re-stimulation is the unprocessed energy of the event still trapped in the body. When the trauma of the event is over, we discharge the energy through a sort of epileptic quaking movement. At least, we should. The problem is that humans have an evolutionary disadvantage when it comes to traumatic experience. We think.

We tend to use *thinking* to override our feelings. Rather than discharging the energy of the event we hold onto it. This locks it into the body. We then try to use reason and logic to deal with the traumatic memory. This just never works.

What Greenwood and Nunn had discovered is a way to help the body *unfreeze*. Myoclonic shaking is a physical releasing the trauma of the event. Releasing the trapped energy will activate the body's own healing system and the body will discharge the trauma of the event.

Sometimes it happens spontaneously. The energy in the body will reach ignition and all the kindling will burst into flames. The body will then start to burn off all the biochemical stress hormones. That's the energy of the event.

I have experienced this in my own body during a regression session. It felt like cold waves flowing down my legs and out the bottoms of my feet. I have also witnessed it in sessions with clients.

I had one client whose legs were shaking so much that the chair was vibrating! That was a more profound experience of myoclonic shaking. If your client is working through a traumatic event that has significant emotional intensity to it, and their body starts to quake - *let it*.

Make it safe for the client to allow this natural process to happen. They're healing. Encourage the client to just let the body do what it is doing. Give the suggestion, "The body knows how to heal." Give the body permission to release the energy trapped in the event. When this natural process completes of discharging the trauma of the event completes, the client will notice a profound internal shift.

Abuse

Grownups may find it easy to blame others, but what about children? What happens when a child gets hurt? What happens if the child gets hurt by a parent? What about sexual abuse?

A Child is dependent upon its parents for two things: love and protection. When a parent hurts the Child, there's going to be fear *and* anger. The problem is that there's nowhere for the feelings to go. Especially the anger. When anger gets trapped inside, it takes the form of self-abuse which can find expression in any number of ways including negative self-talk, self-sabotaging behaviors, bullying, trash-talking, wallowing in self-pity, righteousness, contempt, and more.

The Child can't blame the parent because the Child is dependent. That would put them at risk for abandonment or punishment. This just increases fear.

A Child needs to be able to make sense of its environment. The Child will often reason, "I must have done something wrong." This turns the anger inside. Taking the blame means the Child doesn't have to lose the love. But when anger gets turned inside, it takes the form of self-loathing.

Self-blame serves a positive purpose. It's basic survival. Safety and security. Survival may be the subconscious mind's Prime Directive, but it comes at a cost. When there's no one there to support the Child, the Child gets stuck in feeling scared, alone, and angry. The Child needs to have a sense of control in life. Without it they will experience ongoing, unresolvable anxiety.

A way for the Child to get a sense of control is to decide, "If I can change myself this won't have to happen again." The Child can then conclude that, to avoid getting hurt, "I have to take care of myself." Or "The only person I can rely on is myself."

Remember, it's not what happened that's causing the Pain. It's the *meaning* the Child gave to what happened that is the source of the pain. Children are making decisions all the time. They're making decisions about themselves, others, how relationships work, how the world works, what they can expect in life, and what they deserve. These decisions form a person's world view. It becomes their point of view on life. This forms their expectations of what life is going to give them.

If you are dealing with abusive behavior, there are likely going to be multiple events contributing to the client's presenting issue. Parent's behavior tends not to be a one-time event, and abusive behavior can easily be accepted as normal by the Child. There are usually multiple events calling for resolution. That means compounding.

Compounding is a process of building and reinforcing the underlying perceptions, thoughts and feelings involved in those events, making them stronger. It also reinforces the neural pathways that are still under development early in life. As a result, the younger the Child is the deeper those impressions are going to be. Uncovering decisions regarding identity will be particularly important.

If what happened was not perceived by the Child as loving, the experience will be interpreted as abandonment. Abandonment is a biological threat to survival because every child knows that it cannot survive on its own. This will generate fear.

This fear is rational and logical. It's reasonable to feel fear in the face of a life-threatening threat. If the Child concludes, "I'm going to die!" there's going to be intense fear rippling through the nervous system of the body.

Dissociation is Nature's way of protecting the body from experiencing pain. When there's no way out, the Child will check out of the body. It's Nature's Way of protecting. Just like the bunny who can't escape from the clutches of the hawk. There's no way out. It can't run. It can't fight. The nervous system then goes into a Freeze Response which causes the body to go numb. This ensures that the bunny won't have to experience the pain of being eaten. Like that bunny, the Child can't run away. It can't fight. There's no way out except to checkout of the body.

During the uncovering process, watch for dissociation. If the client reports viewing the scene from a distance, or their point of view on what's happening is as a witness, this could be where the client is stuck. They could be stuck in the Freeze Response because numbing out can become a habitual coping strategy. It's a conditioned response to a specific traumatic experience that, over time, becomes a way of being in the world.

Add a few pharmaceuticals to the mix and you can end up with an emotionally flat individual.

Complexity

Working with sexual abuse can be tricky. Multiple episodes of abuse add both complexity and emotional intensity because the feelings stacked up inside have been compounded through repetitive events. There can be more than one ISE.

Remember, the ISE, or Initial Sensitizing Event, is considered the "the seed planting" or the "causal" event. This is the first event or experience responsible for generating the client's presenting issue. This is where things can get confusing. Some people mistakenly think that there is just one causal event. But the ISE is just the causal event for one "thing". The question is, the first time for what?

What if the first sexual encounter felt good to the Child. What if the Child interpreted that experience as "good"? It's not what happened that is the problem. It's not the adult interpretation of the event that's the problem. It's how the Child interpreted the event, *at that time*, and whatever decisions were being made.

Remember, all the Child wanted was love. If what was happening was perceived as a way to get attention, it might have been experienced as loving, in which case it would be interpreted as good.

What if what was happening was confusing for the Child? Even when the event was perceived as loving, to get attention from a loved one, there is always an element of secrecy attached to these situations. This can generate confusion.

Confusion is often a signature of an ISE. This is especially true in infancy because confusion is usually an infant's first response. The younger the Child is, the more you need to watch for confusion because there's less personal history with which to compare and evaluate new experiences.

Guilt and Shame

Confusion is an inability to make sense of what's happening. It's not about what's right or wrong. Young children get their sense of right and wrong from their parents by borrowing their parents' Critical

Faculty. It's the things that are said and done that establish the rules for good/bad, right/wrong. What can happen is that there's confusion at the ISE, but there's nothing "wrong" with what happened. Then, the Child goes to school and gets introduced to social morality. This can form a second ISE.

The first ISE is rooted in confusion. The second ISE involves the shock of social disapproval. When the Child realizes that what seemed loving and good was actually wrong that's when guilt gets installed.

The first ISE is about not being able to make sense of what's happening. There may be some fear attached to it because not being able to figure out what's happening will naturally generate a biological conflict. We need to be able to make sense of our environment to survive. But the second ISE will have some juice in it because it involves guilt and shame.

The perception of love includes love-ability, i.e., how loveable I am. The second ISE shatters self-worth and can have a retroactive effect by rippling back into the first ISE. It then contaminates the event of confusion with guilt and fear. The guilt and shame are not based in the *Child's* interpretation of the initial experience, they are based on the opinions of others. This can seed a lifelong pattern. If you get a client who has a strong concern about the opinions of others, needing to please others, this fear can be rooted in guilt and shame.

Guilt and shame are two sides of the same coin. Guilt says, "I must have *done* something wrong." Shame says, "I *am* wrong. I'm intrinsically flawed, defective, broken and irreparable." Guilt is about doing. It's about behavior. Shame is about being. It's about identity. You need to address both to get a complete healing.

You need to deal with both sides of the coin. Pulling the pin on the self-blame may require addressing multiple events and there can be complexity. That can take time. But resolving those events will allow the client to heal. And it can transform their life in unexpected ways. Just know that the client's story will tell you everything you need to know to find the path to healing for that individual.

When is a factor. Parents (or primary caregivers) have the greatest influence on a Child's development. These are the people the Child has the most contact with during the formative years. What happens in the first five years of life will decide how life will be viewed and experienced.

The problem isn't what happened. What's causing the adult client pain is how the Child *interpreted* things *at that time*. It's the decisions the Child made as a result of those things. What you're dealing with is basically a betrayal. Betrayal is about anger and a loss of trust. But it's also about Love. It's just that being vulnerable is what got the client hurt in the first place. And now the pain of fear, anger, guilt, and shame are all mixed up with the love.

The Child needed to be loved to survive. Clients who have a history of childhood abuse – emotional, mental, physical, sexual – are often conflicted because they needed the person who hurt them to survive. This can result in relationship conflicts in adult life. If you release the anger that's trapped in the event, you'll find the love. There's always love under the anger. Find the love and you'll find the forgiveness. Find the forgiveness and you'll find the healing.

Abuse isn't always bad. What qualifies as abuse to the adult mind is not always perceived as "bad" by the Child. It could have been satisfying an important need. For example, closeness or attention.

An ISE in early Childhood involves confusion. Confusion is usually a good indication of a new perception. Because the Critical Faculty has not yet formed, there was no sense of "right" or "wrong" attached to it. Avoid the temptation to impose your grown-up judgments onto the event. Your job is to stay neutral and support the client as you uncover the perceptions and decisions of the Child. Remember, young children cannot think critically. They get their sense of "right" and "wrong" from their parents.

The *first time* may not have been traumatic. It was just the first encounter of this kind. It may not have been until later, when the Child was confronted with social morality, that the client experienced the signature shock of the ISE. The second ISE is the whammy because it involves the opinions of others. That's shame which then acts retroactively, rippling guilt and shame back into the first event[63]. This then contaminates the original perceptions of goodness, love, and love-ability. *This* is what shatters self-worth and trust.

Abandonment is a biological threat to survival. If what happened was *not* perceived as loving, if it was painful or involved threat, the Child would interpret that as abandonment. Abandonment is a biological threat to survival which generates fear because a child is incapable of surviving on its own.

Taking the blame allowed the Child to keep the love. Self-blame can provide the Child with a much-needed sense of safety and security. But when a Child decides that *they* need to change to avoid being hurt again, it seeds the belief, "There's something wrong with me." This is shame. Shame gives fear a reason.

---

[63] Remember, memory is not static. Every time an event is reviewed, it changes.

Shame says, "I'm bad, flawed, and broken. I'm worth-less and cannot be repaired. In fact, I shouldn't even exist." This reason for fear is a lie because there is nothing wrong with the Child. There is nothing the Child could ever do to deserve such ill-treatment. The Parent is responsible for ensuring the well-being of the Child. The Child needs to know this.

When there's no way out for the Child, there's intense fear. Terror and panic lead to dissociation. If the Child cannot run or fight, or if the Child thinks, "I'm going to die!" there's a freeze response. The body goes numb.

While hypnotherapists don't work with psychiatric conditions or diagnoses, it doesn't hurt to have a basic understanding of what dissociation can look like when it shows up in your office.

Dissociation

French neuropsychiatrist Pierre Janet (1859 - 1947) believed that intense emotional experiences (i.e., trauma) can cause the memories associated with them to be dissociated[64] from consciousness and stored in the body as physical sensations or as visual memories such as nightmares or flashbacks.

Dissociation is defined as "the disconnection or separation of something from something else or the state of being disconnected." This is nature's way of protecting the body from experiencing the pain of being eaten by a predator. But repeated disconnection from the Child's Core State of Being (safe, loved) can condition a person for dissociative disorders.

---

[64] When the mind perceives that what is happening is too much for us to handle, it has the ability to protect us by 'hiding' all or parts of the event from conscious recall.

Common Dissociative Disorders include:[65]

Dissociative amnesia: memory loss; the inability to recall traumatic periods, events, or people in life, especially from childhood.

Dissociative identity disorder (DID): formerly known as multiple personality disorder (MPD); characterized by "switching" to alternate identities (a.k.a. "alters") when under stress. Alters can also be experienced as internal voices or personalities[66].

Dissociative fugue: (a.k.a. psychogenic fugue) is a rare psychiatric disorder characterized by amnesia for personal identity. The state typically lasts from a few hours to a few days but can last months or longer. Fugue states can also be brought on by psychotropic substances, physical trauma, dementia, bipolar disorder, or depression. This state is usually precipitated by a stressful episode.

Depersonalization disorder: This is where consciousness leaves the body; the sudden sense of being outside yourself, observing your actions from a distance as though watching a movie. Time seems to slow down, and perceptions are distorted. Symptoms may last only a few moments, or they may come and go over many years.

The Aftermath of Abuse

The aftermath of an event of abuse is emotional upheaval. There was no one there to support the Child or help the Child deal with the feelings of confusion and fear. Because the Child wasn't able to make sense of what was happening to her, the energy of the event didn't get

---

[65] Mayo Clinic
[66] John and Helen Watkins' study, Ego State Therapy, explores this condition and provides practical reading for hypnotherapists.

discharged. As a result, that energy has been trapped inside, ever since. This is what German New Medicine[67] calls a "hanging conflict"; an unresolved conflict that continues to generate unconscious internal stress.

Following a traumatic event, the Child does not know that the event is over. She doesn't know that there isn't more hurt on the way. This leaves the Child suspended in time. Because the subconscious mind doesn't know that the client isn't still a Child, the fears and misperceptions trapped in the event continue to generate pain.

Trauma sets a person up for symptoms later in life. All it takes is for the right set of circumstance to arise and it acts like a match. The kindling then bursts into flames and symptoms appear. Psychology calls it "priming." Like priming a pump, once the emotional content has built up enough internal pressure it will begin to gush out. Hypnotherapy calls this "Sensitizing."

During a traumatic event, the person becomes hyper-sensitive to specific things. Each Subsequent Sensitizing Event (SSE) that, in some way resembles the first time or Initial Sensitizing Event (ISE), acts as a reminder of the original event, re-stimulating the pattern of thoughts and emotions formed in the ISE.

When this happens, the energy disruption occurring in subsequent events flows back into the original trauma, adding strength to it. This reinforces the overall pattern, making it stronger. This is called "the compounding effect."

---

[67] Dr. Gerd Hamer, The German New Medicine

The more subsequent events there are in the person's life, the more the pattern is reinforced, and the sooner symptoms will come to the surface of consciousness. If there's a lot of compounding early in life, symptoms will appear sooner. For example, in childhood or teen years.

When the internal pressure gets strong enough, the person starts to experience emotional and physical distress. That's when they will show up in your office with some kind of emotional or physical distress. Physical symptoms associated with abuse include headaches, sleep problems, weight problems, miscarriages, digestive problems, addictions.

The goal of regression therapy is to locate the causal event so that you can release the energy that has been trapped inside the traumatic memory. Reframing the event will then allow learning to take place. That's when healing will happen.

In an event of child abuse there's always confusion. The younger the Child is, the more likely it is that their first response will be one of confusion. In fact, this can be a sign that you have landed in the ISE. This is because the Child lacks the ability to make sense of what's happening. And not being able to figure out what's happening in your environment registers as a biological threat to survival. This is an old-brain response which triggers fear.

The subconscious mind is programmed to response to any perceived threat by stepping in to protect. As a result, following an event of abuse, the subconscious mind starts ruminating. It keeps going over and over that experience trying to come up with a survival strategy. Because it only has the resources of the Child at the age the event occurred, this unconscious ruminating has a compounding effect which makes the fear worse.

If the abuser was a primary caregiver, there is also going to be guilt and shame. The Child is dependent on that person to meet important needs for nourishment, safety and security. Rather than blaming the parent for causing them pain, the Child will take the blame because blaming the parent would mean losing the love. Instead, the Child will internalize the blame and anger. This generates more fear. This means that there are going to be layers of fear, and anger, and confusion, and more fear, and more anger feeding into the underlying cause of the problem. This creates complexity.

The Child naturally wants to make sure that this experience never happens to them, again. It's not uncommon for a Child to decide, "I'm the problem." The decision that follows is, "I need to change myself so that this won't happen, again." This provides a much-needed sense of control for the Child. But this decision is not reasonable because the underlying decision is, "There's something wrong with me." This is a false belief based on misperception. There is nothing wrong with the Child. The Child is innocent. The Child's worth is independent of the things that happened to it.

Decisions made in childhood can (and do) wreak havoc in a person's adult life. Reframing the ISE will change the perceptions underlying the problem to allow relief from symptoms. This is the essential function of Inner Child Work.

When a client regresses into an event of childhood abuse, recognize that they are in an extremely vulnerable state. They are showing you their tender, emotional underbelly. They are trusting you with their deepest, darkest, most shameful truths by exposing a wounded Child that they've been keeping hidden within themselves. Often, this is something they have never shared with another living soul.

Sometimes, it is something they haven't faced themselves; they've been avoiding it. It is vitally important that you listen. Make it safe for the client to tell their story because that's what the Child most needed. That Child is still alive.

Show the client that you're not going to judge them. Show them that they can tell you this stuff and it's not going to freak you out. You're not shocked by it. You've seen it all (even if you haven't) because this helps to show the client that there's nothing wrong with them.

Keep your tone matter of fact, like it's no big deal. Often, I'll say to the client, "Well, now we know what we're dealing with. Realize this is where your healing lies. You're not the first person to go down that path. Sadly, you probably won't be the last. But I want you to know that this is where your miracle lies. You realize that don't you."

I want to educate and empower the Adult Part of the client before I start working with the Child Part because I need a Grownup who can be present and loving toward the Inner Child. Grownup needs to do the reprogramming because anything the client might say to themselves has far more power than anything I might say. The Adult Part is going to take on the role of a loving parent for the Child that they once were and provide whatever that Child needed. That way, the Child can grow up feeling good about him or herself.

It doesn't matter what happened. It doesn't matter that someone they trusted hurt them. It doesn't matter that there was no one there to step in and protect. They might have wanted those things to happen, but they didn't. The only thing that matters is what's going to happen *next*. Bring the Adult Part of the client in to prepare the Child for what's going to happen.

Teach the client how to be a loving support to their Inner Child. Identify what the Child needed at that time. Then, help the client to decide what needs to happen *next*.

What needs to happen next will really depend on what is revealed through the uncovering process. But The Devil's Therapy gives you a simple, four step protocol you can follow.

1. Find it.

This step is the discovery process. You need to do the uncovering work to find out what you're dealing with. What is the actual problem?

The most important information is what was missing for the Child. Once you identify what was missing, you can find a way to provide it. What core needs were not met? What understanding or resources did the Child lack? What was most wanted or needed? Who wasn't there to support the Child?

Remember, we're not there to change what happened. We're not there to reconstruct history. The goal is to change how it feels. That's where the healing lies.

2. Feel it.

Releasing the feelings that got trapped inside the event sets the client free of the pain story. That story got started long before the client was old enough to know how to with feelings and emotions including:

- Confusion
- Fear
- Isolation
- Anger toward the Perpetrator

- Love toward the Perpetrator (if not a stranger)
- Anger toward self (blame turned inward becomes guilt and shame)

3. Heal it

Healing happens every time you celebrate a release. Validating every improvement, every insight, every shift for the better creates space for healing to occur. Parkhill called this, "creating a void" into which you can install new believes, understandings and learnings. Validate change! Celebrate insights. Recognize better feelings. Reclaim freedom of choice. Build new resource states out of old grievances.

Guilt is not a feeling. It's a thought based on misperception that becomes a belief over time. Guilt says, "I have done something wrong." This is a thought that always generates fear. The client needs to understand that there's nothing wrong with the Child. The Child is innocent. The person who hurt them had the problem.

The Child was not the problem. They didn't deserve to be treated badly. The person who hurt them had the problem. And the client doesn't have to suffer for the rest of their life because of the things that were done to them. This is the understanding that allows change to happen.

Even if the Child did something "wrong," it's because they didn't know any better. But the Child did nothing to invite or deserve getting hurt. The person who hurt them was a Grownup. *They* had the problem. Not the Child.

Shame is another misperception. It's not a feeling. It's a thought that says, "There's something wrong with me." This thought also generates fear because if you can't fix it, you're stuck. There is nothing intrinsically wrong with the Child. The Child is innocent. The Child didn't deserve to get hurt. But it happened.

If your client has a spiritual view on life, you have a greater Source of Love that you can call upon. Love heals. Even without a spiritual belief, most clients are open to a higher perspective. Just frame your suggestions to fit with the client's belief system. For example, whatever happened cannot change who and what the Child is at her core. This means that she is, and she remains, as she was created - whole and complete, and completely love-able. This restores the client's sense of security.

The Creator/Universe/Life doesn't make mistakes. Everything works. (Just not always the way we think.) Science is still discovering deeper and deeper layers of the mystery of Creation/Universe/Life. We just haven't got it all figured out yet. Fortunately, we don't *have* to. Because everything works, the Child/Client could never be "broken." This is a valuable concept to reinforce because "broken" translates to "unforgiveable." But being vulnerable isn't a crime.

Even if the Child did do something "wrong", it was just a mistake. Human beings make mistakes. That's how we learn. Mistakes are forgivable. The problem is that a Child can make decisions and form opinions about how life works without the benefit of adult consciousness. This means that mistakes are bound to be made.

What the uncovering procedure will reveal is that the client made some decisions as a Child. These decisions were based on the knowledge they had at that time. They might have been appropriate to the Child, at that time. But are they appropriate to the client's adult life?

Healing is a self-empowerment process. With awareness the client is empowered to choose differently. They can allow those past experiences to become a source of strength and wisdom for them in adult life. In other words, a source of empowerment. But they must choose. The choice is to continue either to hold on to the pain of the past, or to let go of the old pattern and make a newer, better decision for themselves.

This is what it means to forgive. Forgiveness is the healing.

4. Seal it.

To "seal" is to make adamant. To make all changes permanent the Adult consciousness of the client needs to connect the dots between the ISE, SSEs and the problem they have been struggling with. That's why they're seeing you, right? For example, how might this event/experience relate to the client's presenting issue? How might aspects of this event have been impacting them in daily life? How might those events in the past contribute to creating the problem?

When the client starts experiencing insight into the cause of the problem, and how those past experiences have been creating symptoms, they start to delete all the connections. This effectively neutralizes the problem. You can then start to generalize change throughout their entire life.

Brain research shows that traumatic memory is healed when all the aspects of a traumatic event are linked together and then moved from present memory to past memory. This is because trauma shuts down the hippocampus.

The hippocampus is the part of the brain responsible for moving present experiences into past memory. When the hippocampus doesn't complete this function, the memory stays stuck as a present event. That's the basic problem: the client is still stuck in the event because their subconscious doesn't realize it's over and that they survived. Connecting all the dots allows the subconscious mind to realize that the event is over. It's in the past, now.

Help the client to connect all the dots. Then, weave them a new story based upon meaning that empowers the client in some way. Turn it into a new story where the client is the hero, where they have overcome a challenge and, as a result, have become something "more". Then, generalize all the changes by sending send them both forward and backward in time along their timeline. (I like to send those changes "throughout all dimensions of time and space".)

Stephen Parkhill offered a beautiful suggestion in a lilting tone, "Washed and rinsed and cleansed and healed." Isn't that lovely?

Guilt and shame leave a person feeling dirty. When you wash them clean, they have a new sense of self. So, really fill them up with all the good stuff. As you bathe the client in all the positive energies of change, you'll witness transformation occurring.

Bring it all home by growing the Child up through the SSEs. Then, allow the client to embody those changes by sending the newer, better feelings through the nervous system of the body.

If you have time, send it forward into future situations – either anticipated or unexpected – and test the results.

If the client is feeling fine, reinforce the realization that change has really occurred. For example, "You've changed! You're not the same person anymore! You've put the past behind you. The past is just the past. Now you know …"

Reinforce the theme of "renewal" and give the client a new story.

If the client bumps into something while future pacing, it just means that there's still work to be done. You're not done yet. That's okay. Healing is a process. Some people just need more time to clear up all the contributing aspects.

Remember, the client doesn't have to do it all at once, and neither do you! Just work at whatever pace is right for the client. If there's still work to be done, you will have discovered the next step in the client's healing journey.

The aftermath of abuse is a person's entire life. It's not isolated to just one area of their life. They embody the trauma. It forms as part of their identity. It decides what they deserve in life. It can take a while to undo all the contributing factors. It can take time for the client to realize just how much those events have impacted them in their life. But once they realize that it's over, it's over.

Before wrapping up a session, I elicit a Statement of Commitment by having the client state out loud their agreement to *keep* this level of change. For example, "I have changed! I choose to keep this level of change."

To polish things off, offer a few suggestions to encourage positive expectancy. For example, looking forward to even greater levels of healing, and enjoying even more profound shifts in daily life, etc.

Commitment to Change

- "I keep this change."
- "I am (put an ending on it)"
- "I can (put an ending on it)"
- "I will (put an ending on it)"
- "I choose (put an ending on it)"
- "I keep this change because (put an ending on it)"

When change occurs, and you seal it in, you have made a profound change in that person's life in ways you may not realize. This is because changing one thing can have "domino effect" in the client's life. Other areas of their life will begin to heal, even though you never address them.

There is nothing more rewarding than transforming a person's life for the better. But you may never know just how much you helped your client because the ripple effect continues for many years to come.

Birth Trauma

Birth holds a lot of "firsts" that can influence a person for life. A great deal of learning takes place during the birth experience. Fears and misperceptions formed at this time can have a lasting effect if left unresolved.

The thing to keep in mind is that it's just a story. Like every story, it has a beginning, middle, and an end. It's just that it hasn't reached "the end", yet. You can change that. When a client lands in the birthing event, stay right there. Clearing this important life event can have a lasting, positive influence on the client's life. This can include areas of their life that may not be directly related to the presenting problem.

Segmenting

When the birthing experience is traumatic, segmenting the event into three parts – beginning, middle, ending - will make it much easier for you to manage the many aspects that can arise during the birthing experience. This will also help you to be more thorough when it comes to resolving the various perceptions, thoughts and feelings that got trapped in the event.

The Beginning

The birthing experience begins when the contractions start to come on. Before this, the Child is floating around inside Mom, then something changes. It's often subtle to begin with but, when the contractions get stronger, they can be frightening to the child. What's happening as the contractions come on?

Common perceptions to watch for when the contractions come on include feeling pushed, the thought, "Don't want to go", fear of the unknown, sense of "no way out", helplessness, hopelessness, trapped, alone. Provide support. Make it safe for the Child to proceed.

The Middle

The middle is when the child begins moving through the birth canal. The sensation of being pushed forward can be frightening, however. And there is a moment during that passage where the child is unable to breathe (asphyxia). Usually this doesn't last very long but when it is prolonged it can result in claustrophobia later in life. What's happening as the Child moves through the birth canal?

Common perceptions to watch for as movement through the birth canal occurs involve fear and rage. The most common perception is an inability to breathe. This usually doesn't last long but when it does, rage emerges. You may have to poke around a little to find it, however, because anger is frightening to infants and young children.

If birth is delayed, this may set a pattern of inability to "get through" anything. Watch for feelings of being trapped or frustrated.

Provide support. Make it safe. Prove that the Child will make it through this ordeal by fast forwarding to just *after* the sensations of not being able to breathe pass. This shows the Child that they can get through challenging experiences. Celebrate success! For example, "You made it! A moment ago, you were feeling (pressure), but now you're okay! You made it through! Good job!" Remember, forgiveness is the antidote for anger.

Common birthing complications include Breech birth, Caesarian Section, Mom being drugged, and premature birth. With Breech birth, forceps are frightening and are often associated with torture. This will generate intense fear/terror.

Caesarian birth is perceived as violence, an act of aggression. Nightmares in childhood can often reflect this terror as the subconscious mind attempts to find a resolution.

Use a dissociative technique for the uncovering procedure. Restore peace and clarity by reminding the client that this is just a memory and that she didn't die. Then, bring the Child back into the event *before* anything bad happens and support Grownup in preparing the Child to move through the experience knowing that s/he will make it through. This will allow you to uncover any unresolve aspects and release them.

Premature birth is always a crisis involving abandonment, isolation, and fear of dying. This can be the root-cause of eating disorders and a lifelong struggle with obesity. Premature birth can be complicated by other factors such as Mom being in distress, medical emergency, and drugs.

Chunk down. The biggest problem is one of overwhelm. Slow things down to uncover the individual aspects. Titrating will allow you to clear one thing at a time before moving onto the next aspect. This helps to restore balance to the body-mind system.

When Mom is drugged, the baby is drugged. This can result in a client who is incoherent or unable to describe what's happening. This is not resistance. They are revivifying the actual experience of the effects of the drug. Realize that the loss of control is terrifying to the Child.

You can move *after* the drugs wear off to clear things in hindsight. Or you can clear the symptoms of not being able to think, feel, or communicate clearly.

If what the Client is experiencing seems to be too much for them, move the client *forward* to a point after the distressing experience is over. Let the Child experience what it's like to know that s/he made it through. The realization you need to instill is that *it's over*. It's just a memory.

Then, gather up all the insights, and better feelings, and bring the client back *before* the scene plays out. This allows the client to come back into the event with some clarity and understanding. Go through the process again to clear any residual aspects.

Alternatively, you can Bridge back to an earlier time.

The End

Birth is both an ending and a beginning. This moment of separation from Mom is inherently traumatic for a Child because the Child doesn't have anything to compare it to. But birth is also the beginning of life. It is the moment of emergence into the world.

What happens at this moment of emergence sets a pattern for handling stressors later in life. (In Astrology, the birth chart is based on this moment of imprinting on the physical world.) What's happening during the Child's emergence into the world?

Your objective should be to shift the Child's perception from that of separation (pain), to one of celebrating emergence into the world, and of becoming one's own person.

The Most Important Factors

Birth is the ISE for a lot of things and often involves confusion. Remember, confusion is the inability to make sense of what's happening and is often the first disruption in the Initial Sensitizing Event. Fear follows confusion because not being able to make sense of your environment is a threat to survival. The most important factors are:

1. Where is Mom?
2. Does bonding occur?
3. Does Mom express love for the Child?

The most important person in the Child's life is Mom. Separation from Mom is confusing and scary for the Child. Where is Mom?

Does bonding occur? If there are problems immediately following birth, it will delay the bonding process. This will put the Child in distress. If Mom is in danger, the child will experience separation anxiety. Disrupted bonding can seed a host of emotional problems that can surface later in life.

Does nursing take place? How soon? Love, nourishment, and bonding provide a sense of safety and security for the Child. Is there eye contact? Stroking? Words of endearment. Physical touch paired with loving words are programming the Child with safety and security.

Does Mom express love for the Child? How is the Child received into the world? Lovingly in celebration? Or with medical disinterest? Love equals survival for the Child. If Mom is ambivalent or rejecting the Child, find out what decisions are being made by the Child.

What is being said? And to whom? These are suggestions that are being accepted by the Child without the benefit of critical thought.

The sex of the child can be a big issue in many cultures! How is the sex of the Child being responded to? With celebration? Disappointment? Something else?

Dad is important to the Child. The Child needs to know that s/he is important to Dad. Where is DAD? What are Dad's feelings toward the Child? It can be reassuring to the Child to know that Dad is nearby or on his way.

Remember, it's never too late to have a happy Childhood. Uncover what was missing for the Child, then find a way to provide it. Provide a bonding experience with Mom that includes eye contact, physical stroking, and words of endearment. For example, "I love you, I accept you, I'm so glad you were born, you matter to me," etc.

Test for Dust-bunnies

Once you have cleared the event, run it again. Test for any residual "dust-bunnies!" Then, when the client's Inner Child is a bubbling happy wee-one, gather up those good, positive, happy feelings of being loved, and accepted, and wanted, and valued and send them ahead so that they flow into and through all events growing up. This will act to neutralize many subsequent events, allowing the Child to have these energies available growing up, (which just makes your job easier.)

Polishing Technique

The following script is adapted from Circle of Stones by Judith Duerk. It is suitable for use after clearing up a traumatic birth experience, or as an imagery exercise to give a client the experience of what they wanted or needed coming into this life.

******

How Might Your Life Be Different?

How might your life have been different … if you had been born into loving hands? … if there were conscious, caring people present to welcome you into the world? … And prepare you … and accept you … and love you … as they themselves had been loved and accepted and welcomed at *their* birth …?

How might your life have been different … if you had easily moved from inside Mom … and gently LET GO your connection to the womb ... to become more fully yourself ... as you embraced ... enthusiastically ... your first vital breath ... as you entered into a world of light and sound and sensation and smell and taste?

And what would it be like to then be lifted ... oh-so-gently ... lovingly ... onto your mother's belly, still connected ... umbilical cord still intact .... and simply rest ... warm, comfortable ... just breathing it all in ... just breathing ... easily and effortlessly .... with a sense a being and knowing?

And as your breath grew strong ... *so connected now* ... to your *own* life ... that as the umbilical cord was severed ... you were lifted into eagerly awaiting arms ... to at-long-last gaze into the eyes of love ... appreciation ... welcome?

How might your life be different?

How might your life be different if ... the first time, as a tiny child, feeling feelings of anger coming together inside yourself ... someone, a parent or grandparent or older sister or brother said, "Bravo! Yes, that's it! You're feeling it!" ... and then hugged you ....

And what if, in that anger, you were affirmed by someone able to see that ... you were taking your first tiny baby steps toward feeling your own feelings, of knowing that ... you are you ... You are your own person ... so it's RIGHT that you see life a little differently from those around you?

And what if you were helped to experience your own uniqueness ... to feel the excitement of sensing for the very first time ... your own awareness of life ... having someone to help you own all of this ... to own your own life? All of it. Just as it is ....

How might your life be different?

And as a young (woman), the first time you felt feelings of depression, a Grownup came to BE with you ... someone who knew you better than anyone .... to simply sit, quietly, perhaps wordlessly ... to BE with *you* ... Simply accepting your feelings ... accepting them *so completely* and fully that ... you realize it's okay to feel your feelings? You could feel safe with them ... knowing there was no need to judge or question, no need to attempt a smile, or deny your feelings, but simply to BE ... in that silent acceptance ... of you ... And have a glimmer of faith that ... there is meaning and truth, even in darkness ...

How might that have changed things?

If deep within ... ever since you were a little girl ... you carried an image of an old nursemaid, a simple, large woman ... who was comfortable with herself? ... A woman in a rocking chair, perhaps, who nurtured you in a gentle way ... who provided an ample lap to crawl into ... warm, full arms to hold you ... and who rocked you ... back and forth ... back and forth ... saying, "There, there, now.... There, there... Oh, all those tears, yes. You feel so bad........Oh. Oh. Oh ... All those tears ......You just cry it out. Cry it all out. We'll just sit here and rock while you cry it all out. That's it. That's it. There. There. There. Let's put this sweater 'round you. There. There."

A voice to hum, to croon, while you cried it all out ... and were comforted. A voice that said, "It's going to be all right. You just have a good cry. And soon, you'll be right as rain. That's right. It IS going to be all right. We'll just sit here and rock until you feel better. You just cry it all out till it is better." And rocking, stroking, "There, there, now. There, there."

How might your life be different?

How might your life be different if, long ago, when you were still a tiny child, long before you began to come to this Healing Place, this Place of Feeling and Healing, there had been a place for you, a place where you could be loved and accepted, just as you are ... where you could find order to your moments and your days ....?

A place where you could learn a quiet centeredness ... to help you ground yourself in daily patterns ... and gentle rhythms that would nurture you? A place where, at the ending of a task ... you could know stillness ... and feel your connection to a deeper ... more ancient ... loving presence within... and flowing out ... to sustain you ... And you learned how to receive ... and sustain it in return?

How might your life be different?

And in that place, in those safe surroundings, you could feel the truth of your feelings ... the dread and panic you sometimes felt in your life ... and there was someone to listen to you? ... Another (woman) to listen quietly, intently, as you experienced those fears, as you experienced your own shame and abandonment .... And <u>let it go</u>.

If there had been stillness in that moment ... and you felt that (she) really WAS there, present to your suffering ... that (she) was there, so present to your pain and woundedness that ... (she) helped you ... to embrace *all* your feelings ... even the bad ones ... even your own anguish ... and give it a place to rest ...

How might your life be different?

How might your life have been different if there had been a place for you ... A place where ... there was a deep understanding of the ways to nurture yourself … in every season of your life… A place of feeling and healing … to help you grow into your own true nature … and help you prepare … and know when … YOU ARE READY.

A place where you would finally claim your NAME. And as you spoke it, hearing the sound of it, it brought you full circle into the timeless perfection of your True Self.

How might your life be different?

I invite you to *speak your name now* and notice how that feels. (wait)

Say it again, realizing that you are reclaiming yourself and reconnecting with your own True Nature and worth. (wait)

Always remember that you are you … You are a worthy soul on an important journey. It has always been so. (pause)

Optional: Autosuggestions

Now, repeat after me and put an ending on it.

(*Repeat each statement three times, putting a different ending on each one.*)

- I AM ….
- I CAN …
- I WILL …
- I CHOOSE …
- I HAVE …
- I LOVE …
- I CREATE …
- I ENJOY …
- I FEEL …

CHAPTER 17:
Why Diets Don't Work

If you've ever been on a diet it's probably not the first time. Dieting is hard. Dieting takes willpower. You have to consciously remember to stay with it. Dieting makes you feel tired and cranky and leaves you feeling deprived. When you're on a diet all you can think about is food. Is it any wonder that your motivation gives out? Before you know it, you've gain all the weight back – and then some. Now you're worse off than when you began! This can be a real source of frustration for a lot of people. And feeling frustrated only makes things worse.

You already know this. Diets don't work. Dieting only works as long as you stay on your diet. Eventually, everybody falls off the wagon. Dieting isn't sustainable over the long-term. 50% of Americans adults are dieting. 80% are trying to do it on their own. And somewhere between 90 and 95% percent of all dieters will regain the weight they lost within five years.

Think about that. 95 percent of all diets fail. If your cell phone company had a 5% success rate putting through calls through, would you continue to renew your contract with them?

Why is it that the typical dieter makes four attempts to diet every year? That's the definition of insanity - doing the same thing over and over again expecting a different result. Stop the insanity! The problem is not *losing* the weight; it's keeping the weight *off*.

Most people will initially have some success with a diet. This is because motivation is usually quite high at the beginning of a program. This is why a lot of weight loss programs have a Quick-Start program. It's to take advantage of the higher level of motivation that's there to begin with. The problem is that, after a while, dieting gets old. Old behaviors start to slip back in. Before long, you're right back where you started – only worse because you've added a few extra pounds.

Usually, it's because something will happen to sabotage your success. Temptation will rear it's ugly head. You'll be at a party or a restaurant and you'll forget about your weight goal. You'll promise yourself it's just this once. You deserve it. It's only one. Tomorrow you'll go right back on your program. And tomorrow never comes.

Worse, you'll go totally unconscious and go on a binge. You'll eat everything in sight. Then hate yourself for it in the morning.

It's not your fault. It's just how the subconscious mind works. The subconscious mind drives behavior. And it's primary concern is with keeping you safe. As a result, it will do anything to keep things safely in the Status Quo Zone because that's what's normal. That's who you are. That's how you learned to cope. If the status quo happens to be eating a quart of Hagan Daz every night, your subconscious is going to do it's best to ensure that you keep up that behavior. This makes it difficult to create change.

Depressing, I know.

Consciously you want to do the right thing. You want to make healthy choices on an ongoing basis. And you know what you need to do to sustain a healthy weight. *You just can't do it.* This is because of the pain-pleasure principle. Human beings are hardwired to seek pleasure and avoid pain. Food is pleasurable. Food can numb pain. Changing your diet won't change this most basic of human drives which is to feel good - and avoid feeling bad. This is the territory of your subconscious mind.

The subconscious mind is the emotional mind. It's the part of you that holds onto feelings, and memories, and beliefs that shaped your identity and your expectations about life. That's what drives behavior. So, when you try to use conscious willpower to try to override *all that*, you're destined to join the 95% of dieters who are doomed to fail. So what do you do?

First, realize that your subconscious mind is never the enemy. It's there to help you satisfy your most important needs. It wants you to be happy. And it always has a very good reason for doing what it's doing. If your subconscious mind is driving you to overeat, then that behavior is meant to be helpful. It's either helping you to soothe upset feelings. Or it's giving you a way to self-medicate the pain. Or it's protecting you by holding onto the weight.

Your subconscious mind is not trying to make you miserable. It actually wants you to be happy. And it's doing it's best to help you satisfy important needs – based on your history. If you're feeling down in the dumps, your subconscious mind is always going to be your best friend and come up with ways to help you feel better. It will find a way to help you soothe upset feelings, or get some relief from physical or emotional pain. And what better way than food?

Food is easily accessible. It's safe. We've been enjoying food since the day we were born. Every happy occasion in our lives is celebrated with food – Christmas, Easter, Birthdays . . . If you're feeling down, what better way to bring more joy and pleasure into your life than food?

Your subconscious mind will even try to protect you by holding onto the weight. That's it's Prime Directive – to protect you from harm. The truth is that if you've tried and failed at losing weight more than once, it's probably because there's an underlying need for the behavior that caused you to gain weight in the first place.

If you've lost weight before, you know what you need to do to lose weight. That's not the problem. The problem is that the conscious mind just doesn't have the power needed to override a subconscious directive. And weight is seldom just a problem of behavior. That's why diets don't work.

Diets don't work because you can't diet your way out of an emotional need. You can't out-exercise your ability to over-eat, either. But most people don't know this. This simple fact keeps them buying diet books and magazines, and exercise equipment, all in the hope that somehow, they'll find the key that will finally set them free. All this does is *add* to the weight of the problem because much of the information conflicts. The "facts" keep changing. Low calorie or low carb? High fiber or high fat? Vegan or Caveman?

All this adds confusion which increases internal stress. And *stress* makes the body hold onto the weight. Then there are all the false beliefs about what causes a person to be overweight. They think they've been cursed with bad genes. They think that they're "big boned." They think they have willpower deficiency. Most of the time, none of these things are true. Only 5% of all health conditions are truly genetic.

If you weren't born obese, your genes are probably not out to get you. There's no such thing as "big bones." Bones are bone sized. And if you have *ever* been successful in taking the weight off, you have all the willpower you need to succeed. It's just that willpower isn't enough to over-ride the subconscious need to feed. So what's the solution?

The solution is to gain access to the subconscious mind and change the internal drive. How do we do that? Hypnosis. Hypnosis gives us access to the subconscious level of mind. And it can make it a lot easier for you to create the kind of change you want. For example, it can help to increase your motivation which will make it easier for you to stick to your program. Or help you to change unwanted habits by locating and resolving the underlying emotional drivers. When you pull the plug on the underlying pattern, then there's nothing there to drive unwanted behavior.

All hypnosis is not equal. There are different approaches to creating change with hypnosis. The approach *you* need will depend on the nature of the problem. It's different strokes for different folks. The two most common approaches are (1) relaxation hypnosis, (2) regression hypnosis.

Relaxation hypnosis is where a hypnosis practitioner guides you into a relaxed state. They then deliver suggestions to encourage the kind of changes you want. This can be very effective when you're dealing with a simple behavior problem.

If the weight problem is simply the result of having learned some bad habits, relaxation hypnosis can be highly effective because anything that has been learned can be un-learned.

If you learned how to overeat, or eat the wrong things, or eat too quickly, you can change that. It's really just a process of re-learning what you always knew. For example, every child knows when she's had enough to eat to stop eating.

Research shows that children will binge on sweets when they're available but then they get tired of them. It's nature's way of keeping us healthy. If you've just fallen out of alignment with your genetic programming for healthy eating, hypnosis can make it easier for you to change those old behaviors and replace them with healthier choices to maintain a healthy body weight. Often, relaxation hypnosis is all that's needed to get you back on track. But sometimes a weight problem points to a deeper issue. That's when a deeper technique is needed.

When unwanted behaviors like overeating serve an underlying subconscious purpose, willpower won't work. And surface techniques like imagery and suggestion alone will fail to have a lasting effect. So, if you have already tried hypnosis, and the results didn't last, it's not that hypnosis doesn't work. It's that you probably need a deeper technique. This is where regression hypnotherapy can help.

If you're at a place where nothing else has worked, it's not your fault. If you've tried hypnosis and it didn't last, it's not that the hypnosis failed. It's often just a sign that there's a deeper issue calling for resolution. This means that you need a deeper approach to get to the underlying cause of the problem. You need to find out why your subconscious is doing what it's doing because, once you understand what's causing the problem, you can find a way to correct it.

Regression hypnosis allows you to get to the underlying *cause* of a problem and resolve the problem where it got started. Once you understand how the problem got started, and what purpose the excess weight serves, you can change it. That will put you back in control of your eating choices.

The important thing to realize is that it's not your fault. There's nothing wrong with you. It's just how the mind works. And diets don't work. Statistically diets fail 95% of the time. That doesn't mean that *you're* doomed to fail.

What the mind expects tends to be realized.
~ Gerald Kein

CHAPTER 18:
Conclusion

Little River Band wrote a song that says, "There are so many paths up the mountain. Nobody knows all the ways." Regression hypnotherapy is just one of many paths to healing. It's not THE path because no therapy is suitable for every client. But when the client has already tried everything else, or when surface techniques have failed to achieve a lasting result, or the client's issue clearly has roots in unresolved emotions from the past, you're probably dealing with a deeper issue.

Deeper techniques require a deeper technique. If your goal is to get a lasting result, regression to cause therapeutic hypnosis may just be the right solution.

Despite the many objections to regression, the facts remain: clients are going to regress whether you want them to or not. They're going to experience uncomfortable feelings and emotions. And every problem is the result of a life experience. Uncomfortable feelings and memories don't just come out of nowhere! Something happened to cause the problem. That's where we must go to resolve it.

When a person doesn't know how to deal with their uncomfortable emotions, their coping strategy is often to try to avoid their feelings. As a result, problems tend to get worse over time. While repressing unwanted memories and emotions is an effective coping strategy in childhood, in adulthood, it's a problem. Because the situations responsible for causing unwanted thoughts, feelings or behaviors haven't been processed and brought to completion, the person is vulnerable to being triggered by situations in daily life which act as reminders of the causal event.

And people who get triggered are going to get triggered again.

The feeling is never the problem. Feelings and emotions are how the subconscious mind communicates with the conscious mind. When memories and the uncomfortable feelings they generate are allowed to be experienced and expressed fully, they don't last very long. It's only when we judge against our feelings and deny them expression that they become problematic.

Because most people are resistant to facing uncomfortable memories and emotions, phase one of the Devil's Therapy focuses on laying the foundation for regression to happen very easily. Allowing the client time to prepare for the deeper work of regression hypnotherapy can help to reduce their resistance to "going there" which will save you precious time in subsequent sessions. This is the purpose of the Ready for Regression First Session.

By the end of the Ready for Regression First Session, your client will have experienced much more than just hypnosis and you'll have a client who is truly ready for regression.

You'll have a client who can:

- Return to the state of hypnosis quickly and easily,
- Follow your instructions to regress into past events,
- Respond quickly during the uncovering procedure,
- Be a source of loving support for the Inner Child,
- Participate in a Dialogue Process,
- Forgive Inner Child and Parent Parts

That's a lot.

Time Management Tips

The Ready for Regression First Session approach involves the following five distinct phases. The following tips will help you to manage your time more effectively so you can feel more in control of the process.

First, there's the **preliminary intake**. This is where you gather the information you need to guide the healing process. Usually, the intake takes about 20 minutes. But when a client is in distress, allowing them more time to talk during the intake can be a valuable investment of your session time.

Remember, you can always wrap up your session following the Conditioning Session. This gives you total time control in your first session, allowing you to relax and simply respond to the needs of the client.

Second, you need to make the client a partner in the healing process. This is the purpose of the **educational pretalk**: to establish a therapeutic contract that allows both hypnosis *and* regression to happen. This ensures that you have a client who is willing to proceed with the hypnotherapy. Allow about 20 minutes.

If you decide to incorporate the Potty Break Protocol into your first session, you'll need to allow about 10 minutes to complete the Session Worksheet. The Session Worksheet provides all the information you will need during every session to guide the process easily.

Third, you're going to guide the client into **hypnosis**, test for somnambulism, provide proof to the client that hypnosis is happening, and then install a trigger for a rapid induction. Utilizing a rapid induction will save you precious time in subsequent sessions. Allow at least 20 minutes to give the client time to experience some hypnotic depth.

Fourth, you're going to guide the client through the **Ready for Regression Session**. This will allow you to assess the client's readiness for regression and then teach them how to work with you in a regression. Introducing the client to the uncovering work, Inner Child work, and Forgiveness work of regression hypnotherapy *before* you start asking them to go back into painful past events makes the processes familiar. Remember, subconsciously familiar is safe. Allow 35 minutes plus an additional five minutes for your session wrap up review.

Finally, give yourself about 10 minutes to conduct a post-hypnosis debrief. Remember, the client is still processing. Help them to make sense of what's just happened and ensure that they're feeling good before sending them out the door.

While the Conditioning Session and the Ready for Regression Session are designed as stand-alone protocols, they're designed to work back-to-back in the first session.

To complete all the phases, you'll need to allow two to two and one-half hours for the first session. That may sound like a long time, but it will save you time in the long run.

Phase 1	Phase 2		Phase 3	Phase 4	Phase 5
Preliminary Intake Process	Educational Pretalk Process	Potty Break Protocol	Hypnosis Conditioning Session	Ready for Regression Session & Wrap Up	Post-Session Debrief
15-20 min	15-20 min	10-15 min	20-25 min	35-40 min	10-15 min

Ready for Regression Phase Checklist

1. Preliminary Check-in
2. Blanket/Permission
3. Hand Drop Re-Induction
4. Deepening (Snow Falling)
5. Pseudo Regression (Hypermnesia Exercise)
6. Finger Pinch Anchor (Optional)
7. Regress to Childhood
8. Regress to Womb (Inside Mom)
9. Uncovering Procedure
10. Pseudo Inner Child Work
11. Future Pacing
12. Anchor State
13. Mental Rehearsal
14. Emerging
15. Debrief/Homework

Stand-Alone Protocols

Most of the time the first session will go like clockwork. But some clients are going to need more time during the intake process. This is especially true when you're dealing with a client who has been to counseling. Clients who have been through the medical mill are usually frustrated with not being listened to. Clients who have been to counseling *need* to talk because that's what's familiar. Giving your client a little more time to talk will allow them to feel heard, providing much-needed safety.

It's all about being client centered. If the client needs more time during the intake, that's okay. Prove that your approach is different by honoring their feelings. This will give you a more cooperative client to work with.

If you find that you're running short on time in the first session, that doesn't need to be a problem. Just make sure that you guide the client through the Conditioning Session.

Remember, the client thinks they're paying for hypnosis. Leave yourself enough time in the first session to provide the client with an experience of deepening relaxation. Install and test the trigger for re-induction. (This doubles as a great Convincer!) Then in the next session, you can pick up where you left off.

The next session would then begin with a preliminary check-in, followed by the hand-drop induction, followed by the Ready for Regression Session. Simple, right?

Conditioning Session	Ready for Regression Session
- Three Ps - Intake Process - Educational Pretalk - Potty Break/ Session Worksheet - Three Permissions ---------------- - Formalize the Induction - Covert Test - Overt Test - Body Tour - Emerge (Not really) - Time Distortion Test - Install Trigger (Gift) - Proceed to Ready for Regression	- Test Trigger - Deepen - Imagery Deepener - Hypermnesia - Regress to Childhood - Regress to Womb - Uncovering - Inner Child Work - Future Pacing - Anchor State - Mental Rehearsal - Emerge - Debrief/Homework

Ready for Regression Session

When you use the Ready for Regression Session as a stand-alone program, you will have already completed the intake, educational pretalk, and conditioned your client for a rapid induction. This means that you're going to have plenty of time to continue into the deeper work of regression hypnosis.

Once you have converted the Hypermnesia exercise into a real regression and have guided the client into an actual event in childhood, you could begin working on the client's issue. For example, let's say you have a client who comes to you to resolve a fear of spiders.

During the positive regression, the client goes back to a pleasant event where they're two years old. Give the client a few minutes to enjoy the experience of feeling safe and happy. Fill their tank with all the good feelings. Then, offer a few suggestions to remind them that …

- They still have this ability to feel good about themselves,
- They're allowed to change,
- They're allowed to feel good again,
- This is why they're seeing you; to get their *good* feelings back.

Next, find out if the problem the client came to see you about is a problem for the two-year-old. For example, how does the 2-year-old in that event feel about spiders?

If spiders aren't a problem at age two, you know that the problem got started sometime *after* the age of two. The next step would then be to move forward along the timeline until you locate the first time that they felt "that fear".

If the two-year old already knows to be afraid of spiders, just mentioning spiders will bring up the fear. This will give you a feeling you can Bridge back on to an earlier event.

If that feeling is strong enough, it could even cause a spontaneous regression. (The best kind!) Because you already have the client in the ballpark for the causal event, the subconscious mind could automatically associate into the situation or event that has everything to do with that fear. When that happens, all you need to do is conduct the tests for the Initial Sensitizing Event (ISE).

Nice, right?

Remember, if you instruct the client to go back to a positive event and their subconscious mind bounces back into a painful event from the past, Yay! You're right where you need to be. All you need to do is begin the uncovering procedure.

Find out where the client's mind has taken them, how young they are in that scene, and what's happening to cause them to feel "that feeling". Then, test for the ISE. Continue the process until you locate the ISE. Then clear the causal event.

If you don't have enough time to locate the causal event, or there's too much going on for you to get a complete resolution to the problem, no problem. Button up the client for the next session. Then, wrap up the session by making whatever happened in that session relevant to the client's issue and you'll be all set up for the next session.

That's all you ever need to do. When you're facilitating a multi-session healing program, all you ever need to do is set the client up to take the next step. Make it safe for the client to take the next step and it will happen easily.

So that's it. Once you have completed both phases of the Ready for Regression first session, you'll be set up to get to work on the client's presenting issue without any unnecessary resistance. Subsequent sessions will then follow the standard regression hypnotherapy protocol.

A standard regression-to-cause hypnosis takes about 90 minutes. A 90-minute session gives you plenty of time to conduct a preliminary check-in, induce hypnosis, bring up a feeling for Affect Bridge, Bridge back to a past event, guide the client through the therapeutic process, and emerge and debrief the client following the session.

Standard Regression Session Checklist

1. Preliminary Check-In
2. Blanket/Permission
3. Hand Drop Induction
4. Deepen Immediately
5. Provoke Feeling
6. SUD Test/Amplify the Feeling
7. Affect Bridge
8. Preliminary Uncovering/ Test for ISE
9. Uncover the Story (ISE)
10. Release Trapped Emotions
11. Reparent and Educate Child
12. Test ISE (Is it clear?)
13. Test SSEs (Grow the Child Up)
14. Integrate Changes at Adult Level
15. Future Pace/Mental Rehearsal (Optional Test)
16. Test Results in Real Life

Wendie Webber

With over thirty years of experience as a healing practitioner, Wendie brings a broad range of skills to her unique approach to regression to cause hypnosis.

She is an Omni-Hypnosis graduate, 5-Path practitioner, Transactional hypnotherapist, Alchemical hypnotherapist, Satir Transformational Systemic therapist, and Regression Hypnotherapy Boot Camp participant.

Before hypnosis, Wendie owned a self-help bookstore where she explored spirituality, psychology, and energy-based healing.

Wendie is the recipient of the 2006 5-PATH Leadership Award and the 2019 Gerald F. Kein OMNI Award for Excellence in Hypnotism.

She enjoys an eclectic lifestyle on Vancouver Island, British Columbia, Canada, surrounded by nature, oracles, and cats.

Ditch the Pitch! Digital Free Client Attraction Guide for Hypnotists is a beginner's guide to marketing yourself and your services *without* having to do that dreaded sales pitch, figure out how to game the algorithms on social media, or stay on top of SEO. This is an old-school, hands-on approach for healers who want to take care of business by connecting with real people who truly need your help. That's it.

"I've paid a lot of money for business courses and never completed them. I felt overwhelmed and lost in all the content. This course was easy, simple to follow, and taught me so much. I feel confident and ready to change my current system and start implementing what I've learned in my own practice". ~ **Nicole Dodd, UK**

The Devil's Therapy: *Hypnosis Practitioner's Essential Guide to Effective Regression Hypnotherapy.* Discover how a 200-year-old fairy tale reveals a complete system for facilitating effective regression hypnotherapy. Learn the "Why" behind the "How-To" of regression to cause hypnosis. Turn your hypnosis sessions into healing programs and get results that last. This practical guidebook gives you a step-by-step map you can use to facilitate successful regression therapy. It's much simpler than you might imagine.

This is absolutely amazing work. It's so clear and precise, just like a laser. It leaves no doubts about what to do, how to do it, and the best part: Why to do it!! - **Zoran Pavlovic, Belgrade, Serbia**

The Devil's Therapy provides a simple three-phase, seven-step protocol for facilitating regression to cause therapeutic hypnosis. The first phase is comprised of three steps which effectively set up for a multi-session healing program. The second phase is comprised of two steps which make up the core work of regression to cause and inner child work. The third phase involves the final two steps of testing/integrating all changes followed by the forgiveness work. Available on Amazon in English, German, and French versions.

Ditch the Script: *Get Everything You Need from the Client for Successful Hypnotherapy and Set Up to Wrap Up with Results* reveals simple strategies you can use right away to set up to facilitate effective Regression Hypnotherapy. Wrap up your sessions powerfully without ever needing a script. Break free of 'scriptnotism' and start facilitating client-centered Regression-to-Cause Therapeutic Hypnosis.

Make room in your toolbox for Wendie Webber's brilliant new book, put down your scripts, and become more adept at using regression successfully. In the words of Dave Elman, "Want it to happen, make it happen and watch it happen!"
~ Cheryl J. Elman - President of the Dave Elman Hypnosis Institute

---

Radical Healing: *Hypnosis Practitioner's Guide to Harnessing the Healing Power of the Educational Pretalk.* Learn how to prepare your clients for a body-centered approach to healing the mind. Discover how every phase of the healing process involves a contract – from the initial call with a prospective client, to the first session, for the hypnosis, and for regression.

Wendie's lessons have been invaluable in helping me to understand the subconscious mind and I feel like I really get it now. I used what I learned right away to great effect with my clients, and it has taken my practice to a whole new level of learning. My clients are seeing results faster! The insights and healing just come more naturally, now – it just seems to flow easily. – **Craig Homonnay, Australia**

The Devil's Little Black Book: *Regression Hypnotherapist's Troubleshooting Guide with Tips, Tricks & Even Scripts to Tweak Your Therapeutic Technique.* Where *The Devil's Therapy* answers the question, "Why do we do what we do when we do it?" *The Devil's Little Black Book* answers the question, "What if?" What if sh*t happens in a session and you don't know what to do? This companion guide to *The Devil's Therapy* provides proven strategies for dealing with some of the more predictable ways resistance can show up in your sessions with client – and what to do when it does.

After almost 40 years of doing hypnosis, I discovered your phenomenal books and online videos very recently and it opened up the floodgates of memories in my career. Your history of hypnotherapy, your trials and tribulations, parallel mine . . . I am going to recommend your books to all those people who've been bugging me to put to paper these principles. I wish I had heard of you years before when I was active, and an industry turned against me because I refused to take shortcuts and jump on the latest bandwagon of change-work for the month. – **John Petrocelli, USA**

Dream Healing Practitioner Guidebook: *A Healer's Guide to Uncovering the Secret Messages of Your Dreams.* Learn deceptively simple techniques you can use – yourself and with others – to uncover the meaning of your dreams. If you're a healing practitioner, *Dream Healing* gives you an insight therapy you can offer to clients. *Dream Healing* can help you to develop valuable skills that can support you in your healing sessions with clients. Working with your own dreams can help you to develop intuition while bringing balance and harmony to your mind-body system.

Makes Things So Simple

I have thoroughly loved working with dream healing tools. Wendie makes things so simple and easy that learning new skills such as dream healing become easy to apply and implement from the start. I have absolutely loved uncovering my dream meanings and then putting what I've learnt into action because understanding a dream is not enough; it also needs some change/action for resolution to happen. It's been such an interesting and fun experience. Thank you, so much! – **Nicole Dodd, UK**

www.ingramcontent.com/pod-product-compliance
Lightning Source LLC
Chambersburg PA
CBHW050326010526
44119CB00050B/697